# The DOG BEHAVIOR PROBLEM SOLVER

Teoti Anderson
CPDT-KA, KPA-CTP

**Project Team**
Editor: Jeremy Harwood, Sarah Bloxham
Copy Editor: Joann Woy
Design: Mary Ann Kahn
Index: Elizabeth Walker

## i-5 PUBLISHING, LLC™

Chairman: David Fry
Chief Financial Officer: David Katzoff
Chief Digital Officer: Jennifer Black-Glover
Chief Marketing Officer: Beth Freeman Reynolds
Marketing Director: Will Holburn
General Manager, i-5 Press: Christopher Reggio
Art Director, i-5 Press: Mary Ann Kahn
Senior Editor, i-5 Press: Amy Deputato
Production Director: Laurie Panaggio
Production Manager: Jessica Jaensch

### Library of Congress Cataloging-in-Publication Data

Anderson, Teoti.
 The dog behavior problem solver : step-by-step positive training techniques to correct more than 20 problem behaviors.
    pages cm
 Includes index.
 ISBN 978-1-62187-115-6
 1. Dogs--Behavior. 2. Dogs--Training. I. Title.
 SF433.A535 2015
 636.7'0835--dc23
                          2015030606

This book has been published with the intent to provide accurate and authoritative information in regard to the subject matter within. While every precaution has been taken in the preparation of this book, the author and publisher expressly disclaim any responsibility for any errors, omissions, or adverse effects arising from the use or application of the information contained herein. The techniques and suggestions are used at the reader's discretion and are not to be considered a substitute for veterinary care. If you suspect a medical problem, consult your veterinarian.

i-5 Publishing, LLC™
www.facebook.com/i5press
www.i5publishing.com

Printed and bound in China
18 17 16 15    2 4 6 8 10 9 7 5 3 1

# CONTENTS

# PART I

# A LOOK AT BEHAVIOR AND TRAINING

*Trust between owner and dog is an all-important essential.*

**Y**ou do NOT remember signing up for this. You distinctly remember the original dream. You wanted to add a dog to your family. You wanted a furry friend to love you no matter what. You wanted a sweet, loving companion—smart, friendly, and well-behaved enough to take anywhere. It was supposed to be perfect. It was going to be fun. It probably started out that way. But somewhere along the way, your dream of the perfect pet faded. You're waking up to the fact your dog has some problems. And now you're getting worried.

What happened? You know other people who have dogs like yours, and their dogs seem just fine. Your coworkers often laughingly share stories about their dogs' funny antics. You have relatives who brag about their dogs' accomplishments. Maybe you've had dogs before who were so easy to live with. Why did this dog turn out differently? How did living with an adorable, beautiful dog turn into such a hassle? Is your dog just … broken? More importantly, can you fix him?

You're not alone, even though it surely feels like it sometimes. Please don't despair. You already made the decision to help your dog, and that's a positive step!

## Dog Differences

Any time you bring a different species into your home, you're going to encounter challenges. You see the world very differently from the way your canine friend does. You certainly have different distractions. You have better sight, he has better senses of smell and hearing. The way you perceive the world around you affects your actions in it. For example, you might be distracted by the sight of a friend in the distance, while your dog becomes obsessed with the scent of a steak grilling two blocks away.

You process information differently as well. People primarily communicate verbally, while dogs are much more adept at reading and signaling through body language. Humans are capable of saying one

thing while meaning another, while dogs are unfailingly honest creatures. You always know where you stand with a dog. People, not so much. Is there any wonder miscommunication occurs?

You have different priorities. You may be obsessing over a business deadline while your dog lives for you tossing him a tennis ball. Dogs also have different skill sets than we do ... skills that involve chewing, pulling, jumping, digging, and other behaviors. We adore dogs for what they are while at the same time getting annoyed at what they do. Sometimes problem behaviors are minor. Sometimes they are quite serious.

Studies have shown that behavioral problems are a top reason why people relinquish their dogs to shelters and other rescue organizations. Common problems cited include aggression toward people and other pets, a tendency to escape, destructiveness indoors and outdoors, hyperactivity, house soiling, and disobedience. This doesn't mean that all shelter dogs have problems. Far from the case! There are other reasons for relinquishment, such as people moving and unable or unwilling to take a dog with them, divorces, deaths in the family, lack of money to care for a dog adequately, and more. But behavioral problems frequently top the list.

Some people get in over their heads with a dog who has problem behaviors. Sometimes, a dog's problem is much more than his owner bargained for, while other times people make the mistake of not doing their research before bringing a dog into the home. Whatever the motive, the fact that behavioral reasons are a prime reason for relinquishment should tell you that problem behaviors are fairly common with our canine friends. Don't be fooled by all those perfect dog stories you compare your dog to ... it may be that you just hear the nice Fido stories and not the naughty ones!

*Smell is your dog's most powerful sense.*

Just because your dog has a problem behavior does not make him "defective." Each and every dog has a unique personality and individual characteristics all of his own. He's one of a kind. Your dog just happens to have some problem issues you need to address. It also doesn't mean that you're crazy for loving him. He may pose challenges, but he's still the fluffy bundle of joy you brought home. There was a reason why you chose this dog. There was something about his spirit ... his eyes ... the way he interacted with you ... that spoke to your heart. He's taken up residence there now, even though he does try your patience.

So what do you do about it? Take positive steps to figure out what is contributing to your dog's behavior and how to address his specific issues.

*Dogs and laptops don't always mix.*

*With time, patience and training, you can have a well-behaved dog.*

# 1 What Is Problem Behavior and What Causes It?

Having a dog with behavior problems is very frustrating. When your dog does something you don't like, it's easy to take it personally. Doesn't he love you? Doesn't he realize how good he has it? Both are typical human responses. Dogs see things differently. Your dog probably doesn't see his behavior as a problem at all. Many of the things that annoy people about dogs, such as jumping, digging, growling, and chewing, are very typical examples of canine behavior. This doesn't mean you have to put up with such behavior, but in order to fix any problems you need to understand that you and your dog may have different definitions of what a problem is. Heck, people don't always agree on what is a problem and what is not!

For example, you have a strict policy of no dogs on the furniture. Your cousin lets her dogs up on every piece of furniture in her house. You don't want your dog to jump up on you. Your cousin encourages her dog to jump up on her all the time. Which of you is correct? You both are!

Many canine behaviors are only problems if they bother you. The rules you have in your home can be completely different from those in someone else's home. That's completely OK.

## When Behavior Becomes a Problem

Behavior becomes a problem when it annoys you, your family members, friends, or the neighbors. It's a problem if your dog is destructive. If a behavior is unhealthy or dangerous to the dog, other people, or other animals, then it is definitely a problem behavior. Aggression, for example, is a serious problem behavior. It puts people or other animals at risk. It's also a risk to the dog who is aggressive because it could mean euthanasia if it can't be resolved.

If you are struggling with problem behaviors, there is one important thing to understand right away. The problem is not likely to go away on its own. You can't ignore it and hope the dog outgrows it. Please don't make excuses for your dog, either. It's one thing to try to understand why your dog behaves the way he does and another thing to find excuses for his behavior. Saying "Oh, he growls over his food because he was a stray" isn't going to calm down anyone the dog bites.

*A dog on your couch is only a problem if you don't want him to be there!*

Postponing treating the problem will just make it worse. The more a dog practices a behavior, the more ingrained it becomes, until it becomes a habit or your dog's preferred response to a situation. Ingrained behaviors are harder to fix.

A growling puppy can grow up to be an adult dog who bites. A dog who starts to dig will just learn to dig more or bigger holes. Unruly dogs will not magically turn into perfect ladies and gentlemen overnight. Luckily for you, you're not ignoring a problem, or you wouldn't be reading this book! You've already taken a positive step in the right direction.

*Aggression behavior is always a problem, but it can often be helped with positive training.*

## Why Problems Arise

Choosing to share your life with a dog means you're bound to encounter a problem sooner or later. Maybe your dog won't stop barking, pees in the house, drags you down the street, or won't let you take a bone away from him. Maybe he runs away from home or hides when you try and groom him. Why?

There are many reasons why problem behaviors arise. Some are inherent simply because dogs are a different species to us. Dogs love to follow their noses, even if it means dragging their human along with them in the quest to find the source of the scent. They dig holes. They are born to chew on things. They also have to pee and poo, and they don't understand why you don't want them to do either in the house. We bring dogs into our lives and expect them to live by our rules, but we're not always very good at explaining the rules to them in terms they can understand.

*Digging holes is a habit that can easily turn into a problem if left unchecked.*

## Physical Problems

Having a "problem dog" can be disheartening and frustrating. You brought a dog home to be a pet, not a problem! Where did things go wrong? Why did your dog develop problems in the first place?

Many owners mistakenly put down changes in behavior to simple stubbornness. For example, your dog normally loves walking in the neighborhood, but one day, near the end of your walk, he balks and refuses to budge. This soon turns into a habit. Walks start out great, but after a while your dog just stops and won't go any farther. Before assuming your dog is just being defiant or stubborn, it's time for a veterinary examination.

If there is a physical reason for your dog's behavior, then trying to get him to modify it will not be practical until the physical problem is treated. Fixing that may resolve the behavior altogether. This is why many modern trainers will suggest you take your dog to a veterinarian for a physical exam before starting a training program. Unexpected changes in behavior, especially, are a red flag for physical issues. If your dog suddenly develops a behavior problem, your first move should be to take him to a veterinarian to rule out any physical cause. For example, if your dog has been housetrained for a long time and suddenly starts peeing in the house, he could have a urinary tract infection or other related illness.

*A vet will check for any physical causes of problem behavior.*

## Medical Problems

That's by no means all. For instance, your dog could be developing an orthopedic problem, such as hip dysplasia. This is an abnormal formation of the hip socket that is both crippling and painful. (It's also a common genetic disease in many breeds, including Bulldogs, French Bulldogs, Rottweilers, Shih Tzus, and Golden Retrievers.)

While hip dysplasia usually affects older dogs, it can occur in very young dogs as well. Like other orthopedic and joint diseases, it can cause a dog to limit his activity. So can a pulled muscle or a torn muscle or ligament. If your dog stops wanting to jump in the car or on the bed, or he refuses to climb up and down stairs, there may well be a physical issue at the root of the problem. It's not defiance at all—it's pain.

When a dog is in pain, he can be withdrawn or even aggressive. For example, the little dog who snaps when you pick her up may have arthritis. The dog who is normally social and friendly might snap at the veterinarian who examines his ear to treat an ear infection.

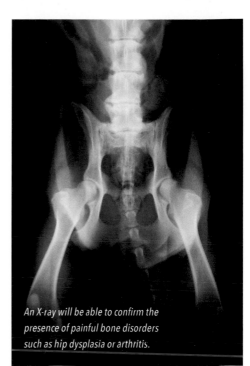

An X-ray will be able to confirm the presence of painful bone disorders such as hip dysplasia or arthritis.

## Chronic Conditions

Other diseases, such as diabetes, can also impact on behavior. A diabetic dog can get very thirsty and will naturally drink a lot of water as a result. This may cause him to pee more frequently. If he can't get outside in time, he may pee in the house. Arthritis or other painful joint conditions may lead a dog to pee and poo in the house as well. It's just too hard and painful for him to get outdoors.

## Watch Your Dog's Body Language: It Hurts!

Have you noticed that when petting your dog, he tenses when you reach a certain spot? Maybe he looks away or starts licking his lips? Or, he's panting and when you reach a specific spot, he stops panting and closes his mouth tight shut? Once you move on from that spot, he relaxes again.

Do you have an older dog who used to love your younger dog, but recently has started lifting his lip when the younger dog gets near to him? Are you starting to see squabbles when they used to be best pals? These and similar situations call for a veterinarian visit. Your dog may be getting stressed or aggressive because he's in pain.

With some dogs, it's easy to tell when they are hurting. Others may be more subtle with their signals. You may have to play detective to find out what's really going on. Your veterinarian can help you rule out any physical issues that may be causing a problem.

An older dog may find it harder to get around if his joints are painful.

## Deafness

Deafness can be a problem, too. As a dog ages, he may lose his hearing, so he can't hear you when you call him or give him other spoken cues. He's not being stubborn, he's simply deaf.

# Lack of Training

Many problem behaviors are simply due to lack of training. If you've never taught your dog, then he doesn't know what you expect from him. You also have to instruct him in terms he can understand.

Remember, dogs aren't born automatically understanding your language. Yelling at your dog to "Come HERE!" isn't going to mean anything to him unless you've trained him to come when you say those words. Shouting "Sit, sit, sit, SIT! SIT!" over and over again doesn't teach your dog how to sit.

Dogs learn body language before they learn verbal language. This is why it's normally easier to teach a dog hand signals than verbal signals. Dogs just understand them more quickly. This doesn't mean you should only communicate to your dog using hand signals (although if your dog is deaf, this makes perfect

Learn to read your dog's body language. A dog who rolls over for a belly rub is at ease with you.

## Positive Training

You may have very clear ideas about what your dog should and shouldn't do, but you need to communicate those expectations to your dog in terms he can understand. You can absolutely do that with positive training.

Every teacher also has to adapt to his student if he wants to communicate effectively. Can you imagine being taught how to drive by an instructor who didn't understand or speak your language? How would you ask him questions when you were confused? How would you know if you were getting something right or wrong? Would you be nervous about driving in a city rush hour under this teacher's guidance? It would be very frustrating, and you would learn at a really slow pace, if at all.

You can't speak dog. But you can learn how to understand your dog better so you can communicate with him more effectively. This will make you a better trainer and give you a better chance of teaching your dog what standards of behavior you expect from him.

This may sound like having a dog involves a lot of training. It does! If you want your dog to be a good family companion, training is important. And for a dog who has problem behaviors, training is critical. Positive training can help resolve them.

*You do not have to use physical punishment to get your dog to learn.*

sense). It just means you will need to be more patient with your dog as he learns to catch on to your verbal cues. Just saying a word doesn't communicate what it means to your dog. You need to teach him what words mean.

Dogs don't know automatically how you expect them to behave. You have to teach them this, too. For example, it's normal for a dog to follow his nose. Sometimes that might mean following a nose right up on top of the kitchen counter if there's food on it. Your dog doesn't realize the kitchen counter is off limits unless you teach him that it is. A dog will bolt out the door, happy just to get outside. He doesn't know he should wait at doorways unless you teach him. Puppies are notorious for putting everything in their mouths. They don't know what's appropriate to chew on and what's not until you teach them.

*Understanding your dog will make training so much easier.*

## Lack of Proper Socialization

During puppyhood, from birth to anywhere between 12 and 16 weeks, puppies form their view of the world. The experiences they have during this time will impact on them for a lifetime. The late Dr. R. K. Anderson, DVM, Diplomate, American College of Veterinary Medicine and Diplomate of the American College of Veterinary Behaviorists, was a strong proponent of early puppy education. He stated "breeders, new puppy owners, veterinarians, trainers and behaviorists have a responsibility to assist in providing these learning/socialization experiences with other puppies/dogs, with children/adults and with various environmental situations during this optimal period from birth to 16 weeks. Many veterinarians are making this early socialization and learning program part of a total wellness plan for breeders and new owners of puppies during the first 16 weeks of a puppy's life—the first 7–8 weeks with the breeder and the next 8 weeks with the new owners. This socialization program should enroll puppies from 8 to 12 weeks of age as a key part of any preventive medicine program to improve the bond between pets and their people and keep dogs as valued members of the family for 12 to 18 years."

What if you didn't get your dog as a puppy, so you have no idea what happened during his critical socialization period? Or what if you didn't realize how important the critical socialization period was, and you missed this window of opportunity? A lack of proper socialization can cause problem behaviors.

For example, a puppy who doesn't have positive experiences with children during his socialization period may be fearful of children when he meets them as an adult dog. He may growl or snap at them because he is afraid of them. A puppy who never leaves the house or only goes out to visit the veterinarian's office may be fearful as an adult of strange environments. A puppy who isn't properly socialized with other dogs may growl and lunge on leash at them as an adolescent dog. Puppyhood is a vital formative time. If your dog didn't get the benefit of proper socialization, it could be the prime reason for the problems you're seeing now.

## Owner Miscommunication

Many folks think they are good communicators. It's often the case, however, that while your directions would be clear to another person, they're easily misunderstood by your dog.

*An adult dog will be more likely to enjoy children if positively introduced to them as a puppy.*

For example, Roman the Bull Terrier loves to jump on his owner, Dan. Dan yells at Roman when he does this and pushes him off. Dan thinks he's being very clear: "Roman, don't jump on me!" Roman keeps jumping up, though. Why doesn't he understand what Dan wants?

One possible reason is that Roman likes attention, even if Dan is yelling. Roman also loves it when Dan pushes him. It's like enthusiastic petting to him. It's fun! So Roman bounces off Dan, thinking it's a great game. Dan meant to teach his dog not to jump up. What he actually taught Roman was to jump up more often. Bounce! Bounce! Bounce! What started as a minor behavioral problem is now a major one.

### Puppy Options:
### The Power of Proper Socialization

Socialization is not just making sure your puppy has a lot of different experiences. It is ensuring that your puppy has a lot of different, *positive* experiences. If he meets people who scare him, or things happen to him that he perceives as frightening, he could be fearful of similar people and situations as an adult.

Also note that socialization doesn't just stop at 16 weeks. Even though the critical socialization window closes at about that time, if you stop socializing your puppy altogether he may have difficulty retaining the benefits into adulthood. Socialization is a continuing process, especially with some dogs who are prone to being fearful or shy.

It is true that some dogs have lousy childhoods and still end up saints. They are the lucky ones! The great debate over nature versus nurture is never ending; no one really knows why some dogs with rough starts thrive while others falter. Your best bet for the future of your puppy is to make the most of the socialization period while you can to best influence his adulthood.

*If you encourage your dog to jump up in play, you may have trouble controlling this behavior in other situations.*

Some people also tend to mix and match words, intending them to have the same meaning. This can be very confusing to a dog. If you say, "Get down!" a couple of times when your dog jumps up on you but "Off!" at other times, this is not consistent communication. Remember, dogs don't understand verbal language unless you teach them. Have you taught him that both "Get down" and "Off" mean the same thing? What if you then also expect him to lie down when you say "Down?" What's the difference to your dog between "Down" and "Get Down"? Are you confused yet? So is your dog!

## Inconsistent Direction

Inconsistent behavior occurs when there is inconsistent direction. For example, you have a dog who doesn't come to anyone consistently when he is called. It turns out that when you want your dog to come to you, you say, "Come here!" Your spouse uses "Come!" Your oldest son uses "Get over here," and your daughter uses "C'mere!" To top it off, every time family members want your dog to do this one action, they use a different term for it. This is very confusing for people, let alone a dog. It results in a dog who doesn't come consistently when he's called because he's called differently each time.

If you or your family are using inconsistent cues, your dog's problem behaviors may be due to confusion. At a minimum, inconsistent communication is going to make problems harder to solve.

## Vague Communication

A classic example of vague communication is the common use of the word "No!" If your dog steals your socks, you yell, "No!" You intend "No" to mean "Don't steal my socks." But he might interpret your "No" to mean don't chew the sock or don't lie down with the sock on the couch. So he still steals your socks. Worse, he brings you a sock and your sharp "No!" could teach him not to bring you a sock. So he will still go on stealing your socks, but now he'll hide them. "No" can certainly indicate to your dog that you're displeased, but it's not very specific. It doesn't tell him what you want him to do instead.

This doesn't mean you shouldn't ever say "No" to your dog. If you haven't trained your dog and he's doing something wrong—and definitely if he's doing something that can hurt him or someone else—go ahead and use "No." Just be aware that it's not the best way of communicating. For example, if you teach your dog to sit, you could cue "Sit" to prevent him from jumping up on the kitchen counter. If you teach your dog to leave things alone, you could cue "Leave it!" when he's headed for your socks, and he would understand he's to leave them alone. "No" is just vague—it isn't instructional communication.

## Unpredictability

Another example of miscommunication is when you reward your dog for performing behaviors sometimes but not others. For example, when Linda plays fetch with her terrier mix, Fritz, he barks until Linda throws the ball. He barks and Linda tosses the ball. Linda is paying him for barking with the reward of chasing the ball. Fritz starts barking for other things—his food, his leash, and Linda's attention, for example. Linda yells at him for this. Well, she's already taught Fritz that barking is a good thing. She's been paying him for it. He doesn't understand why he gets paid sometimes for barking and not for other behaviors.

It's simple. Linda accidentally has miscommunicated to her dog that she likes a certain type of behavior. He doesn't understand it's only appreciated within a specific context. If you reward behavior sometimes but not others, the unpredictability can only make behavior get worse.

There are a lot of other ways that people can miscommunicate their expectations to their dogs. Until everyone in the family gets on the same page and starts communicating consistently, problem behaviors will not go away.

# Unrealistic Expectations

Do you have realistic expectations based on your dog's species, age, and breed (or breed combination)? If not, this can often lead to problem behaviors. Here are some common examples of unrealistic expectations:

- An 8-week-old puppy can hold his bladder and bowels all night without a potty break.
- A 4-month-old puppy can hold his bladder and bowels during a typical eight-hour workday without a potty break.
- Dogs should be able to tolerate any behavior from children, including when kids climb on them, pull their ears or tail, or hold their heads and stare into their eyes.
- Dogs should know not to chew on certain things, like couches, cabinets, children's toys, shoes, etc.
- Dogs who have taken a training class on leash should always come when called off leash.

*Make sure your dog knows that stealing socks is not a game.*

*For some dogs, play can be even more rewarding than treats.*

- Dogs should always do what they're told no matter what's going on around them.
- Shy dogs will get over their fears just given time.
- A dog should just work for you for praise—that's all the motivation he should need in order to comply.

Do you get frustrated when your Retriever puts everything in his mouth? Or your Border Collie chases your children? Or when your Boxer has so much energy you think he's nuclear? These are breed-specific traits. You may or may not want to do the things your dog was bred to do, but that won't shut off his DNA. If you have a mixed-breed dog, he will share a combination of breed traits.

Having unrealistic expectations can make inherent problem behaviors worse because your dog can't live up to them. Before you start any training plan, make sure you fully understand what your dog should be able to do. If necessary, talk to a professional trainer or your veterinarian to be sure you are setting realistic goals. Take a look at the more realistic picture of these expectations:

✗ An 8-week-old puppy can hold his bladder and bowels all night without a potty break.

✔ A normal puppy this young will need to pee and poo at least once, maybe twice, during the night.

✗ A 4-month-old puppy can hold his bladder and bowels during a typical 8-hour workday without a potty break.

✔ A normal puppy this young will need at least one break mid-day for a potty break. In general, you take a puppy's age in months and add one to determine the amount of hours he can hold it when confined. So four months plus one is five. That's the maximum time he can spend in confinement until he needs to potty.

✘ Dogs should be able to tolerate any behavior from children, including when kids climb on them, pull their ears or tail, or hold their heads and stare into their eyes.

✔ While some dogs do tolerate these types of behaviors, and some even enjoy it, not all dogs do. Dogs are not jungle gyms or horses. They should not be ridden or climbed on. It is cruel to pull a dog's ears or tail. Holding a dog's head still and staring into his eyes is also an extremely assertive gesture in canine language and could be interpreted as a threat. That's why children get bitten. We certainly don't tolerate being manhandled by everyone we meet, so why do some people expect their dogs to put up with it?

Also note that while this is unfair on the dog, it's also unfair to the child. A child who grows up crawling all over a dog and grabbing at the dog's body parts ends up thinking it's OK to do this to all dogs. Young children have difficulty understanding that their dog may behave differently from other people's dogs. A dog is a dog is a dog to a toddler or small child. Allowing a child to interact with the family dog inappropriately can cause that child to do the same to another dog who is far less tolerant. This can have disastrous consequences.

✘ Dogs should know not to chew on certain things, like couches, cabinets, children's toys, shoes, etc.

✔ Dogs can learn not to chew on specific items, but you need to teach them. They will not automatically know what is off limits for chomping. Chewing is a natural canine behavior. While you see your leather shoes as stylish, your dog sees them as delicious.

✘ Dogs who have taken a training class on leash should always come when called off leash

✔ Just as we learn new things, dogs learn by starting with the basics and gradually moving on to more challenging lessons. There is too great a gap between on-leash and off-leash behaviors. Your dog can learn to respond to you off leash, but you need to build up to that level of learning with transitional steps. If you haven't trained your dog with the intermediate steps, this is an unrealistic expectation.

✘ Dogs should always do what they're told no matter what's going on around them.

✔ This is another example of something that needs to be taught. It's not automatic. Your dog may sit when you cue him, but will he do it when the doorbell rings? If you dropped a plate of hamburgers next to him? If a squirrel runs across his path? Teaching your dog to perform behaviors while experiencing different distractions is called "proofing." If you haven't proofed your dog's behaviors, then it's unrealistic to expect him to perform around distractions.

*Dogs love praise and attention from their favorite people.*

What Is Problem Behavior and What Causes It? 21

✘ Shy dogs will get over their fears just given time.

✔ Fear is a powerful emotion. Dogs need help overcoming their fears. They won't go away without proper intervention. Instead of time, a dog may need behavior modification and maybe even medication, depending on the severity of the problem.

✘ A dog should work for you just for praise—that's all the motivation he should need in order to comply.

✔ If you give a dog the choice between food and praise, or a squirrel and praise, which do you think is more likely to grab his attention? Praise is a good reinforcer, but it rarely can compete with other items that a dog naturally finds of higher value. This is humbling, but normal. While your praise may mean a lot to another person, it may not rank as highly with your dog.

## Environmental Influences

Dogs can easily be distracted, especially puppies. It's completely normal for dogs to be distracted by things going on around them. Such distractions, however, can cause problem behaviors. If your dog is so obsessed with squirrels, cats, or cars that he lunges on his leash and won't listen to you, it could be a problem.

When you go out into the neighborhood, you can sense many things around you. Your dog can sense a lot more. Dogs can smell things you can't. Did you know, for instance, that dogs can smell 100,000 times better than humans and smell something up to 40 feet underground? They can hear things you can't as well. Dogs with erect ears hear better than a dog with floppy ears, but, in general, dogs can hear about four times greater than humans. This means that your dog is being bombarded with many more environmental distractions than you are.

*Dogs love praise, but a pocketful of treats is better!*

In order for dogs to perform reliably, behaviors need to be trained to fluency. This means they need to be trained with a variety of distractions, under different circumstances, in order for dogs to perform them consistently. If that training hasn't been done, then what's going on around him will have a greater impact on a dog's performance.

The environment especially impacts on a frightened dog. A shy or fearful dog constantly monitors his surroundings for danger. It is much more difficult for a dog like this to concentrate on learning since his energy is dedicated to keeping safe. For example, you take a fearful dog to a park festival. Your dog jumps up on you, trying to get some comfort. You tell him to sit. He continues to

*It's a natural instinct for dogs to investigate all sorts of scents, especially since their sense of smell is so well-developed.*

jump up on you because he is afraid. He's too scared to sit. The problem behavior is not disobedience or jumping up. It's simply fear.

The environment is always competing for your attention. With positive training, you can trump the environment's temptations. You can even learn to use the environment to your advantage. For example, if your dog loves to sniff, you can use giving him the opportunity to sniff as a reward. Instead of the environment causing problems or making problem behaviors more challenging, you can put it to work for you!

*It can be hard for a dog to focus amid many distractions.*

What Is Problem Behavior and What Causes It?    23

## Anxiety, Shyness, and Fear

Anxiety, shyness, and fear can cause many problem behaviors. Shyness can prevent a dog from bonding. If a dog isn't bonded to you, he doesn't have a vested interest in doing things you ask of him. If he's so shy you can't pet or even touch him, you will have problems grooming him, cleaning his ears, doing his nails, or tending to him if he is sick or injured. If he gets loose, he's not likely to come to you if he has no relationship with you. This is why modern trainers will often have you work on basic foundational behaviors before you even try to tackle advanced problems of fear. Your dog has to have a solid, positive relationship with you—a relationship of trust—before you can help him overcome his anxiety.

A dog who is anxious and fearful may growl, snap, or bite. Most aggression is based in fear. For example, a dog who is frightened of children may growl or snap if a child goes to pet him. A dog who is afraid of other dogs can act aggressively if another dog enters his personal space.

Some dogs only experience anxiety in certain settings. For example, a dog who is happy and outgoing at home may be fearful outside the home or around the neighborhood. Or a dog who has never been to the groomer may panic and bite in self-defense when put on the grooming table for the first time. Some anxiety is situational. For example, a dog turns destructive only when left alone. Or a dog will pee in the house only during a thunderstorm. The destructiveness and house soiling are both problems rooted in anxiety.

Illness or injury can also cause anxiety. A dog who has broken out in an itchy rash isn't comfortable, and he may pace restlessly or bite at his skin. A dog developing arthritis in his forelegs can start licking obsessively at his skin, causing open sores. Similar behavior can occur because of fleas or ticks. For some dogs, a single fleabite sends them into a frenzy of biting and scratching themselves.

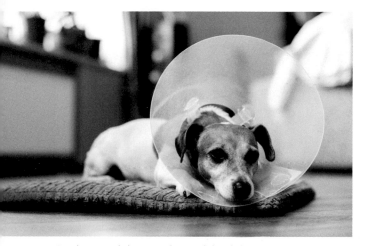

*A neck cone can help to stop obsessive licking behavior.*

Illness or injury can also cause a dog to become aggressive. A dog who is otherwise social and friendly may cower or growl at the veterinarian's office during examination. He doesn't feel well, so he's less tolerant of handling. He's trying to protect himself.

If your dog has behavior problems rooted in anxiety or fear, you will need to address them on several fronts. These dogs can learn. You just need to understand their challenges so you can have patience while helping them overcome their problem behaviors.

## Breed-Specific Traits

Dog breeds were created for specific purposes. Certain dogs were developed to retrieve, herd, hunt vermin, help people hunt other animals, guard, be companions, and more. These traits were cultivated on purpose, but they can sometimes cause problems in the average family household.

A Golden Retriever who puts everything in his mouth can be annoying. A Collie who chases the children can be frightening. A Fox Terrier who attempts to "kill" your children's precious toys can be frustrating. A German Shepherd who won't let your friends come into the house can be dangerous.

Do you have a mixed-breed dog? If you know his parentage, you can better understand why he behaves in the way he does. If you have no idea what breeds make up your dog, you can sometimes determine the types they are from his behavior. Does your dog love to chase children, often nipping at their heels? There may be some herding in his genetic makeup. Does he stare at birds and lift one foot in point? There could be a sporting breed in the mix.

Hopefully, you researched your dog's breed or breeds thoroughly before bringing him home, so you knew what to expect. If not, you might have been in for quite a surprise.

Your dog can't help his DNA. While there are some dogs who are not interested in or adept at living up to their genetic inheritance, most dogs are fairly good at following the breed plan. If you're not going to pursue the task for which your dog was bred, your dog's DNA still wants to try. This doesn't mean you have to put up with problem behaviors, but it's important to understand that your dog is not trying to be a pain. Instead of getting angry at your dog for being who he is, you can teach him other behaviors you prefer.

*A Golden Retriever will mouth almost everything he comes across, including the remote!*

# 2 Training Philosophy and Methods

If you're sick and the doctor says you need a prescription, don't you want medication that gets results with the fewest possible side effects? Of course you do! There are many ways to train a dog. While many will get you results, there are some that also can have unpleasant side effects. This book focuses on positive, reward-based training techniques. These effective techniques are based in science and not on myth. They do not have the side effects of other, more old-fashioned types of training. They are especially effective in solving problem behaviors.

This comes as a surprise to some people. A prevalent myth is that positive training only works for minor problem behaviors. You can use reward-based training to teach a dog to stop jumping on you, but it'll never work with a dog who bites. Not true.

Another popular myth is that positive training only works with "easy dogs"—breeds known to be gentle or easy to work with. You can teach a Cavalier King Charles Spaniel using cookies, but that'll never work with a German Shepherd. Also not true.

With positive training based in science, the laws of learning apply to all dogs. They apply to all organisms with a nervous system, for that matter. Learning is learning, whether you're dealing with a Maltese, a Chow Chow, or a walrus!

## What Is Positive Training?

At its core, positive training rewards behaviors you like. The laws of learning dictate that behavior that is rewarded is repeated. So when your dog does something you like, you give him a reward. The reward is a paycheck for a job well done. Your dog is very likely to do the same again since he got a paycheck for it the last time.

For example, Leo the Labrador is about to stick his head into the kitchen trash can. His owner, Philip, calls him to come. Instead of pursuing the temptations of the trash, Leo trots over to Philip instead. Philip rewards him with some popcorn he's been munching and makes a big fuss of him, telling him he's a great dog. Later that day, Leo is once again heading for the trash, but this time he stops, turns away from it and trots over to Philip instead. Philip is out of popcorn, but gives him lots of praise for making a good decision. Soon Philip begins to notice that, although Leo may glance at the trash can as he walks by, he prefers to come and sit by him. Philip has been rewarding Leo's behavior of coming to him instead of the kitchen trash can, therefore he comes to Philip more frequently. Behavior that is rewarded increases in frequency.

In order for reward-based training to work, the reward must be just that—a reward. If your dog doesn't find your paycheck to be very valuable, then you won't see an increase in the behavior. For example, if your dog hates popcorn and doesn't really like being petted, then popcorn and petting are not going to be as rewarding to him as they were to Leo the Labrador. Every dog is different. You need to learn what your dog finds rewarding so you can use it as a suitable paycheck.

Marker training is a type of positive training that uses a marker to indicate to the dog that he has done something correctly. The marker is immediately followed with a reward. The dog

*For many dogs, receiving a small food treat will reinforce good behavior.*

learns to associate the marker as meaning he is going to get paid. Clicker training is a popular form of marker training. It is extremely effective because it's precise. It marks an exact instant in time when your dog does something you like. It's also transferable. As long as everyone in the family uses it consistently, the dog will understand training from Mom just as much as from Dad.

You can also use a specific verbal marker, such as "Yes." Studies have shown, however, that a verbal marker is not as effective as a clicker. It is useful, though, when both of your hands are busy or if you don't happen to have a clicker on you when your dog does something you want to mark.

*A clicker, quickly followed with a reward, is a very effective training tool.*

# Rewards versus Punishments

Positive, or reward-based training, has been around for some time. Many trainers (including this author) who started out training dogs using punishment-based methods have switched to positive training because of the results. It's fast, it works, and it's easier for dogs and people.

Old-fashioned training techniques are fairly confrontational. There's a whole "us vs. them" attitude behind this approach to training. Dogs are out to rule the world! Every time they try to get your attention, they're manipulating you to get you to fall in with their plots for global domination! Don't let them be the boss of you!

As a result, such training methods involve a lot of physical force. If you want your dog to sit, you push his rear end down. If you want him to lie down, you stand on his leash, close to his neck that has a choke chain round it, and then force his front legs flat on the ground. If your dog jumps on you, you are supposed to slam your knee into his chest.

Discipline was even more severe. Can you believe one of the most popular dog-training books of the 1960s recommended practically drowning your dog to break him of the habit of digging holes? If your dog dug a hole, you were supposed to fill the hole with water, push your dog's head into it and wait as he struggled to breathe. The theory was that this would teach your dog to never dig a hole again. What it more likely did was teach your dog that you were a homicidal maniac.

These old-fashioned techniques are pretty physical. Using your muscles can work well if you are stronger than your dog, but what if you're not? A petite woman with a bouncy adolescent Golden Retriever is going to have a hard time physically pushing him into different positions. A child certainly can't do it. Not everyone is able to slam a knee into a large dog's chest effectively. You might hurt your knee before you hurt your dog! If you want your dog to perform just as well for your family members as for you, old-fashioned methods can be problematic in achieving that goal. With positive training, you don't need to use physical force to make your dog do what you want.

This is not to say that punishment doesn't work. The laws of learning also state that behavior that is punished decreases in frequency. A challenge is that it has to be truly adverse to the dog in order to get results. For example, your dog jumps on you. You knee him in the chest. He keeps jumping up on you anyway. The behavior does not decrease. Therefore, the knee slam was not punishment. You need something more aversive in order to achieve the goal. What will it take to find something unpleasant enough to get the dog to stop? It can be

*You want your dog to look to you for direction and positive reinforcement.*

*You can positively train your dog to stay out of the trash can.*

difficult to figure out with some dogs. For some, your knee is going to suffer long before the dog does! Do you really want to go there? Especially when you can achieve the same goal through a less forceful method?

What can also happen is the behavior returns when the punishment stops. For example, your dog heads for the kitchen trash can and you spray him with a squirt bottle full of water. He flinches and runs away from the trash. Later that day, he heads for the trash can again and looks at you … only to see you don't have a squirt bottle handy. So he rummages in the trash while you run around trying to remember where you left the bottle. You didn't teach him to leave the trash can alone. You taught him to avoid the squirt bottle.

You will often hear modern trainers talk about the "fallout" of punishment-based methods. They are referring to the baggage that comes along with using physical force to train. For example, if you "pop" or spank your dog, you are teaching him that hands are unpredictable. Sometimes they pet affectionately and sometimes they punish. So the next time you go to brush him, he may cower or avoid you. Or, the next time you call him to come to you, he may run the other way. You didn't mean to teach him this, but you did when you used your hands for punishment. It's the fallout that occurred because of the physical punishment.

Another challenge with using physical punishment to train is that it doesn't teach your dog what you *want* him to do instead. It's like using "No!" It indicates you don't want your dog to do something, but it doesn't tell your dog what you do want him to do. Would you rather your dog sit politely to be petted by guests, instead of jumping all over them in exuberant greeting? Great! Teach your dog to sit automatically for petting. You'll be teaching him appropriate behavior, rather than just punishing him for behavior you don't like. It's better communication.

*This dog has been trained to sit for petting.*

Training Philosophy and Methods     29

*Vets recommend positive training methods.*

## What the Experts Say

Positive training is backed by respected organizations in the field. The International Association of Animal Behavior Consultants (IAABC) "supports a Least Intrusive, Minimally Aversive (LIMA) approach to behavior modification and training. ... LIMA requires that trainers and behavior consultants use the least intrusive, minimally aversive technique likely to succeed in achieving a training [or behavior change] objective with minimal risk of producing adverse side effects."

The statement continues: "Positive reinforcement should be the first line of teaching, training and behavior change program considered, and should be applied consistently. Positive reinforcement is associated with the lowest incidence of aggression, attention-seeking, and avoidance/fear in learners. ... We seek to prevent the abuses and potential repercussions of unnecessary, inappropriate, poorly applied or inhumane uses of punishment. The potential effects of punishment can include aggression or counter-aggression; suppressed behavior (preventing the consultant/trainer from adequately reading the animal); increased anxiety and fear; physical harm; a negative association with the owner or handlers; and increased unwanted behavior, or new unwanted behaviors." (For the complete statement, see http://iaabc.org/about/LIMA.)

Veterinarians also recommend positive training. According to the American Veterinary Society of Animal Behavior (ASVAB), "AVSAB's position is that punishment (e.g. choke chains, pinch collars, and electronic collars) should not be used as a first-line or early-use treatment for behavior problems. This is due to the potential adverse effects which include but are not limited to: inhibition of learning, increased fear-related and aggressive behaviors, and injury to animals and people interacting with animals. AVSAB recommends that training should focus on reinforcing desired behaviors, removing the reinforcer for inappropriate behaviors, and addressing the emotional state and environmental conditions driving the undesirable behavior. This approach promotes a better understanding of the pet's behavior and better awareness of how humans may have inadvertently contributed to the development of the undesirable behavior." (For the complete statement, see http://avsabonline.org/uploads/position_statements/Punishment_Position_Statement-download_-_10-6-14.pdf.)

Luckily, as science has revealed more about canine behavior and training has evolved, we've moved away from pushing, shoving, kneeing dogs, and cutting off their air supplies in attempts to educate them. This is good news for both people and our canine friends.

## Rewards, Bribes, and Lures

It's important to note that positive training has a foundation of rewarding dogs for desired behavior, not bribing them. If you use a treat to lure your dog into his crate—that's a bribe. Continuing like this will soon make the relationship between you and your dog dependent on always having a treat in your hand,

and that's not good! Instead, you should teach your dog to go into his crate, after which he gets a treat. This is a reward—the difference between a paycheck and a bribe.

For some training exercises, though, it does help to use a treat in your hand to lure the dog into performing. For example, when teaching a dog to sit, hold a treat in your hand close to the dog's nose, slowly move it above his head between his eyes, and then backward toward his rear.

Using a treat in this manner is called a lure. It helps establish some behaviors faster. In order to avoid dependence on the lure, however, you "fade" it. You get the dog performing the behavior several times, and

Getting your dog to like his crate is easy with positive training.

then try it again without a treat in your hand. You use the same hand motion as before. If done in quick succession, most dogs will still perform the behavior. You are not fooling your dog into thinking you have a treat in your hand. Dogs can smell there is no treat. They are now responding to the corresponding hand signal you have taught them, rather than just following the treat. You would still give the dog a treat after he performed the behavior   his paycheck—but you have faded the use of the treat as a lure.

Control how and when you use treats so your dog does not come to always expect them.

## Keeping Control

Being a positive trainer does not mean that you let your dog do whatever he wants, whenever he wants. It's true that for some behaviors, it's best to ignore them in order to get rid of them. Remember, the laws of learning state that behavior that is rewarded increases in frequency. So if it's not rewarded, it should go away. The only way this will work is if there is absolutely no reward in it for the dog. If your dog barks at the neighbors and you try to ignore it, your dog is still likely getting paid. Barking is fun! There is still a paycheck in it for the dog, so the behavior will increase in frequency.

## Why Trainers Are Up with the Chickens

All over the world, modern dog trainers are paying to attend workshops–to train chickens. Why on earth would they do this, and what does training a chicken have to do with training a dog?

While dogs love us, chickens are not as enamored. Your dog is very forgiving at your attempts to communicate with him. Because of this, it's easier to train a dog. It's much more challenging to train a chicken. Chickens just aren't as invested in making you happy.

Your timing has to be excellent to train a chicken, including your speed of delivering reinforcement. If you tell your dog you're going to give him a treat, he will generally get all excited. If you fumble around with the treat bag and take a while to get him the treat, he'll wait. Chickens are not as patient–they'll just fly away! You also can't use harsh training methods with a chicken. If you do, you might kill it. Chickens can die of fright.

Training chickens improves a trainer's skills. If you can train a chicken to navigate a small agility course or differentiate between colors, training dogs is much easier in comparison!

Positive training is used with all different species. From marmosets in zoos to sharks in aquariums to your beloved family dog, all different types of animals can learn using positive training.

*Although it's natural for a dog to bark, excessive uncontrollable barking is undesirable.*

There are also some behaviors that you just can't ignore. When a puppy mouths you with his needle teeth or a dog jumps up and might cause a fall or injury, ignoring him isn't always an option. What about a dog who barks incessantly in an apartment building? Or a dog who growls over his food? You shouldn't ignore these behaviors. It's just not practical. It's also a myth that if you want to use positive training methods, ignoring undesired behavior is your only choice. Instead of ignoring your dog or getting mad at him, you teach him what you want him to do instead.

Set consistent rules in your house. Have boundaries for canine behavior you will and won't accept. You absolutely can do these things and still use positive methods. You can be positive without being a pushover!

Positive training methods are non-confrontational and do not require physical harshness. This often makes them actually better to use with dogs who have serious problem behaviors, such as aggression. They are safer. Can you imagine getting into a battle with a Great Dane over a food bowl? Sure, you might win if you are strong enough, but you are also likely to get bitten pretty severely. And if your Great Dane weighs more than you do, it's not going to look good for you in a match. The best part about the training methods in this book is you don't have to fight with your dog in order to win. You can teach him to do what you want without ever getting into a battle at all.

Positive training has a lot of benefits. It teaches you how to better communicate with your dog so he will better understand you. It teaches your dog what you want him to do. It will also enhance the relationship you have with your dog. After all, you brought that little cute pup home in order to be a part of your family. You want him to love you, not be afraid of you.

## Using Reinforcement

To successfully train your dog and fix problem behaviors, you need to learn what is rewarding to your dog. What motivates your dog? What does he like? Find out. Once your dog learns you are in charge of all the things he likes, he is much more likely to pay attention and listen to you.

This can be a fairly humbling realization. Ever take your dog on a walk and he stops dead in his tracks, fascinated with a clump of dirt and completely ignoring your requests to continue? At that moment, the clump of dirt has a greater value than your attention. Ouch! That's normal, though. Dogs can easily be distracted, and since many of their senses are more acute than ours, they have a lot more distractions to deal with than we do.

Review these different types of reinforcement and rank them for your dog. What does he like best? What does he like least? When training your dog, use a variety of reinforcements your dog likes so you don't become predictable. You can also mix reinforcements during a training session. For example, you may use treats as you're building a new behavior, but for the very last repetition in your training session, you might reward your dog by letting him play with his favorite toy or enjoy a game with you.

## Food as Reinforcement

Food is often the fastest way to your dog's brain. For training purposes, you should have a variety of treats on hand. They should be small and thus easy for your dog to swallow quickly. In general, the more scent a treat has, the more rewarding it is to your dog. Crunchy kibble, for example, example, doesn't smell as enticing as a soft liver treat.

Try to choose healthy treats for training. Choose ones with natural ingredients and avoid ones that have added sugars and dyes. Try small pieces of grilled or baked chicken, string cheese, or hot dogs.

When training with few distractions, you may be able to use your dog's regular food as reward. For example, if you are working in your living room on a simple behavior, your dog's regular food might be a good enough paycheck to ensure he repeats the behavior more frequently. If you are working in an environment with more distractions, however, his regular food may not be good enough. For example, your dog is bad about jumping on guests, so you are training him to settle on his bed when the doorbell rings. For the early part of this training, when you teach your dog to settle on his bed, his regular food may work fine as a reward. Once you add door knocking, the doorbell, and actual guests entering the home, however, that may not be rewarding enough. Your dog may get more out of greeting your guests than by going to his bed. So, for this phase of training, you will need higher value treats.

When training your dog, especially when working on problem behaviors, you will find you go through a lot of treats. You may have to adjust your dog's food intake accordingly, so he doesn't put on too much weight. If your dog will work for his regular food, incorporate a portion of his regular meals into his training portion for each day. For example, if your dog gets two cups of food a day, you could use up to two cups of his food as part of his training rewards; just stop feeding him out of a bowl. Instead, he will be eating his meals while he learns new behaviors. He may still get extra treats, but it won't be as much as extra treats plus two cups of regular food.

## Treats, Praise, and Physical Attention

If your dog eats kibble, and you don't think it will be rewarding enough, measure out a portion of his meal and bag it with some enticing treats. Let it marinate for a few hours or, better, overnight. The treats will impart scent and flavor to his regular kibble, making it more desirable.

Praise can be a great reward. Just make sure you have a realistic gauge of how much it impacts on your dog. It's humbling to realize that if your dog was given a choice between a piece of grilled chicken or a "Good boy!" he would choose the chicken first. Please don't let your feelings be hurt by this because it's completely natural.

Praise can often be an added reward to a dog, on top of another one. When you do use praise, mean it! Make a big deal of it. If your dog is not happily wagging his tail in response, your praise may not be rewarding enough.

If your dog does enjoy physical affection, it can be a great reinforcement. Find your dog's favorite spots for petting! Some dogs melt into a happy puddle when you pet them. Others are not big fans of petting. Some dogs have special spots on their bodies where they enjoy being petted, such as behind an ear, on the chest, on their bellies, or right above their tails. It depends on the dog. This, too, is normal.

Don't assume that your dog loves being petted. How can you tell? Watch his body language. Does he lean into you or away? Does he avert his eyes and look worried? Does he struggle to escape a hug? Many dogs don't really like hugs. They also don't always like being petted on the top of the head. It's a personal preference, just like some people aren't really huggers.

Keep in mind that some dogs love exuberant physical affection, but others do not. For example, some dogs may enjoy when you thump them on their sides, but the same action could cause another dog to be afraid of you. One dog loves it, the other one thinks you are being too rough. Adjust your actions based on the dog's perception of what is rewarding.

This is especially critical if working with a shy or fearful dog. If this is a new dog to you, such as one you recently adopted, he may not find physical attention reinforcing. As the human with a big heart who brought this dog home, your inclination may be to cuddle him and pet him to comfort him when he is afraid. But if he is not bonded to you or is afraid of you, your touch is not a comfort to him. It is punishment, and it can make him more fearful. The same goes for your friends. Perhaps your dog loves

*Petting your dog can help you build a bond with him.*

you and enjoys being petted by you, but is fearful of others who come to the house. Asking them to pet your dog will not cure him of his fear. It's like allowing monsters to come grab your dog. It's just not reinforcing.

## Toys and Games

Does your dog go bonkers for a tennis ball? Do his eyes light up when you bring out his favorite tug toy? If you have a dog who enjoys toys and games, they can be strong motivators. Using toys and games as reinforcement can be a good idea depending on what behavior you are trying to solve. Just keep in mind that playing with a toy takes longer than eating a treat, so it will impact on the length of your training session. If you are working to build behavior by rapidly repeating it, toys and games also may not be ideal options.

You also wouldn't want to use toys if the problem you are trying to solve is that your dog growls over his toys! But sometimes a rousing game of fetch or a quick game of tug can be more satisfying to a dog than just a cookie.

Here are some other games your dog may enjoy. Be sure to choose ones that won't make your dog's problem behaviors worse. For example, if your dog is chasing your children and nipping at their heels, don't choose to play chase games. Or, if your dog is overly mouthy, don't roughhouse with your dog. You don't want to accidentally teach him to carry on with his problem behavior. Your goal is to find an appealing reinforcement for your dog, not to give him mixed signals.

Playing fetch can be a rewarding part of training for dogs who enjoy this game.

## Chase Games

Rather than chasing your dog, encourage your dog to chase you. You want your dog to learn to run toward you and not away from you. You can also use a flirt pole—a long stick with a cord at one end, at the end of which is a toy. You flick the pole so the toy bounces around for your dog to chase. (A flirt pole looks very similar to a fishing pole toy for cats.)

Getting your dog to chase you is a great game for both of you to enjoy.

## Wrestle Games

Some dogs adore a good wrestle! Be sure your dog is gentle and doesn't bite down hard on you. Also make sure your dog enjoys the game as much as you do, or it won't be a reward. Also be careful with some dogs who get too riled up if you wrestle with them.

## Playtime with Other Dogs

If your dog loves playing with other dogs and plays with them appropriately, this can be a powerful reward. Proper play between dogs is give and take by both parties. One dog may chase for a while, and then the other will chase. One will be on top of the other for a while, and then they will switch. Dogs who are very good at playing with other dogs will also initiate time outs. This interrupts play before it gets too intense. They may stop and sniff something or momentarily disengage to go visit you. For a dog to be a good play buddy with your dog, he should also have a similar play style. Some dogs love to chase, while others like to wrestle. Some dogs like to "jaw spar," in which they clash their muzzles together in a fierce display that results in a lot of slobber exchange, but no injury at all. If two dogs have dissimilar play styles, it can cause conflict and even a fight. For example, a dog who likes to wrestle and body slam other dogs may become alarmed when another dog starts to chase him. He could snap at what he perceives to be inappropriate behavior.

Not every dog loves playing with all other dogs. This is normal. We don't want to go to parties with every person we meet. If you want to use dog-dog playtime as a reward, make sure all the dogs involved are having a good time.

Sniffing at each other like this is all part of natural dog play.

## Life Rewards

These are rewards your dog finds enjoyable just from living with you and being a dog. Letting him sniff the base of a tree, taking him for a car ride, letting him run off leash in a safe place … all these can be extremely satisfying to your dog. Just as with toys and games, life rewards don't make for speedy training. Used judiciously, however, they can be effective additions to your training sessions.

## Body Language Overview

When you are working on fixing behavior problems, it is extremely important that you pay attention to your dog's body language. Dogs communicate extensively through their ears, eyes, mouth, tail, and body position. Your dog will tell you what he is feeling, but you have to learn how to understand him. If you misread his communication, you could actually be making a problem worse.

*These dogs are really enjoying playing a game of tug, but take care not to let it get out of control.*

For example, Darcy just started dating a new guy, Blake. Blake is 6' 5" tall and is losing his hair, so often wears a baseball cap. Darcy invites Blake over to her apartment to meet her Beagle mix, Lily. Lily takes one look at Blake and growls. He leans over her, trying to make friends. Lily won't look straight at him, but turns her head away, eyes wide. She has a tight, closed mouth. Blake reaches to reassure her and

Lily snaps at him. Darcy is mortified. Lily is not being rude. She's not jealous of Darcy's new man and trying to sabotage their fledgling relationship. She is exhibiting signs of stress and fear. Darcy could make this problem worse by yelling at Lily. Will yelling help a fearful dog? Not at all.

When reading a dog's body language, look at the overall context. You need to put together different parts of the puzzle in order to get the entire picture. For example, a dog who is growling but backing away from you is afraid. His growl tells you he's upset about something. His desire to get farther from you tells you that he's afraid of you (or something you are holding).

When a dog licks his lips it can be a sign of stress. If your dog is licking his lips while staring at the bacon cheeseburger you're eating, though, he's probably just hungry! Look for clusters of signals—if a dog yawns, looks away, and cowers, then he is stressed. If he just looks away, it doesn't mean he is necessarily stressed. So when you see signs of anxiety or stress in your dog, look at what's going on around him and how it might be impacting his reaction.

*If a dog lowers his body like this, it is usually a sign that he is trying to make friends with you.*

Dog communication also can be very fluid. A dog can lower himself in friendly greeting when you enter the house but, a second later, be standing upright with hackles raised when someone he doesn't know follows you through the door. Your dog's dialog will change based on who he is interacting with, his surroundings, and what he is experiencing at the time. For example, your dog could be all wiggly greetings at the veterinary clinic for most visits, but all stiff and menacing when taken to have a broken leg treated. Dogs who are raised primarily by women may have curved body positions and lowered ears, with low wagging tails, when approached by other women. But when a man tries to pet them, they may lean backward, turn away, and start licking their lips, indicating nervousness.

Once you learn about a dog's body language, you may be surprised to find that your dog has been talking to you all along! It will open up a whole new way for you to understand him.

## Eyes and Ears

It is said that the eyes are the windows to the soul, and it's certainly true that dogs convey a lot of emotion with their eyes. Some people get concerned when their dog stares into their eyes, but it's usually not a problem. A soft, squinty look is one of happiness and often affection. A hard, direct stare, with little to no blinking, is a sign that a dog is highly aroused or fearful. He could be ready to attack. When a dog's pupils are dilated, it's a sign of high arousal (excitement) or fear. For example, when a dog first enters a veterinary clinic, his pupils may be extremely dilated.

If a dog turns his head away from something but keeps his eyes on the object, you will see mostly the whites of his eyes. This is called "whale eye" and is another sign of fear and stress.

When trying to assess what your dog is feeling, be careful about monitoring the eyes, especially if you are dealing with fear or aggression issues. You certainly don't want to get in his face to get a better look—

*Ears pricked forward usually signal the dog's interest in something.*

that's too close to his teeth! Dogs with dark faces can often be harder to read when it comes to the eyes, but with practice you should be able to better assess what those windows to the soul are telling you.

If a dog's ears are laid back and flat against his head, this can be a sign of fear and stress. Your dog may also lay his ears back when he greets you affectionately, so it's not always a sign of stress. Look at the overall context.

If ears are forward, it's a sign of interest. Your dog will prick his ears up when he hears something that interests him.

Of course, with the shape of some dogs' ears, they can't move them as much as others. Many spaniels have long ears that can't move forward much and already lay flat against their heads. The ears do still move, though, so you may be able to observe subtle movements.

## The Mouth and Panting

The mouth is the scary part! That's where the teeth are, and if you are dealing with aggression then you are probably very wary around it. Your dog's mouth can tell you a lot about what he is feeling. If a dog has a relaxed, open mouth, he is at ease. A tense, closed mouth is a sign of stress.

Panting can mean several things. Of course, a dog will pant if he has been exercising. Panting can also mean a dog is in pain or overheating. Sometimes it can mean stress. If a dog is panting but suddenly stops, this can indicate interest, an escalation of excitement, or sometimes pain. For example, your dog is in the backyard with you while you have several guests over for a barbeque. He's panting. As a small child toddles over, reaching to touch him, your dog stops panting and closes his mouth tightly. This means your dog is getting concerned about the toddler's approach. This would be a good point to intervene.

When a dog's lips move forward over his teeth so they look puffy, it is a warning to stay away. The lips can also curl up in a snarl, retracting to expose his teeth. This is another warning.

There is another kind of lip retraction that can be startling if you've never seen one. It's called a *submissive grin*. It can be mistaken for a snarl, but it's not a warning to stay away, it's a sign of happy excitement. In a submissive grin, the dog's lips pull up vertically to expose the front teeth. It's almost always accompanied by submissive body posture—curved body, low wagging tail, frequent look-aways, and squinty eyes. A submissive grin is a sign of happy greeting.

Yawning can be a sign of stress in dogs as well. You might see dogs yawning in the veterinarian's office. They're not suddenly sleepy, they're stressed.

# Mind Your Dog's Body Language: Canine Signals and Children

You may be surprised to learn all the nuances of canine body language described in this section. What you thought was just a yawn or your dog licking his lips may turn out to be signs of stress. There are probably several signals, though, you instantly recognized.

For example, when a dog lifts his lip in a snarl, most adults recognize it for what it is—a warning to stay away. Children are not as good at reading dog signals. A dog may start with lifting his lip, then go to a full snarl, and then start to growl to warn a small child to stay away. Meanwhile, the child continues interacting with the dog, oblivious to the escalating warnings. When this happens, a dog may feel the need to escalate his communication even further. This could result in the dog biting the child.

To the dog, it's not personal. He told the child to back off and the child didn't, so he bit him to show he was serious. To us, it's very personal! And extremely dangerous.

Children and dogs should never be left unsupervised together. When kids and dogs are together, watch them carefully and pay attention to their interactions. Dogs are dogs. Even the kindest, sweetest dog could be put in a situation where he reacts negatively. This can especially occur when dogs get older. As they age, they can become less tolerant of being poked and prodded by little fingers. For example, a dog who might have enjoyed hugs when he was younger may not appreciate a child hugging him as he develops arthritis in his golden years. You might notice him wince or look away when you approach his sore spots, indicating something is wrong, but a child is not likely to pick up on the dog's signals. Read the signals for your child to keep everyone safe. And as your children grow older, teach them how to understand what dogs are telling them, too!

## Tail Language

A dog's tail can indicate many things. If it's tucked under him, he's afraid. If it's straight up, held high, he is excited.

A wagging tail is not necessarily a sign of a friendly dog. A dog who is holding his tail high, wagging it back and forth rapidly, is highly aroused and excited. He could be getting agitated and deciding on his next actions. This means that a dog could be wagging his tail while he bites you.

If the tail is low, and wagging back and forth rapidly, he could be stressed and trying to appease. For example, you sometimes see a puppy hold his tail very low, wagging rapidly, when examined by a veterinarian. The nervous puppy is trying to appease the veterinarian, "Please don't hurt me!"

Generally, if the tail is held mid-level or low and swishing back and forth, a dog is relaxed and happy.

Some dogs will not be able to hold their tails in all positions. Some have tightly curled tails, and some dogs have no tails or docked tails. Even a stubby tail can be a good indicator of a dog's interest or intent. Look at the base of the tail for signs. Notice the difference when your dog is at rest or when he is alert. When your dog is relaxed, the base of the tail will be set mid-level or low. When he is alert, you'll see the base stand straight up.

*When a dog wags his tail like this, he is usually relaxed and happy.*

## Body Position

A dog's body position can tell you a lot about what he's feeling. If he leans or moves toward you, he wants to close the distance between you and engage. This may be a good or a bad thing! If a dog leans or moves away, he's trying to increase the distance between you. He could be nervous or afraid. If a dog goes back and forth, shifting his weight forward and backward, he could be conflicted. For example, you pull out the vacuum cleaner, and your dog backs away from it. You encourage him to examine it, and he moves closer, then away again, then closer still, then away. Your dog wants to examine the vacuum cleaner, but he is stressed about it. He's conflicted.

When a dog has a curved body position, it indicates appeasement or friendliness. You may notice this when your dog greets you after you've been at work all day. Friendly dogs will greet people with curved bodies. They often curve one way and then the other. Some dogs are so good at this they seem to wag with their entire bodies. Alternately, a dog who has a straight body posture, with no curve, is more assertive. You can see this sometimes when dogs greet each other. For example, a puppy may approach an older dog all curvy and low, while the older dog stands straight and stiff. The older dog is on alert while the puppy is trying to appease him.

Lifting a paw can indicate appeasement, or it can be an invitation to play. You may see a dog paw at another dog's face or front paws. This is a friendly gesture. Some dogs use their paws more than others. Boxers, for example, are aptly named!

When a dog lowers his front end with his rear remaining upright, it's called a *play bow*. It's an invitation to play. This dog is lowering his teeth and making himself look smaller and less threatening. Dogs who are very good at playing with other dogs will often play bow to entice more hesitant dogs to engage. You may also see it in older, larger dogs when they are trying to be less intimidating to younger, smaller puppies.

A dog who does the opposite, who makes himself as tall as possible, with a high neck and standing on his tiptoes, is trying to appear bigger. He is not trying to make friends but to display that he might be a threat.

A dog who has a stiff body position but lowers his head is also in assertive mode. His body weight will be forward, with intent to threaten. He may look as though he has "locked and loaded" on a target. He may or may not bite.

If you see the fur rising up along a dog's hackles, this is a sign of arousal. The technical term for it is *piloerection*. Although it can indicate aggression, it doesn't always do so. For example, an adolescent dog may be over-the-top excited to greet another dog, and his hackles will rise. This dog is just really excited.

When a dog rolls over to expose his belly, it can be a sign of appeasement. It can also be a request for a belly rub!

## Mind Your Body Language: People Aren't Dogs

Understanding that dogs communicate better through body language, can you communicate with them with your body as well? You already do. Your dog is very good at reading you. He can tell when you are about to leave the house, when you don't feel well, or when you are angry. It's in a dog's best interests to understand you, so dogs have become pretty good at reading our body language (and vocalization tones). While you can accurately mimic some dog language, your dog is also very aware that you are not a dog. You can't possibly convey the same intention with every behavior.

For example, when a dog lowers his front end but keeps his rear in the air, it's called a play bow. If you do this with some dogs, they will get very excited and approach you. They recognize it as a signal for play. Some dogs, however, may look at you like you are nuts.

If you live with a shy, nervous dog, and you stare at him directly, you will unsettle him. But if you turn your head away from him frequently, and approach him at a curve instead of directly on, you may soothe him. This is how dogs with good communication skills approach strange dogs, to ease the introduction and demonstrate that they are not a threat. So, mimicking these types of behaviors can sometimes be helpful.

Other behaviors just can't be reproduced accurately. For example, there is still advice floating around that if your dog nips you, you should growl at him and even bite him back! These techniques will not work the way you intend them to and can backfire and cause aggression. It will not help you communicate to your dog that he is doing something wrong. It's a great way to get bitten yourself. It's not that the dog is fighting your leadership. You are just not communicating the same way a dog would. You may think you are going for an acting award with your dog impression, but your dog is fully aware that you are not the same species.

You are also not a wolf, nor is your dog. So flipping a dog over, upside down, into an "alpha roll" is not effective. It can cause your dog to struggle and even pee on himself, a sign of terror. If you watch dog play, you'll see that they take turns being upside down voluntarily. They also don't use their front paws to flip each other. When you use your arms and hands to force a dog into position, this is not mimicking wolf or canine behavior, and they know it. It's just not effective communication, and it can make problem behavior much worse.

*Confronting a dog like this is never a good idea.*

## Vocalizations

Some dogs are very vocal. This especially can be the case with herding breeds, bred to use their voices to help move livestock. Whining can indicate excitement or worry. For example, some dogs will whine in the car because they're excited to go for a ride, whereas some will whine in stress when you pick them up and put them in the bathtub.

Barking can mean many things. It can be a sign of excitement or alarm. It can be a greeting, as with the dog who barks when you come home. It can also be an attempt to make something the dog perceives as scary go away.

Howling is another canine vocal communication. Dogs howl to announce their presence, to make contact with others, and sometimes to attract attention. Some dogs only howl when they hear sirens, certain musical instruments, or specific songs.

# Making Adjustments in Your Training

When employed correctly, positive training methods work with all dogs. There are some things in the program you may need to adjust with certain types of dogs.

## Adjustments for Puppies

Puppies have no attention spans! Keep your training sessions very short. Also understand that up until about 16 weeks, puppies are in a critical socialization period. The experiences they have during this time can impact them for life. It's very important that they have positive experiences with a variety of people, environments, other dogs, sounds, and especially your training sessions during this critical period.

Keep puppy training sessions short and simple; otherwise, your puppy will lose concentration.

The good news about puppies is that you are catching problems early. Waiting until a puppy reaches adulthood, having all that time to practice his problem behavior, will make the behavior harder to fix.

## Adjustments for Seniors

Senior dogs have greater attention spans than young puppies, but they also have had longer to build up bad habits. If you've been dealing with a problem behavior for years and now want to fix it, or if you've adopted a senior dog with a long-established problem behavior, you will have your work cut out for you. Habits are challenging for any species to break. Have you ever tried to quit smoking? Stop biting your fingernails? Quit eating fast food? Working with a long-ingrained problem behavior in a senior dog will require consistency and patience.

You may also need to adjust your expectations based on a senior dog's physical condition. As dogs age, they can develop arthritis and other conditions that can impact their ability to perform behaviors. Seniors also lose their hearing, so they may not hear your cues as well. You may have to adjust your training to rely on hand signals if your dog is going deaf.

Older dogs may need to pee and poo more frequently. If your senior dog suddenly starts urinating in the house, it may be because he just can't hold his bladder as long as he used to.

Depending on health issues, senior dogs may also have diet restrictions. This may affect the types of treats you use in training.

As dogs get into their golden years, they can also grow more anxious about things that didn't used to bother them. For example, you've been leaving for work for 10 years at the same time, but as your dog gets older you've noticed he starts to whimper when you go and seems more agitated. He doesn't seem to want to be left alone. Older dogs can also be less tolerant of handling. Tackling a mat of tangled fur on a fluffy

## Puppy Options: When Will My Puppy Grow Up?

In general, the size of the dog will determine how long he stays in puppyhood. Toy breeds are considered adult dogs at about 1 year of age. Medium- to large-sized breeds, such as Golden Retrievers or Boxers, are not adults until about 2 ½ years old. Giant breeds, such as Great Pyrenees or Newfoundlands, are considered adults at about 3 years old.

*Senior dogs can have physical problems to contend with as well as bad habits that have become ingrained over the years.*

older dog may result in a growl or a snap. Or when you try to trim his nails, he pulls his paws away. If he has physical issues that cause him pain, having you tug on a mat or hold a paw may be painful to him.

If you have concerns about your older dog's ability to participate in a training program, consult your veterinarian. A quality, reward-based trainer will also work with you and your veterinarian to design a behavior modification program that accommodates your older dog's physical capabilities while dealing with his problem behaviors. It's another great benefit to using positive training methods—they can be very effective and gentle on an older dog's body!

## Adjustments for Small Dogs

Small dogs can learn just as well as their larger counterparts. But keep in mind that they have smaller stomachs, so training sessions with food should be brief. Just because your little guy wants to train longer and acts like he's starving doesn't mean that he won't have an upset stomach if you stuff him too full. Some dogs are better at regulating their appetites than others. While some dogs will refuse treats when they are no longer hungry, other dogs would happily demolish an entire bag of them even when their stomachs are full.

## Senior Dog Options: When Is My Dog a Senior Citizen?

Most dogs enter senior status between 7 to 10 years. Larger dogs do not have as long a lifespan as smaller dogs, so a 7-year-old Toy Poodle will not be considered as geriatric as a 7-year-old Saint Bernard. For example, the average lifespan of a toy breed dog, such as a Papillon or Yorkshire Terrier, is 12–15 years. The average lifespan of a medium- to large breed dog, such as a Labrador Retriever or Australian Shepherd, is 10–13 years. The average lifespan of a giant breed, such as a St. Bernard or Great Dane, is 8–10 years. The American Animal Hospital Association (AAHA) applies senior guidelines to dogs who are in the last 25 percent of the predicted lifespan for their breed.

You should also realize that behaviors that may seem cute in a small dog can still be problem behaviors. If your toy-breed dog displays aggression, it's not adorable. It's a problem. Even small dogs have teeth and can bite. So if your small dog growls over food or toys, or if he growls when you're holding him and someone approaches you, this should be addressed. It will not solve itself on its own, and in fact, it could get worse.

Other dogs may also not care how small your dog is, if he is aggressive toward other dogs. If your dog barks, lunges, and growls at other dogs, even dogs twice his size, other dogs may not find it amusing. A dog could answer the challenge, and, due to your dog's small size, it could lead to a tragic outcome.

Working with a small dog can also involve some extra coordination on your part. For example, when you want to give your dog a treat as a reward for a desired behavior, you'll have farther to bend, especially if you're tall. You still need to deliver the treat when your dog has four paws on the ground. Otherwise, if you allow him to jump up to meet you, you will also be rewarding him for jumping.

You might consider using a cooking spoon or spatula to feed peanut butter or cream cheese to your dog—it will provide you extra reach so you don't have to strain your back by continual bending. There are also tubes of paste treats sold commercially that can be very handy for treat dispensing. They look similar to toothpaste tubes and are used to stuff rubber chew toys. They come in a variety of flavors, including peanut butter and yogurt. Or purchase your own tube and fill it with baby food or pureed wet dog food. There is also a treat dispenser that has a ball end that your dog can lick to get a taste of liquid treat. This is similar to a water bottle for rabbits or other small animals—they lick the ball at the end of the water bottle to get the liquid. To find these and other ways to extend your reach for treat delivery, check your local or online pet supply stores.

## Training Tools

To build behavior, you need the right tools. Here are the recommended positive tools for fixing problem behaviors.

### Collar

A flat quick-snap or buckle collar. You should just be able to get two fingers, laid flat, between the collar and your dog's neck.

### Harness

Front-clip harness. Attaching the leash to the front of the harness, on the dog's chest, gives you greater control over the dog's forward motion. If you have a dog who pulls while on walks, lunges or jumps, a front-clip harness is an excellent, humane management tool. Harnesses are also recommended for brachiocephalic (flat-faced) dogs that have difficulty breathing,

*A small dog may look cute, but this doesn't mean he is incapable of behaving badly.*

*A dog wearing a front-clip harness like this is easier to control if he lunges and jumps unexpectedly.*

especially when excited, upset, or hot. Using a harness helps prevent added pressure on the dog's neck and airway.

When you purchase a front-clip harness, check that it fits properly. A common error in fit is tightening the front chest strap too tight, so that the strap that goes around the dog's torso pushes forward against the back of his front legs. This could chafe behind your dog's legs. Most dogs take little time to acclimatize to a front-clip harness, so if your dog balks and pulls backward when you try to walk him in it, it may just not be fitted properly.

## Head Halter

If you need greater control, consider a head halter. A head halter offers you a management solution that does not put pressure on a dog's trachea, unlike a choke chain or a prong collar.

As with the front-clip harness, make sure that the head halter is fitted properly. Get a knowledgeable sales associate or professional dog trainer to help you if needed.

## Muzzle

If your dog gets easily scared or turns aggressive, having him wear a muzzle can help keep people safe while you work to resolve his problem. Choose a secure, basket-type muzzle that will still allow your dog to drink water and take treats. Avoid nylon or other restrictive muzzles. These can interfere with breathing and will make it hard to feed your dog treats during training.

You will need to teach your dog to get used to wearing a muzzle. If you don't desensitize your dog to the muzzle and just put it on him, he may be frightened and react badly. It may then be harder to get him acclimated to it afterward. Introduced properly, dogs can learn to love wearing their muzzles just as much as they do a collar or harness. (See the Muzzle Training section.)

## Leash

A 4- or 5-foot cotton, nylon, or leather leash. Do not use retractable leashes. Even if you lock them it's hard to manage your dog, and if you drop one it will "chase" your dog and could frighten him. As for thickness, you want a leash that is sturdy enough to manage your dog but still feels comfortable in your hand. Note that if you are working with a very small dog, choose a leash that has a small clasp. Some leashes are thin but still have regular clasps that can hang heavy on a tiny dog's neck.

## Crate

The problem you are working on with your dog will determine the size crate you need. If you are working on housetraining, the crate should just be big enough for your dog to stand up, stretch out and lie down. (Note that this will not work if your dog is a crate soiler, which is common for puppies born and raised in puppy mills. You should still get a crate to teach this dog confinement, but you cannot use it for

## Getting Used to a Head Halter

The head halter has a nose loop that can be annoying to some dogs. It is better that you take the time to get your dog used to the head halter before you start using it regularly in your training. Here's how:

1. Hold the head halter up at your dog's nose level, with the nose loop open. Offer your dog a treat through the nose loop so that he has to put his nose through the loop to get the treat. Do this for several days.

2. When your dog is eagerly putting his nose through the loop, you are ready to move on. Hold the head halter up and offer your dog a treat through the loop, as before. Quickly clasp the head halter closed for a few seconds. Give him several treats rapidly in succession. Remove the head halter. Repeat this for several days.

3. Gradually increase the amount of time your dog wears the head halter. Also, before feeding him all his meals, put on the head halter, feed him his meal, then remove the halter. This will help him eagerly anticipate wearing his head halter.

housetraining.) For all other dogs, get a crate appropriate for their size, with room to spare. If you have a small puppy who will grow up to be a large dog, consider choosing a crate that comes with a divider, so you can gradually increase the amount of space in the crate as the puppy grows.

You don't just purchase a crate and put your dog in it, assuming he will be comfortable in there. You need to teach him to love his crate. You can use the "Settle" exercise (see the Foundation Behavior section) to teach your dog to be comfortable with confinement. Don't use the crate for punishment. The goal is

A leash should be sturdy enough to help you to manage your dog while still feeling comfortable.

to gradually get him used to longer and longer periods of confinement while pairing it with something reinforcing. Crates can be wonderful tools as long as they are used correctly. They should be used for management and safety, not as a crutch to avoid dealing with a problem behavior.

## Baby Gates

Use to contain your dog in a confined area. These are good for transitioning a dog from a crate to a larger area. They are also good to contain your dog safely behind a barrier if your dog is fearful or aggressive toward other dogs or people.

There are a variety of baby gates to choose from. Some have easy-open doors so you don't have to step over them. If you are dealing with aggression and are using the baby gates for safety, you might want to choose a model that mounts to the wall for extra security.

## Clicker

Used as a marker to indicate to your dog that he has performed a desired behavior. A click is a promise that a treat is coming. Before he realizes this, however, you have to teach him to associate the click with a pending treat.

To introduce your dog to the clicker, have 10 treats. Do not ask your dog to sit or give him any cues. Your goal is just to teach him to listen to the click sound. Click, immediately feed your dog a treat. Wait a few seconds, then repeat until the treats are finished. Practice the exercise a couple times a day for a few days. Your dog will start pricking his ears at the sound of the click and getting excited. This means he is starting to associate the click with the treat.

Do not point the clicker at your dog. Keep your treat hand still until after the click so it doesn't distract your dog from the sound of the clicker. A click is a promise—it should always be followed by a treat.

If you think your dog will be afraid of the click sound, then start with something that will make a softer click at first, such as a ballpoint pen. Just click the pen once, then follow it by a treat. When your dog starts to associate the soft click with a treat, you can work up to a louder clicker. You can also muffle the clicker in a towel so it's not as loud at first. It helps to have your dog get used to the louder clicker simply because the sound will carry farther when you are in a noisier training environment.

*Always reward your dog with a treat after you click.*

*A qualified dog training professional can help you and your dog deal with problem behavior.*

# When to Call in a Professional

It is much better to call in a professional when a problem first starts, rather than wait for it to get worse. The sooner you get help, the more likely it is that the problem can be tackled successfully. How do you know if your dog's problem behavior needs outside help? If the problem is fear or aggression, it's best to call in professional reinforcements.

If it's simply a manners issue, such as your dog pulling you on leash or jumping up, and it's not a risk to anyone or the dog, then you may not need outside assistance. There are many positive books (like this one!) and videos that can help you. A lot will depend on you. How much experience do you have in training dogs? Of course, it will also depend on your dog. Some folks have had dogs all their lives and then end up with that one challenging pup who seems to defy all training attempts. Don't be afraid or ashamed to get professional help if you need it!

Once you've decided you need assistance, you need to choose the professional who can best help you. There are different types of canine professionals, with different levels of experience and education. It can be confusing to choose an animal behavior professional because, unless it's a veterinarian, there is no one set path to becoming one.

## Trainers

Some trainers attend one course for a couple of weeks and then start training dogs professionally. Some attend one school for several months and gain a certification. Some may not attend any formal education at all but use their life's experiences as a foundation. Some trainers have a background in working with shelter dogs, and others may have a background in competitive dog sports. Trainers' backgrounds can be very diverse. Deciding who is competent and who isn't can definitely give you a headache. There is no licensing. Anyone can claim to be a dog trainer.

When looking for a professional trainer, here are some questions you should ask:

## What is Your Educational Background and Practical Experience?

It's not enough these days for someone to love dogs and have worked with dogs all their lives and then one day decide to call themselves a professional dog trainer. There is an art to working with dogs, and there is definitely science. If a trainer doesn't understand the science, he or she is missing a huge chunk of critical education. Think of a surgeon who skipped his anatomy classes or an accountant who never took math instruction. Would you want that surgeon operating on you or that accountant doing your taxes? Not at all! While some may think all trainers do is play with puppies all day, you know better. You're reading this book because you're experiencing problems with your dog. If they were that simple to solve, you wouldn't be here!

In order to help you, a quality trainer has to have an extensive education in addition to practical experience. Look for a trainer who has an education in learning theory and canine behavior. Ask how the trainer got his or her education. Was it a course that took just a couple of weeks? That is not long enough. Was it a school? If so, find out what kind of training the school specializes in. Does it teach modern, positive methods? Also, was there a practical component of the training? In other words, did the trainer have to actually train a dog or just attend a class and pass written tests?

Practical experience can range widely, but look for a trainer who has experience with a variety of types of dogs. Some people only want to work with trainers who have owned or worked with their particular breed of dog. This may or may not be helpful. An old-fashioned trainer who has worked with your breed but uses outdated methods will not be as good as a trainer who has never owned your breed but is up to date on current learning theory and training techniques. There are thousands of dog breeds—no one trainer could possibly have them all at home! Ask if the trainer at least has experience working with similar breeds of dogs. For example, if you have a Shetland Sheepdog, you may want to know if the trainer at least has experience in working with herding breeds. If you have a Cavalier King Charles Spaniel, you may want to ask the trainer if he or she is experienced with toy breeds. Learning is learning—the laws of learning apply to all species. But there are unique aspects to different types of dogs that are helpful to understand when working with them, especially to change problem behavior.

Don't forget the other end of the leash—you! If you have special needs, ask if the trainer has had experience coaching similar clients. For example, if you have severe arthritis and limited mobility, you will want to work with someone who can modify the lesson plans so you can be successful. A great training plan for a dog won't do you any good if you can't carry it out! Another example would be if there are children in the home and you want them to be part of the learning process. Does the trainer have experience working with children? Ask the trainer to describe the specific experience and outcomes. Please note that, depending on your dog's problem, the trainer may recommend your child not be involved directly in the training program. For example, if you are working on aggression, it would not be safe.

If you want the trainer to help you with a specific problem, ask how much experience that trainer has with that problem and what his or her success rate is. For example, you might find a trainer who has titles in competitive obedience who can't housetrain your dog.

## How Many Years Have You Been Training Dogs?

This may vary. If you are getting help for a simple problem behavior, then it may be OK to work with a professional trainer who has only been in the business a few years. The number of years is not as important as the dedication to learning modern methods. For example, a trainer who has been training for 20 years but never learning something new may not be as effective as a trainer who has been training for five years using the latest knowledge in canine behavior.

For advanced issues, such as fear and aggression, however, you want an experienced trainer. A trainer who works with serious behavior problems before he or she has had education and experience in them can make the problems much worse.

## What Recent Continuing Education Have You Attended?

Quality dog trainers always want to be better trainers. So they attend conferences, workshops, or webinars and are up to date on the latest information about canine behavior. You don't want a trainer who last learned something 10 years ago. Dog training is continually evolving! The way we train dogs today is not the same as it was even a few decades ago because we've learned more about how dogs think and process information.

If the trainer says he or she doesn't attend continuing education because it's too expensive, this is a red flag. A trainer may not be able to travel to a big conference, but there are hundreds of webinars available that are extremely reasonably priced and can fit any budget. Some are even free. There is never an excuse to not want to learn more. Trainers have access to new books, DVDs, academic papers, and more.

You're a great example of pursuing knowledge by getting this book to learn more about how to help your dog! You want a trainer who shares that commitment.

## What Training Methods Do You Use?

Many students don't think to ask this question and then are surprised or horrified when the trainer uses a method that makes them uncomfortable. Always remember you are your dog's advocate. You may need help with a problem behavior, but your dog is still *your* family member. Your dog needs you to keep his best interests in mind and to protect him from harm. Don't turn your dog's leash over to a trainer just because he or she claims to be an expert. You have every right to ask a trainer what he or she will do to your dog.

You want a trainer who uses modern, positive methods based on rewards. If a trainer skirts all around the subject, that's a red flag. If the trainer waffles back and forth with a claim that she is "balanced" and modifies her methods based on the dog, dig deeper. What does that mean? That she uses treats at first but then physically punishes a dog later for noncompliance? This is not necessary to successfully train a dog.

If the trainer talks about "dominance" and you being the "alpha," it's another red flag. Dogs are not wolves. You are not a wolf. Trying to establish yourself as a leader by thinking you need to assert some sort of alpha status can make problem behaviors worse. The ASVAB recommends "that veterinarians not refer clients to trainers or behavior consultants who coach and advocate dominance hierarchy theory and the subsequent confrontational training that follows from it. Instead, the AVSAB emphasizes that animal training, behavior prevention strategies, and behavior modification programs should follow the scientifically based guidelines of positive reinforcement, operant conditioning, classical conditioning, desensitization, and counter conditioning."

So if the trainer you're interviewing heads down the dominance path, look elsewhere. A good professional dog trainer will be very up front about her methods and be happy to answer your questions.

### What Training Equipment Do You Recommend?

Avoid trainers who use choke chains, prong collars, or electric collars. These are not necessary to fix problem behaviors and can make them worse. Look for a trainer who uses regular collars, harnesses, and head halters. Clickers are also a plus.

### What Professional Associations Do You Belong To? If None, Why Not?

Dog trainers have professional associations just like any other profession. Two examples are the Association of Professional Dog Trainers (APDT) and the International Association of Animal Behavior Consultants (IAABC).

Associations are a great way to network, learn more, and get continuing education. If the trainer says he doesn't belong to any of them, why not? It may be that the membership fees are not within budget, which is understandable. If the trainer says he or she doesn't see the need to network with other trainers or sees no benefit to the educational aspects of an association, this could be a concern.

### What Are Your Credentials or Certifications, If Any?

It may sometimes look like alphabet soup when looking at trainer credentials. While certification is not required, it can indicate that a trainer takes his or her profession seriously and is dedicated enough to pursue the knowledge to earn a credential. Just know that all certifications are not the same.

If a trainer has letters after his or her name, ask what they mean and where the trainer earned the title. If it was because the trainer graduated from a specific school, just understand that the title only means

the trainer has attained accreditation based on the knowledge and experience from that one school. Then, make sure you ask about that school's methods and requirements for the title.

The word "certified" is thrown around quite a bit in dog training circles. When it comes to dog trainers, the term "certified" is definitely different from, for example, what "board-certified" means for a veterinarian. In the veterinary profession, to earn board certification you have to complete a specific, set path of rigorous postgraduate training, education, and examination. Not so with dog trainers.

A trainer can complete a two-week course from a corporate office and be "certified." A trainer can be "certified" for attending a dog training school and passing that school's exams. Some trainers will have earned accreditation from an independent certification organization. Others may earn them after passing strict organization guidelines for education, examination, and experience. Unfortunately, some trainers will also claim to be "certified" but actually have no credentials at all.

To date, there is only one independent certification body for dog trainers—the Certification Council for Professional Dog Trainers (CCPDT). The CCPDT is not affiliated with any school or association. To earn a designation, trainers must have a set amount of hours of experience in dog training, have a high school diploma or equivalent, an attestation from an existing certified trainer or veterinarian, sign a code of ethics, and successfully pass a proctored exam. You can't take the test at home or online. You must take it in person to prove you are the one answering the questions. The exam covers a variety of critical knowledge areas. For example, the exam for the Certified Professional Dog Trainer – Knowledge Assessed (CPDT-KA) designation includes questions on animal husbandry, ethology, instruction skills, learning theory, and equipment. To keep the designation once you've earned it, you must attend a set amount of continuing education and renewal courses every three years.

If the trainer you are interviewing has letters after his or her name that you don't recognize, don't hesitate to ask for an explanation of how he or she earned the title. The stricter the requirements, the harder the trainer had to work to achieve the designation.

Here are some common designations and what they mean:

- ACDBC: Associate Certified Dog Behavior Consultant by the IAABC
- AKC CGC: American Kennel Club Canine Good Citizen Evaluator
- CAAB: Certified Applied Animal Behaviorist by The Animal Behavior Society
- CABC: Certified Animal Behavior Consultant by the IAABC
- CCBC-KA: Certified Behavior Consultant Canine – Knowledge Assessed by the CCPDT
- CDBC: Certified Dog Behavior Consultant by the IAABC
- CPDT-KA: Certified Professional Dog Trainer – Knowledge Assessed by the CCPDT
- CPDT-KSA: Certified Professional Dog Trainer – Knowledge and Skills Assessed by the CCPDT
- DACVB: Diplomate American College of Veterinary Behaviorists
- KPA-CTP: Karen Pryor Academy Certified Training Partner
- NADOI: Endorsed by the National Association of Dog Obedience Instructors

This is just a sampling. There are many more. As promised—alphabet soup! If the trainer you are interviewing has earned a designation that isn't listed here, ask what it means.

Another term to watch out for is "behaviorist." Many in the industry use the term incorrectly, claiming to be "behaviorists" when they are actually dog trainers. There isn't a legal standard for the term, but it is generally accepted in the industry that a behaviorist has a college degree at the doctorate level. If you are interviewing a trainer who claims to be a behaviorist, check those credentials.

### Do You Have Client References?

The trainer should be able to provide you with a few names of clients you can call and get the scoop on how well the trainer worked for them. There may also be letters of reference or testimonials.

### Do You Have Insurance?

Any trainer who deals with problem behaviors, especially fear or aggression, should have liability insurance.

### Please Explain Your Contract, Fees, Cancellation Policies.

There are obvious practical questions you should ask as well. A professional dog trainer will have a contract that clearly states his or her responsibilities and yours. It will cover pricing and liability issues and will outline the trainer's policies for cancellations. Some may also include a waiver for photographs or video. In general, you might be able to negotiate the photo and video waiver. Not everyone wants their picture taken. Some parents do not want pictures or videos of their children appearing on a trainer's website, promotional materials, or Facebook page. The liability waiver, however, is non-negotiable, and that is typical for this industry.

When faced with a contract, read it carefully before you sign it. You want to be sure you understand everything. If you don't, ask questions. Remember, the contract outlines your responsibilities, so you want to be sure you understand them. For example, some trainers will charge for a lesson if the client is a no-show or doesn't cancel within 24 hours. This should be clearly stated in the contract. You don't want to be that client who forgot about an appointment and then was surprised at the charge on your credit card bill. You also want to ensure the trainer is living up to his or her end of the contract as well!

What you should NOT find in a contract or in any marketing materials is a guarantee to successfully solve any canine behavior problem. At first, this may seem strange. If you hired a contractor, he would have to guarantee his work, right? You probably wouldn't want to hire a contractor to remodel your bedroom if he didn't guarantee his work. The difference is that a dog is not a thing. A dog is a living, emotional being, with his own mind.

If you hire a business to complete work for you, you depend on that business to complete the task. But it's not just up to a trainer to fix your dog. It's up to you. The trainer doesn't live with you. He or she can't ensure you're doing the homework or doing it properly. The trainer can't guarantee you're doing everything you need to do to help your dog, so the trainer can't offer a guarantee that your dog's problem will be solved. In fact, it's against the code of ethics of several animal training associations to offer a guarantee. For example, the APDT Code of Professional Conduct and Responsibility states that members will strive to "Refrain from giving guarantees regarding the outcome of training, because there is no sure way to guarantee the cooperation and performance of all parties involved and because the knowledge of animal behavior is incomplete. This should not be confused with a desire to guarantee client satisfaction with professional services."

If a trainer does guarantee he or she can solve your dog's problem, then that is a big red flag. A trainer can guarantee customer service, but not your dog's behavior.

## Veterinary Behaviorists

If your dog has a serious problem, especially one that involves fear or aggression, then you may need a veterinary behaviorist. While all veterinarians have some basic education in animal behavior, it is not a primary focus in the veterinary curriculum. Veterinary behaviorists do specialize in animal behavior. There are several benefits to seeing a veterinary behaviorist, rather than a trainer. The veterinarian behaviorist will be able to rule out any physical problems that could be related to the problem behavior. He or she can prescribe medication if necessary. Veterinary behaviorists also have special, advanced education and experience in treating serious behavior problems, from separation anxiety to aggression.

You may need a referral from your regular veterinarian in order to see a veterinary behaviorist. There are limited numbers of these specialists across the country, so there may not be one near you. That doesn't mean you can't get help from one, however. Some veterinary behaviorists will consult with your regular veterinarian. You may be able to go for an initial consult and then follow-up with phone or video consults. So please don't think you have to rule out this extra level of expertise just because you don't have a veterinary behaviorist nearby.

Choosing a trainer isn't as easy as doing a search on the Internet and plucking a name from the Web. It does involve some research on your part to make sure you choose the right one for you and your canine friend. You are going to hire this person to help you find the right path to solving your dog's problem behavior. You want to make sure you get the best guide!

# Types of Training

There are different types of training you can choose from to help solve your dog's problem behaviors.

## Group Classes

A group class consists of several dogs and their handlers. It may be fine for simple problem behaviors, such as jumping up or pulling on leash. Most basic group classes will teach you foundation behaviors that can solve many simple problems. They are not ideal for more detailed problems, such as separation anxiety

*Trained dogs are happy dogs!*

or problems that mainly occur in your home environment. For example, if your dog is barking at people who come into your house but greets them fine in other locations, a group class won't really address this. Remember that an instructor must share time equally with all other students in the class.

Look for a class that has a good teacher-to-student ratio, such as one instructor per 8 to 10 students. You will also want to be sure the schedule for the class works with your schedule. Ask about how the instructor handles absences—can you make the class up or does the instructor catch you up during the next lesson? You just want to be sure you will get the information you missed, whether it's in a make-up class or during the course of the next scheduled class or another option.

It's a good idea to observe a group class before attending. Most instructors won't mind this because they should have nothing to hide. Does the class feel safe? Is there plenty of room for dogs and handlers? Does the instructor treat people and animals with respect? Is the instructor a good communicator? Does the instructor allow time for questions? Does everyone seem to be learning and enjoying themselves?

There are some group classes that specialize in specific problem behaviors. For example, fearful or shy dog classes are tailored just for dogs with those issues. There are also reactive or "feisty" dog classes for dogs that are aggressive. Some are for dogs who are only aggressive toward other dogs, while some accept dogs with some people aggression.

These specialty classes will teach you to work with your dog and to better understand his triggers so you can make progress together. It can be very supportive to go through a group class with other people whose dogs have similar issues. You will find you are not alone! Be sure the instructor has the experience and education to hold the class. Not every trainer is qualified to work with fear or aggression, let alone in a group setting.

## Private Training

Private training involves one-on-one instruction either in your home or at a trainer's facility. Private training is excellent for problems that only occur in your home, such as a dog who counter surfs or is

*One-on-one training can provide a fearful or anxious dog with the positive attention he needs.*

not housetrained. It's also ideal for very fearful dogs who are too skittish to venture outside the home and would be too upset to learn in another setting. It is also ideal for cases involving aggression, especially with dogs who are aggressive toward other people and dogs.

This type of training should be customized for your particular situation. It has a more flexible schedule than a group class that meets at regular times. Private training will cost you more than a group class due to the flexibility, the customization, and especially if the trainer comes to your home. There may also be different private training rates based on the issue, such as one for manners training and a higher one for aggression or fear. This is because fear and aggression require additional education and expertise on the part of the trainer, as well as additional liability. It's one thing for a trainer to take on a dog who pees in the house and another thing entirely to work with a dog who bites people.

## Day Training

Day training involves a trainer coming to your home and working with your dog to solve his problem behaviors, then transferring the training to you. The trainer trains the dog, then teaches you how to get the dog to perform for you. This type of training is appealing for people who find it difficult to train their own dogs or who have schedules that make it challenging to meet for regular lessons.

The trainer has the expertise, so he or she can "jump start" behaviors faster with your dog. It is really important to understand, however, that unless you actively participate in the transfer sessions—lessons during which the trainer trains you—your dog will not work for you. You will need to study with the trainer and learn the correct cues and actions to take in order for your dog to listen and respond to you. Day training is very convenient and enables your dog to learn faster, but it's not like sending your car to the shop for a tune-up and expecting it to run smoothly when you get behind the wheel. Day training will be a more expensive option than group lessons.

## Board and Train

With board and train, you send your dog to a trainer's home or facility for a period of time. The trainer trains the dog, then holds transfer sessions with you so you learn to work with the dog. Just as with day training, board and train can be very convenient for people who do not want or who are not able to train their own dogs. The transfer sessions, however, are critical. Many are disappointed to learn that their dogs don't listen to them at all when they return home. This is because the dog has learned to respond to the trainer. Unless you participate in the lessons and learn how to work with your dog during the transfer sessions, your dog will not respond to you. It's not like sending your dog off to boarding school and expecting a scholar when he comes home—you still have to be a participant when the dog returns.

Board and train programs will be more expensive than other options because the trainer is providing housing and daily care for your dog. Be very careful who you choose. Interview the trainer carefully to ensure that he or she uses modern, positive methods. You will not be there to see how your dog is treated, so you want to be sure it is a quality program based in science and not in punishment-based techniques. Always tour the facility and find out exactly where your dog will be staying. How much confinement time will your dog have compared to training or play time? How many dogs are trained at one time? You don't want a program that takes on so many dogs that your dog doesn't end up getting any more attention than if you opted for private lessons.

# PART II

# COMMON BEHAVIOR PROBLEMS AND SOLUTIONS

*Sticking to your training program is important. Any lack of consistency will easily confuse your dog.*

Do you get embarrassed by your dog when he displays problem behavior? Confused? Frustrated? Angry? Maybe you don't think the problem is that serious, but your spouse or significant other has delivered an ultimatum, so now you're under pressure to sort it out. You're not alone, although you may feel like you are sometimes! Having a dog with problem behaviors is challenging. It can try your patience and be very upsetting. It can also make you worried. What if you can't fix it?

Don't lose hope! Many problem behaviors can be solved. This book gives you all the step-by-step guidance you'll need to ensure that you and your dog can start walking a new, better path together.

Will it be easy? Probably not. You're a dedicated dog owner, so you deserve the truth. It would be great to be able to sit in a recliner and click a remote control to find the right channel to reprogram your dog, but that's not going to happen. The truth is that you can't get rich quick, lose weight fast and keep it off forever, or wave a magic wand and fix your dog. Don't you wish you could?

It will take an effort on your part to fix your dog's problem behavior. The level of effort will depend on a lot of things, such as your dog, you, other people who interact with your dog, your environment, and especially how long the problem behavior has been in place. If the behavior is just blooming, you have a better chance of stopping it from taking root. If the behavior has been in place for a long time, it's going to take a greater effort to fix it.

## The Qualities You'll Need

Helping your dog will take patience, dedication, and consistency. Patience is essential because it will take time for the training to take effect. If your dog has been building up a bad habit for years, it won't go away overnight. Dedication is vital, too. You need to do the homework and follow the training plan. If you don't put in the work, you won't see results. Consistency is also important. You have to stick with the training plan and not improvise all over the place. If you are making things up as you go along, or if you are trying one thing one day and another thing the next, your dog is also going to be all over the map. It will also just confuse your dog if you mix and match methods. Training using positive methods one minute and using physical punishment the next can bewilder your dog. He won't know what to expect from one moment to the next. Consistency is critical when training your dog to do anything, from a simple foundation behavior to fixing a problem behavior.

In some cases, you may have to change *your* habits because they could be contributing to your dog's behavior. It's hard to change our habits, sometimes harder than changing a dog's! A related challenge is that everyone who interacts with your dog must be on board with the plan. If you are working hard to change your dog's behavior but your spouse, significant other, roommate, children, or friends continue to reinforce it, your dog is not likely to improve. If he's still getting paid for that behavior, then it won't go away. So before you implement a training plan, make sure everyone reads these same pages.

With any training plan, you're bound to encounter some road blocks. Sometimes there's an exercise that your dog just can't seem to grasp. Sometimes you get confused following the steps in order, or you'll have difficulty with a new skill, such as timing the click right or holding a leash. It's OK. Be patient with your dog and with yourself. If you knew how to fix the problem, you probably wouldn't be reading this book, so you're learning new things, too! You and your dog will be learning together. It's completely normal to have a few bumps in the road, so don't let that discourage you. If you hit a snag, just stop your training session. Take a deep breath, re-read the plan, and try again. You can do this!

## Foundation Behaviors

There are certain basic behaviors that all dogs should know, especially if you are trying to address problem ones. Some of them will fix problem behaviors all by themselves! By training your dog in these foundation behaviors, you are building up a relationship, one based on your dog listening to you and doing what you want, rather than ignoring you. You will be learning to work as a team. This will make it much more likely your dog will start listening to you when you start to address his specific behavior problem. Without a solid foundation, you can't build improved responses. So start your training with these foundation behaviors if your dog does not already know them. When you read about addressing specific problems in this book, you'll see notes on which foundation behaviors are

*Punishing a dog for doing something you don't like is counterproductive. Work with him to teach him what you want.*

best suited to help fix those problems. Keep in mind that to make these behaviors reliable, you will need to *train them to fluency*. This means you'll need to gradually add distractions and teach them in different locations so your dog performs in a variety of challenging situations. (For greater details on training these and many other behaviors, check out another book of mine, *The Ultimate Guide to Dog Training*.)

## General Tips

- Keep your training sessions short, just a few minutes at a time. For success, it will take several, sometimes many, sessions. Be patient.
- Work on one exercise at a time.
- When you first start a new foundation behavior, work in an area with few distractions. This will help both you and your dog better concentrate on learning.
- Once your dog reliably performs the behavior in a quiet setting, gradually add distractions and work in different environments to make it more challenging.
- Here's a good rule to follow: three strikes and you're out. If your dog fails in performing the exercise three times, you are pushing him too hard. Back up your training to a point where he was successful. Work there for a while, then gradually increase the challenge again.
- First, teach the behavior. Then, add a cue. Using cues before a dog learns a behavior is just cluttering your training sessions because dogs normally do not pick up verbal cues rapidly. If you are using a hand signal for a behavior and then add the cue, your dog will likely respond quickly. This doesn't mean he understands the verbal cue yet—he's still recognizing the hand signal. It will take many repetitions for your dog to connect the hand signal with the verbal signal, so continue to use both during the transition. Some ask why add the verbal signal at all, but your dog will not always be looking at you when you give a hand signal, so it's good to add a verbal cue.
- When you use a cue, say it one time, in a friendly voice. Saying a cue over and over again will not teach your dog to respond the first time you cue him. You also do not need to yell at your dog or speak firmly in order to get him to respond to you.

# Come

**Goal:** To teach your dog to come to you rapidly when you call him.
**What you'll need:** Clicker, treats.
**Preparation:** First, you need to train your dog to touch your hand with his nose. This will teach your dog to approach you and that coming to you is a positive thing. It also has some nice side benefits. It will teach your dog that human hands are wonderful things, which can make it easier to groom, handle, and take care of him if he is injured. It will also

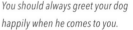
*You should always greet your dog happily when he comes to you.*

*A well-trained dog will perform reliably no matter where you are.*

help you guide your dog to different places when he learns to follow your hand, such as off the furniture or off the kitchen counter.

1. Hold the clicker in one hand. Hold your other, empty hand, palm facing your dog, with fingers pointed down, about one inch from your dog's nose. Most dogs will reach out and nose your hand. The second he does, click and toss a treat on the ground. If he doesn't nose your hand, you'll have to lessen your criteria. So even if he looks at your hand, click and treat.

2. When your dog is reliably touching his nose to your hand, add a cue. If your dog already thinks the word "Come" means run away from you, or if you've ever associated the word with something your dog doesn't like, such as a bath or punishment, you need to use a new word. You can use "Here" or another word that doesn't already have a negative connotation. Give the cue just before you present your hand. When your dog noses your hand, click and toss a treat.

3. Start increasing the distance your dog has to come to reach your hand. Hold your hand out as before, and cue "Come." When your dog touches your hand, toss the treat behind him, away from you. As soon as your dog eats the treat, cue "Come" again, holding your hand out. When your dog noses your hand, click. Toss the treat away again, a little farther each time.

NOTE: When you start working in areas that could be distracting to your dog, put him on leash. Do not use the leash to drag him to you; it's just to control him from running off. Please remember that it is not realistic for your dog to come running to you on cue in an off-leash situation until you have trained this behavior in a variety of different environments with a variety of distractions.

OPTION: If your dog knows the "Sit" behavior, you can add a "Sit" when your dog reaches you. Cue "Come." When your dog reaches you, cue "Sit." Then click and treat.

# Sit

**Goal:** Your dog will sit.

**What you'll need:** Clicker, treats.

1. Hold a treat in your hand, just above your dog's nose. Slowly move your hand in between your dog's eyes, toward the back of his head.
2. Most dogs will lower their rear ends and sit. When he sits, click. Toss a treat to get him up so you can practice the exercise again. Repeat two more times.
3. Repeat the exercise, but keep your hand empty. Be sure to hold it as if you have a treat. This is not to fool your dog. It's teaching your dog a specific hand signal. When your dog sits, click and toss a treat.
4. When your dog is reliably sitting, add the cue. Just before you give your hand signal, cue "Sit" one time, in a friendly voice. Repeat Step 3.

# Down

**Goal:** Your dog will lie down.

**What you'll need:** Clicker, treats.

**Preparation:** Teach "Sit" first.

1. Cue "Sit." Hold a treat in your hand, just under your dog's nose. Very slowly, move your hand down to the ground in between your dog's front paws. Then, again very slowly, move it outward, away from your dog. Most dogs will follow the treat and lie down. When your dog's belly touches the ground, click. Toss a treat to get your dog up, so you can practice the behavior again. Repeat two more times.
2. Cue "Sit." Hold your empty hand as if you had a treat in it, and go through the same hand motion as previously. This is not to fool your dog—he can smell there is no treat in your hand. You are actually teaching your dog a hand signal. By losing the lure of a treat in your hand, you are ensuring that you and your dog don't become dependent on having treats in your hand every time you want him to perform a behavior. When your dog lies down, click. Toss him a treat.
3. When your dog is reliably lying down, add a cue for "Down." Be sure you use a unique cue. For example, don't use "Down" if you want to use "Get down" for when your dog jumps on you. Cue "Down." Then go through the same hand motion. When your dog lies down, click and toss a treat.

NOTE: If your dog lifts his rear end when you move the treat along the ground, try moving it between his front legs toward his rear. Some dogs prefer to fold into the down position.

*Dogs learn hand signals faster than they learn verbal signals.*

# Settle

**Goal:** Your dog will lie down on his bed or in his crate.

**What you'll need:** Clicker, treats, bed, or crate.

**Preparation:** Teach "Down" first.

1. Stand right next to the bed or crate. Look at it and not at your dog. (If you look at your dog, he'll likely just look back at you instead of focusing on the bed or crate.) Click for any interaction with the bed or crate, even if

your dog just looks at it. Drop a treat right next to the bed or crate.

2. Your dog will start interacting more with the bed or crate. Start clicking when he puts one paw on or in it, then two, then three, then four. Always treat after clicking.

3. Gradually work to where your dog will go to the bed or in the crate reliably, then cue "Down." When he lies down, click and treat.

NOTE: This is a perfect foundation exercise for teaching your dog that his crate is a great place to be, but you may have a challenge with this if your dog already has a negative association with his crate. If you have to start from scratch, be patient. Try moving the crate to a different area. You might even try getting a different type of crate. Your goal is to make each interaction with the crate a great experience for your dog.

*Getting a dog to settle happily in his basket, bed, or crate means convincing him it is a nice place to be.*

## Stay

**Goal:** Your dog will hold a sit or down position until you give a cue to release him.

**What you'll need:** Clicker, treats.

**Preparation:** Teach "Sit" and "Down" first.

1. Cue "Sit." Count up to three seconds, then click. Toss a treat so your dog will get up so you can practice the exercise again.

2. Cue "Sit." Count up to five seconds, then click and toss a treat.

3. Cue "Sit." Count up to seven seconds, then click and toss a treat.

4. Cue "Sit." Click and treat. Vary the amount of time you ask your dog to hold the position. Sometimes make it longer, sometimes shorter so that it stays interesting for your dog.

5. During a separate training session, practice Steps 1- 4 with the "Down" behavior.

## Wait

**Goal:** Your dog will wait in position until you cue him to continue forward.

**What you'll need:** Clicker, treats, and a place to practice the exercise, such as a doorway or gate. If you use a door or gate that leads outdoors, put your dog on leash.

1. Stand on the inside of the doorway, with your dog on the same side. Toss a treat over the threshold to get your dog to go outside. (This is a "freebie" just to get your dog in the

*You can use a hand signal to encourage your dog to stay in position.*

*A leash will help you in training your dog to wait, especially if you are working with him by an open door or outside.*

right start position.) When your dog comes back inside, with all four paws inside the threshold, click. Do not pull your dog inside—let him enter on his own. Toss a treat outside over the threshold.

2. When your dog is reliably coming inside and waiting for the click before he goes out again, it's time to add the cue. Cue "Wait." After three seconds, click and toss the treat outside over the threshold.

3. Gradually increase the amount of time your dog has to wait before you click to signal to your dog to move outside.

NOTE: For this exercise, it's not necessary for your dog to be in a specific position, such as "Sit" or "Down." If you prefer your dog to be in a specific position, you can also use the "Stay" behavior to get him to hesitate at doorways or gateways.

## Leave It/Take It

**Goal:** Your dog will leave something alone when you cue him, and he will take something when you **cue him.**

**What you'll need:** Clicker, treats.

1. Hold a bunch of treats in both hands. In one hand, hold the clicker. This will be your delivery hand—the hand with which you will deliver the reward. Put this hand behind your back.

2. Show your dog the treats you have in your other hand. Quickly make a fist so he cannot grab at them. Don't pull your hand away from your dog. Keep it under his muzzle. Your dog will likely try to get the treats. He may even chew or paw your hand. Wait.

3. The second your dog moves his head away from your hand, for any reason, click. From your opposite hand, toss a treat in the opposite direction. You may find that you drop more than one reward because the clicker's also in that hand, but that's OK.

4. When your dog reliably leaves your hand alone when you present the treats, switch hands.

5. When your dog can leave either hand alone, add the cue. Before you present the treats, cue "Leave it." When he looks away, cue "Take it," click, and then toss a treat. After nine more repetitions, you no longer need the clicker. Just use the verbal cues.

6. When your dog responds to the cues when you hold treats in your hands, start practicing the exercise by placing treats on the floor. Keep your hand near the treat so you can cover it if necessary so your dog doesn't grab it!

NOTE: This exercise will teach your dog to leave something alone if you cue him. It will *not* teach your dog to drop something once he already has it in his mouth—that is a separate behavior.

# Release

The click always ends the behavior. So if you cue "Sit," your dog should remain sitting until you click and treat. Once your dog has practiced a behavior successfully in a variety of locations and performs it reliably, wean him off the clicker. The clicker is a building tool. Once a behavior is built, you don't need the clicker anymore. If you take your dog to a new environment, if your dog will experience new distractions, or if he just has gotten rusty, then bring the clicker back out and build the behavior back up again.

The release cue replaces the clicker during stationary behaviors—"Sit," "Down," "Wait," "Settle," and so on—so your dog knows when it's OK to get up or move. If you don't teach a release cue to replace the clicker, then your dog's stationary behaviors may erode. He won't know when to get up, so he may start doing it quickly after you've cued him. Then you end up cueing the behavior over and over. You can also use the cue to end other behaviors, such as walking nicely on leash, just to let your dog know the exercise is over.

**Goal:** Your dog will learn a signal to release him from a previous cue.

**What you'll need:** Clicker, treats.

**Preparation:** Teach a behavior to fluency first. This example uses "Sit."

*A click is a promise. Always give a treat after you click, even if you click by mistake.*

1. Cue "Sit."

2. Give your release cue, such as "All done!" or "Free!" or "Release" or "OK." Choose one cue that you will use for all behaviors that you want to signal when they are done.

3. Click and toss a treat.

4. Repeat Steps 1–3 nine more times.

5. Cue "Sit." Cue "All done!" (or whatever Release cue you have chosen) and then treat. You have just weaned your dog off the clicker to end this behavior.

# 3 Aggression

ggression is a serious problem. It can be tempting to make excuses for an aggressive dog because it's a heart-wrenching situation. "He was a stray and there's no telling how long he went between meals, so that's why he growls over his food." "He was a rescue. Children must have been mean to him, which is why he growls at them." "That woman came up to my dog too fast. She never should have reached to pet him. That's why he nipped her." Excuses like these are common, but they will not solve the dog's problem. They can often help people deny there is a problem in the first place.

Such denials are natural enough. People don't want to admit there is a problem because they're embarrassed, defensive, or worried someone will tell them they have to get rid of their dog or euthanize him. This is completely understandable from a human perspective, but it won't help the dog. Admitting there is an issue is the first step toward resolving it.

## Identifying Aggression

Recognizing aggression can also be challenging. Sometimes it's not a problem of denial, just a problem of not understanding canine body language. For example, if you are playing tug of war with your puppy and he growls at you, he's probably just playing. Does he stop easily? Is his body loose? Is he bowing? Then it's probably just play. Some folks mistake it for aggression, but it's just a dog talking while he plays exuberantly.

Dogs also sometimes growl when playing with other dogs. As long as both dogs seem to be having a good time, it's likely just play. Does one dog look scared? Is one dog trying to get away from the other dog? Is one dog repeatedly body slamming the other dog and not letting him escape if he wants to? If so, it's not play.

Another example is a dog who barks and lunges at the end of a leash. Some people think such a dog just wants to play, but that's not necessarily the case. Depending on the dog's body language, he could actually be afraid of another dog, wanting to attack him, or experiencing leash aggression. If he barks and lunges at people or other dogs, it's a behavior problem you should address.

Dogs growl for a reason. Your dog may be the only one who understands why he's doing it, but he thinks he has a legitimate reason. Please never punish your dog for growling. Growling is excellent communication. If your dog growls, you know there's something bothering him. Yelling at him or physically punishing him won't make what's bothering him go away. Instead, you'll be eliminating his warning system. So, instead of warning you with a growl next time, he may go straight to biting.

Dogs are normally very precise about the signals they give. If your dog snaps at you and misses, he meant to miss you. You're not fast enough to get out of the way. If your dog nips you, he meant to nip you. It wasn't an accident.

Aggression will not go away on its own. Instead, it is very likely to get worse with time. If you are reading this book because you are concerned that your dog is exhibiting aggression, it means you are already taking an important step in getting help.

There are several different types of canine aggression. Here are some common ones.

If your dog growls over his bone, it's a type of aggression called resource guarding.

# Pay Attention to Your Dog's Body Language: Signs of Stress and Aggression

When dogs are stressed, they will let you know. You just need to know what to look for. Dogs will normally give a lot of signals that they are getting upset. These signals are meant to make "scary" things go away or to avoid conflict. If your dog thinks his early warning signs are not understood or respected, he may escalate to stronger signals. Your goal is to recognize the signs of stress at its early stages, before your dog escalates the issue.

### Some Early Signs
- Lip licking
- Looking or turning away
- Yawning

### Increasing Stress
- Panting
- Shaking off (when your dog shakes his entire body as if he's wet, but he isn't)
- Trembling
- Dilated pupils
- Sweating paws (dogs sweat through their paw pads)

- Raised hackles (the fur between his shoulders)
- Whale eye (when the dog's head turns but his eyes fix at a target, so you see mostly the white of his eye)

### Aggression
- Freezing
- Growling
- Showing teeth
- Muzzle punch (when a dog hits you sharply with his muzzle, mouth closed)
- Biting

*Small dogs may become overwhelmed by the big world around them.*

# Dog–Dog Aggression

Charlie is a big, adolescent Boxer. He's the baby of the family, and he grew up with the family's two older dogs. Charlie has always played well with the other dogs in the household, although sometimes he seems a bit much for them. Charlie is full of energy!

One day, his owners decided to take Charlie to the local dog park so he could find some younger canine friends with similar energy levels. When Charlie arrived at the park, he didn't seem to want to interact much with the other dogs. He stuck close to his owners, often whining. His parents kept encouraging him to go make friends. Next thing they knew, a dog came barreling up to them to say hello and Charlie exploded. There was a terrible fight, and the other dog was badly hurt, requiring medical attention. Charlie's owners were mortified! They were also really confused because Charlie had always gotten along well with the other dogs at home. Was it something the other dog did? Or is Charlie really not a friendly dog to other dogs?

Just because a dog enjoys the company of a few specific dogs doesn't mean he will welcome it from all dogs. When Charlie was avoiding other dogs in the dog park and acting clingy, he was actually telling his owners that the place made him feel very uncomfortable. He didn't want to interact with the other dogs. When the other dog got into his personal space, Charlie felt a need to defend himself.

*Do not ignore your dog's signals that he wants to be left alone.*

## Small-Dog Options: Predatory Precautions

Whenever there is a sizeable weight difference between dogs, *predatory drift* can prove to be dangerous. Although you may have heard the term "predatory aggression," predation is actually not aggression. If a dog kills another dog or animal due to predation–hunting behavior–it's not emotional. He is following an instinct to hunt and kill prey. When a dog hunts a mouse, he doesn't hate it. He's not afraid of it, making a big display so the mouse goes away and leaves him alone. The dog doesn't have a personal vendetta against his prey–he's just behaving like the predatory animal he is.

Some larger dogs will see smaller dogs as prey. To some dogs, the sight of a fluffy small dog running full speed might as well be a rabbit–it's a trigger to chase. How do you know if the larger dog is playing chase, rather than hunting? In most normal play, dogs take turns chasing each other. Both dogs will look like they're enjoying the interaction. If the smaller dog has ears back, looks afraid, tries to hide, or comes running to you for help, the smaller dog has recognized he's in trouble. Don't take a chance. This is a serious situation because it doesn't take much for a small dog to get hurt.

If a small dog yelps in pain or struggles to escape, predatory drift can also trigger a larger dog to attack the smaller dog. The larger dog interprets the "Yipe!" or struggle as that of a prey animal, and instinct kicks in to attack.

This doesn't mean that all large dogs will attack small dogs! Some larger dogs are incredibly gentle with their little friends. Just be aware that, for safety reasons, little dogs need extra supervision when around their bigger cousins. Even an exuberant adolescent dog with no control over his body can hurt a small dog accidentally. Play it safe and carefully supervise all interactions. Don't hesitate to remove your small dog from the environment if you feel there is a chance he could get hurt.

Charlie's parents did not recognize Charlie's stress signals and remove him from the park before his stress escalated to a fight. Unfortunately, they learned a hard lesson.

Some dogs do not like other dogs. Sometimes it's specific, like a dog who doesn't like big dogs but can tolerate small ones. Some dogs will get along just fine with other dogs in your household, but not with ones outside your family. Some will be aggressive toward any other dog, no matter the size, gender, or age. Sometimes it seems random—you can't figure out which dogs set your dog off and which don't.

Just because a dog is aggressive toward other dogs does not mean he will also be aggressive toward people. If you are breaking up a dog fight, however, you could incur injury. In the aroused state of a fight, the dogs may not mean to hurt you, but you could get in the way.

## Symptoms

If a dog is fearful of another dog, you may see him lick his lips, turn away from the other dog, curl his lip, have a whale eye, and try to avoid the other dog. Some dogs will react more strongly, barking, lunging, and growling, trying to scare the other dog away. Please know that just because a dog is reacting out of fear does not mean he won't bite or attack if he feels he needs to defend himself.

If a dog wants to attack another dog, you may see a stiff body, a lowered head, and a fixed stare. It's as if the dog is "locking and loading" on his target. This can be especially concerning if dog aggression occurs

*Breaking up a serious dog fight is no joke. Not only can the dogs involved hurt themselves, but there is also the risk of you being bitten.*

between dogs in the same household. Sometimes, dogs have one squabble and it's over, never to happen again. But sometimes, one dog will "target" another dog in the same household and not stop fixating on him. This is a serious cause for concern.

There are always signals before a fight ensues. Fights don't appear "out of the blue." For some dogs, the signals escalate very quickly into a fight. These symptoms can also build over time. For dogs who live together, they may have several instances during which they exchange low-level signals over many months, even years, before it finally turns into a full-out fight. This can lead you into a false sense of security, thinking your dogs may squabble, but they would "never hurt each other." One day, one dog may have decided he's had enough and decide to take his complaint to the next level.

The aggression can range in severity from a dog who just blusters to one who severely injures or kills other dogs. Some dog fights are loud and fierce enough to frighten you, but when you separate the dogs you realize neither one is mauled. This is still serious and warrants immediate intervention and an appropriate behavior modification plan, but it means that the dogs really did not intend to inflict serious damage. Dogs have excellent control over their teeth. If one of your dogs bites another, he meant to do so. It wasn't an accident. Some fights lead to serious damage, requiring medical attention. Some dogs are capable of killing other dogs.

## Why It Happens

Dogs can be aggressive toward other dogs simply due to fear. If a dog has not been properly socialized with a variety of other dogs during his critical socialization period, he could be frightened of them. Dogs react to fearful things differently. Some will actively try to avoid what is frightening them, but others will react more strongly. They can bark, lunge, growl, and bite. When a professional diagnoses such a dog as being afraid, it can surprise his owners. The display of aggression looks very fierce, so you may think of your dog as being the instigator. In this case, however, it's often a dog who chooses to deal with something scary by taking the offensive rather than staying on the defensive. If your dog makes himself

*Dogs may act aggressive and display frightening-looking behavior as a defense mechanism.*

look very scary, then maybe the other dog will run away and leave him alone.

If a dog has a bad experience with another dog, it can cause him to be fearful of other dogs. For example, if a dog is bullied by other dogs at a dog park, he can develop a fear of other dogs. By the same token, if a dog learns to be a bully toward other dogs, he can become aggressive toward them.

Some dogs who were raised with the same breed may be fine with others of their breed, but aggressive toward other breeds or mixed-breed dogs because they were not socialized with them as young puppies.

Canine aggression toward other canines isn't always based in fear. Some dogs simply do not like other dogs and will be aggressive toward them. Some breeds, in fact, have a long history of being bred to specifically fight other dogs. This doesn't mean that these breeds can't get along with other dogs. Many do. But some don't and never will. It also doesn't mean that breeds that are traditionally great with other dogs won't develop dog–dog aggression. Just as an American Pit Bull Terrier can be a complete mush with other dogs, a Labrador Retriever can be extremely aggressive. Don't let a dog's breed blind you to his behavior.

Some big dogs will play happily with smaller dogs and vice versa. Some won't. That's why such encounters should always be supervised.

# Dog–Human Aggression

Bella is a year-old Dachshund who lives with a family that has three children. She is very affectionate with her family members and enjoys playing with the children. When the family has guests over, however, Bella growls and barks at them. Once or twice, she has also growled at the children's friends when they came over and tried to pet her.

Every time Bella growls, family members yell at her. They don't want her to growl at people, so they punish her for doing it, thinking that should make her stop.

One day, a plumber comes to the house to fix a leaky faucet. Bella runs up to him, barking, her body stiff. Embarrassed, Bella's mom yells at her to stop. The plumber reaches down to pet Bella, trying to let her know he's a nice guy. Bella bites him. It's a shallow bite and hardly bleeds, but now her family is concerned she is getting worse.

Bella's family is right to be concerned. The reason that Bella snapped instead of growled may be because they have only been treating the symptom—the growling—rather than the real problem—Bella doesn't like strangers.

Dog–human aggression is one of the more serious reasons why people call in a professional for help. Some people will put up with low-level aggression for years, then suddenly call for help when the dog bites the "wrong" person, such as a child, a neighbor, or significant other. Sometimes they'll cope with it for a while until they're expecting a baby, only then realizing the aggression can be a serious issue.

Sometimes dog–human aggression is only toward strangers, but it can be toward family members. Sometimes it's targeted toward a specific type of person, such as men or children. It can also be location-specific, such as a dog who is only aggressive at the veterinarian's office, in his crate, or in the car.

*Your puppy may nip in play, but you should discourage this behavior.*

## Symptoms

Dog bites do not happen out of the blue. There are always advance signs, although many people just don't know enough about canine communication to recognize them. Dogs will usually give many signals that they are going to bite people before they actually do so. It will start with signs of stress, including lip licking, yawning, and turning away. The dog may have a whale eye, and the pupils may dilate.

Ever see those "cute" photos on social media that people share of their dogs and children? You will see many of these stress signals in those photos. These dogs are not enjoying the close interaction with the children. They are trying to communicate that they are not comfortable. While some may find the photos endearing, professional dog trainers and others who understand canine communication are often horrified.

Escalated signals include curling a lip, growling, freezing, muzzle punches, and then, biting. Not every dog will give every signal. And, if signals have been punished, they may skip them altogether and escalate straight to a bite.

## Why It Happens

If a puppy wasn't exposed to a variety of people during his critical socialization period, up until about 16 weeks of age, he may find them frightening later in life. This can cause an aggressive response. For example, a puppy raised just by women may be afraid of men. A puppy raised with adults may be afraid of children. A puppy who only meets Caucasian people may grow up to be fearful of people of other ethnicities. This is an extremely common reason for a dog who is aggressive toward people—lack of proper socialization.

Many assume that the dog must have been abused previously, but the behavior is often rooted in a socialization problem. Proper socialization ensures that a puppy enjoys a wide variety of positive experiences. So, even if a puppy met someone during his critical socialization period, it needed to be a positive experience. And "positive" is definitely in the eyes of the puppy!

For example, two women adopt an 8-week-old Chihuahua puppy. When Peanut turns 11 weeks old, they introduce him to a male friend. The man is very tall and is wearing a baseball cap. Peanut is hesitant and doesn't seem to want to greet the man, hanging back and refusing to come near him. One of the women scoops Peanut up and plops him in the man's lap, figuring he'll get used to him. As the man holds the puppy up, Peanut frantically, rapidly licks the man's face. The women beam, thinking Peanut has overcome his nervousness.

Months pass by and Peanut is now a teenager. One day, when the family is out for a walk, a tall man wearing a baseball cap reaches to pet the little dog. Peanut growls at him, backs up, and starts barking wildly.

What happened? Peanut's first introduction to tall men wearing caps was not a good one. Peanut demonstrated that he was nervous by actively avoiding the man. By forcing Peanut to be in the man's lap, it made the "monster" unavoidable. He responded with frantic, rapid licking of the man's chin. This type of licking is an appeasement behavior. Peanut was trying to convince the man not to hurt him. So meeting tall men was scary for Peanut. When he met one months later, he remembered that experience and acted accordingly. Except now that he was a teenager, he didn't feel a need to appease so much as get defensive. The women's intentions for introductions were good, but the execution backfired.

Puppies who are hesitant or fearful to approach new things should never be forced to do so. It's one thing if they need to have a veterinarian examination or if you have to do something to them for their own safety. Then, they may need to face a fearful experience. Even then, there are things you should do to make the situation as positive as possible. But forcing a puppy to confront something that frightens him will often serve to worsen his fear.

There are other reasons why a dog can be aggressive toward people. For example, some dogs simply do not like being handled. They have either never been taught to enjoy handling, or they may find it scary or unpleasant. If a dog has arthritis and you pick him up, it may hurt him, so he reacts. If you scoop a small dog up in your arms, it could terrify him, so he stiffens, snaps, or growls. Many dogs have sensitive areas where they don't appreciate being touched. It may be their ears, mouth, paws, or tail.

Some dogs are only aggressive toward humans in certain situations, such as dogs who growl or snap at the veterinarian's office. If a dog is sick or injured, he already doesn't feel well and is not in the best humor. Examining his ears can hurt if he has an ear infection. Taking his temperature is invasive. Manipulating an injured limb is painful. He may warn the staff to back off with an aggressive display. This can surprise

This dog is stressed and angry. If such signals are ignored, biting may be the next step.

*Even a normally placid dog can react defensively when being examined or treated by a vet, especially if he is in pain.*

and embarrass you, especially if your dog has never growled at anyone before. It means the veterinarian's office will indicate in your dog's chart that he might be aggressive when visiting as well. This is obviously embarrassing. But the veterinary staff needs to be safe, so they may recommend you muzzle your dog when visiting.

## Leash Aggression

Amos is a 2-year-old Border Collie mix with tons of energy. His mom is a runner, so she wanted a dog who could run with her. When Amos is at home, he's usually fine. He gets along great with the family and is very affectionate with them. If the family has someone new over to visit, it does take Amos a while to warm up to them. His ears will lay flat and he'll go to the farthest point in the room where he can still see the person. He'll have a worried expression and whine. After about 15 minutes, if the person ignores him, he'll approach and after a few tentative sniffs, he'll be friendly. Amos also has a couple of dog buddies who live next door. The dogs play together very well.

When Amos is off his property, though, he's skittish. It's as if he's listening to everything and watching everything. He's on high alert the entire time. When a car passes by, Amos goes berserk, barking and lunging at the end of the leash, looking like he's trying to give chase. When a person with a dog passes by, he also bark-growls and lunges at the end of his leash. He sounds very fierce. His mom has a hard time controlling him. He's a medium-sized dog, but he's really strong. When he slams at the end of the leash, she feels as though he might get away from her. She's yelled at him to stop, tried dragging him away, firmly told him to "Sit! Sit! Sit!" but nothing is working. She gets embarrassed when people see Amos reacting and they hurry past, keeping their dogs far away from him.

The family is getting very frustrated. They know Amos needs exercise, but how can they take him running when he acts like a maniac out in the neighborhood?

Amos is actually an insecure dog. He's confident at home and with family because he knows this environment and these people very well. His fear shows, however, when introduced to new people who visit his house. He's frightened of them, which is why it takes him a while to warm up to them. The environment off his property is also an intimidating world to Amos. He is a herding breed, which might also be contributing an instinct to chase. While Amos plays nicely with some dogs, it is always off leash. Amos has leash aggression.

Leash aggression occurs when a dog barks, lunges, and reacts on leash. Sometimes, a dog will be aggressive on leash but not off. He may react toward people, cars, dogs, or other animals, or a combination of them. The reaction can be very strong and makes it difficult to take the dog out of the house.

## Symptoms

The dog lunges at the leash, often barking and growling. He may spin. The fur on his shoulders may rise (piloerection). It is typical that he will not listen to you or respond to your instructions. You will usually need to pull him away from whatever it is he is targeting. Triggers will vary and can include other dogs, specific types of dogs, people walking, cars, trucks, motorcycles, skateboarders, cyclists, and strollers.

*Is your dog lunging aggressively on leash, or is he simply pulling you along to check out some interesting scents?*

## Why It Happens

Leash aggression can be very frustrating and confusing for dog owners. Why does your dog go crazy when he sees other dogs or people on leash, but can greet them just fine off leash? One reason could be frustration intolerance. A normally friendly dog who enjoys playing with other dogs or people can get frustrated when a leash prevents him from instantly going and greeting them. Combine that with pressure on his neck from the leash pulling at his collar, which reduces his oxygen flow. This can be compounded by an owner who anticipates an aggressive response and tightens the leash the second he or she sees a trigger approaching. The tight leash and reduced oxygen intake increase the dog's discomfort and frustration. What starts out as an intent to greet tips over into frustration at the inability to do so, and then into aggression.

As with other types of aggression, leash aggression can also be caused by fear. Some dogs will act aggressively to try to get the object that scares them to go away. So, a dog who is frightened of other dogs may posture and bluster in the hopes the other dog will leave. If you physically punish such a dog, you are not getting rid of the problem, which is his fear. This is a common mistake people make in trying to solve the problem. The dog is already afraid, then he is punished for demonstrating his fear. This can teach him to associate what scares him with upcoming punishment, so now the object is even scarier than before.

Leash aggression can be an issue for some herding breeds as well. Herding dogs are born to chase. Sometimes, when a herding dog sees a car zoom by, the herding instinct will kick in and he will want to chase it. When the leash prevents him from doing so, this causes frustration.

# Resource Guarding

Maddie is an adorable Maltese who turns into a growling banshee when she has a bone. She's a tiny thing, so, at first, her owners thought it was hysterical. They even took a video of her growling over a rawhide chew and put it up on YouTube, generating lots of comments from people who agreed Maddie was a hoot. Maddie's dad treated it like a game, pretending to take prized possessions away from her so she'd

*Some dogs are fine with you near their food bowls, while others may guard them.*

work herself up into a frenzy. Then the owners had a baby. Suddenly, Maddie's behavior wasn't so funny anymore.

Resource guarding occurs when a dog protects an object. A dog who resource guards will growl, snap, or bite over food, a toy, a person, a resting place, or other things. Some dogs have even been known to guard odd things, like rocks. The problem may be mild or severe.

Resource guarding is a common form of aggression. It can occur in dogs who have been rescued as strays, but also in dogs who have never known a hard day in their lives. Dogs who guard food can be completely friendly in other situations and very social. Some people think their dogs have "Jekyll and Hyde" personalities, when their loving pup turns into a demon over his food bowl or a prized toy.

For some reason, resource guarding seems to be amusing to many people—until the dog actually bites someone, often a child. A dog who growls over objects is not kidding or playing. Please don't think it's just a display and that he would never escalate to a bite. Even a dog who has only growled for years can decide one day his prized possession is worth a bite.

Sometimes, a dog looks like he's resource guarding when he's not. Although there are some dogs who will guard people, just because a dog growls when someone approaches his owner doesn't mean he is resource guarding his owner. The dog could be afraid of the approaching person. He is actually warning the person away from himself, not his owner. You can tell this is the case if the dog also reacts to an approaching person when his owner is not near him. This is still aggression, but it's not due to resource guarding.

*What dog experts term "resource guarding" should not be encouraged. It can all too easily turn into biting.*

## Symptoms

A dog who resource guards may try to get between you and whatever it is he is guarding. He will stiffen when you approach the object, curl his lip, growl, snarl, snap, and may bite. If he is resource guarding his position on a piece of furniture, he may growl, snarl, snap, and bite if you try to move him.

If the dog is resource guarding you, he will exhibit his aggression toward another person or dog who approaches you. Sometimes this only happens if your dog is in your lap, next to you on a chair or couch, or when you are holding him.

## Why It Happens

Canine behavior experts have not really determined why dogs resource guard. It can be a natural dog behavior. Protecting a high-value item is self-serving to a dog. It doesn't matter if the dog has led a charmed life in your household his entire life or grew up a stray. Is it genetic? Does it happen with dogs who come from large litters that have to compete for their mother's milk? Is it encouraged in dogs who try it once and are successful at it? There aren't any comprehensive research studies to indicate specific reasons.

# Territorial Aggression

Max has a reputation in the neighborhood, and his family is embarrassed about it. He is known as "The Barker of Baker Street" because he barks at everyone who passes the yard. Heaven forbid a cat gets on the property—he's killed one already. Max is outdoors during the day, behind a chain-link fence, so he has a pretty good view of everything that passes by. He goes nuts when a delivery person arrives with a package—growling, lunging at the fence, sometimes leaning over the top and slobbering. Delivery folks make quick work with packages, hustling back to their vehicles while eyeing the fence suspiciously. They

It is a natural instinct for a dog to defend his territory. Problems occur when this behavior gets out of control.

are worried Max will jump the fence. He is a big dog, more than 100 pounds. The vet thinks he might be part Mastiff.

When people walk their dogs past Max's yard, they steer clear for the most part. Sometimes the dogs themselves move to the other side of the street, away from Max. Every once in a while, a dog will stop and bark right back at Max. This never sits well with Max, who explodes with more barking and growling until the person drags her dog out of sight. Max has never gone over the fence yet, but the neighbors are worried it's just a matter of time.

Territorial aggression occurs when a dog is protecting his territory. This could be his yard, his crate, or even his owner's car. Just because a dog guards one area doesn't mean he will guard all areas.

Also note: just because a dog growls when a stranger enters his home, it doesn't mean he's protecting his house. It could mean that he is afraid of the person. So what looks like territorial aggression may be plain and simple fear. He's not protecting an area; he's protecting himself.

## Symptoms

A dog may stand tall, trying to look bigger. His body will be stiff. He is likely to bark and may growl. A dog who acts aggressively while moving toward someone or something that is infringing on his area is taking the offensive. A dog who acts aggressively while moving backward may be fearful. Sometimes, a dog will do both—move toward the "trespasser" and then backward. This dog is conflicted. He may fear the person, but feels a need to guard his territory. Or, he could simply be fearful in the first place.

## Why It Happens

It can be a natural behavior for a dog to protect his territory, especially if you have a guarding breed. Chained dogs have a tendency to develop territorial aggression. The Centers for Disease Control (CDC) has stated that chained dogs are 2.8 times more likely to bite than unchained dogs. This is often because the chained dog has limited territory—just what he can cover to the length of his chain. Chained dogs also often have limited interaction with people (as opposed to a dog who lives inside a house with a family). They are defending the only part of the world they know.

Some dogs may start guarding their territories out of boredom. Territory guarding also can be rewarding. If a dog barks at someone passing by and the person continues moving on, the dog has been successful. The dog doesn't realize that he didn't make the person go away. It's still rewarding. So, the next

## Tough Decisions

Having a dog with an aggression problem is potentially dangerous. It's a tremendous liability that you can't ignore. It may be that you can manage the situation at home, but what if you have friends or family over? What if your dog gets loose? Or, you may do everything right, and a complete stranger approaches your dog without permission, causing an incident. You simply can't control every aspect of your environment, all the time.

It's also extremely frustrating and heartbreaking. Managing a dog with aggression requires careful, constant diligence. You can't have people over as freely as you would like. You may feel like you're a hostage to your dog if you can't board him anywhere due to his aggression. If you're dealing with dog-dog aggression in your home, you may feel torn between two animals you love very much.

What Are Your Choices?

- You can work to solve your dog's aggression issues. This could prove to be the most challenging—and the most rewarding—effort you've ever made.

- You can try to rehome him. How aggressive your dog is will help determine how easy it is to do this. In particular, it is extremely challenging to place a dog who has an existing bite history. Many rescue organizations are already stretching their resources and can't take on such a liability. And professional trainers work with so many dogs with issues that they usually don't want to take on such a project. This doesn't mean it's impossible, but you need to understand the challenge. Rather than postponing a decision to rehome your dog until his aggression gets worse and he starts to bite, if you are leaning toward this decision, it is better to make it early.

- You can have him put down peacefully. This is never an easy choice.

These are extremely tough decisions. That's why it's very helpful to work with a professional who has a background in working with aggression cases. He or she will be able to give you a professional assessment of your dog's condition, a description of the behavior modification plan needed (and, in the case of a veterinary behaviorist, the medication that may be needed), and a prognosis for success.

No matter what you decide, no doubt there will be people in your life who question your choice. If you keep your dog, some will say you're taking on too much of a risk. If you rehome or euthanize your dog, people will wonder why you didn't try harder. Please know that only *you* can make the decision. Do your research. Consult a professional. Then make the choice that's best for your family and for your dog.

time someone passes by, the dog barks again. This can especially happen with delivery people. Someone comes to deliver a package. The dog barks ferociously to scare the trespasser away. The person delivers the package and leaves. The dog successfully chased the delivery person away! This is why some dogs who are friendly with other people will bark and growl at the mailman or delivery person.

# The Training Program

If you are dealing with aggression, it is best to seek a qualified, professional, reward-based trainer, a certified applied animal behaviorist, or veterinary behaviorist to help you in person. The level of expertise you need depends on the severity of the aggression. For example, if it's a dog who sometimes growls over toys or bones, and there are no young children involved, a trainer may be able to help you. Make sure the trainer has a successful rate in dealing with aggression cases and definitely uses modern methods. If the trainer starts talking to you about "being the alpha" or pulls out an electric collar, find someone else! If your dog has bitten multiple people—and especially if there is a risk to children—then please consult a veterinary behaviorist. A quality trainer will also not take on a case that is over his or her head—he or she should refer you to someone who specializes in aggression.

It's best to get help when you first start seeing signs of aggression. Between denial and procrastination, many people wait for a long time before they call in professional assistance. Sometimes the trigger is that the dog has finally bitten someone, bitten someone outside the family, or threatened a child. The problem with waiting is that the longer you wait, the longer the dog builds up a habit of aggressive behavior, making it harder to fix. It is much easier, and there is a greater chance of success, in dealing with an aggressive young puppy than with a dog who has been aggressive for many years.

Sometimes, people postpone calling for help with an aggressive dog because they are afraid the professional will tell them they should euthanize their dog. This is definitely a dreaded and crushing diagnosis. Dogs with aggression problems can be sweet, smart, and loving to their families. You adore your dog. He's a part of the family, and you can't imagine having to put him to sleep because of his aggressive behavior. This is completely understandable, but please don't let it deter you from seeking help sooner rather than later.

*Training a dog for guard or protection work should only be done by a professional.*

There's no telling what a professional will recommend until you call and get a thorough assessment. Done properly, you'll give a thorough history about your dog. The professional will ask you a lot of questions. Be honest, even if it's painful. Concealing information will not help your dog. It may very well be that the professional will give you a poor prognosis or painful recommendation,

## Pay Attention to Your Body Language: Children and Aggressive Dogs

Children should not participate in a training program for aggressive dogs. The risk of serious injury is too great. First, adults in the family need to help the dog learn how to make better choices. They need to work to reduce or eliminate the dog's reactivity. Then, if there are children in the family, they should only work with the dog under the direct supervision of a qualified, reward-based professional, preferably a veterinary behaviorist or certified applied animal behaviorist.

Having your child shout commands at a dog or use physical means to comply will not make the dog respect your child as a "leader." Dogs know children are different from adults. Children are shorter, often at eye level with the dog, which can be dangerous. A direct stare is confrontational to a dog, and children often want to grab a dog's head and stare into his eyes. The child sees this as a sign of affection. Many dogs will not.

Depending on their ages, children can be more unpredictable than adults. Toddlers, especially, flail their arms, have poor balance, and randomly squeal. When a toddler grabs a dog, those little fingers can grip like steel. Middle-school-aged children dash around, flop on the ground unexpectedly, and leap on furniture like acrobats. Some dogs may find this behavior too rambunctious and unpredictable. They may act aggressively to defend themselves. If there are kids in the picture, make sure you are working with the right qualified professional so your entire family can enjoy success.

but many times there are things you can do to help your dog get better.

Although there are different forms of aggression, several common treatments can be used to help alleviate them. Some may or may not apply to your specific situation— when you consult a professional, he or she will be able to guide you to the right behavior modification program. Some of the behavior modification techniques also require expertise in recognizing and understanding canine behavior, so a professional will help you perform the techniques correctly. Performing them incorrectly could make the aggression worse.

## Research

**Goal:** To determine your dog's triggers.

**What you'll need:** Before you can tackle an aggression problem, you need to have a solid understanding of what triggers your dog's aggression. With some dogs, this will be very clear. It may be a specific person or animal. It may

*It may look cute, but it is never appropriate for a child to sit on a dog. In this case, the dog is also chewing on what could be a valued item, and may not appreciate young hands near his prize.*

be a specific thing, such as the vacuum cleaner. You may not be able to be specific with some dogs. For example, you may not be able to tell if your dog reacts to men or women if sometimes he reacts to one but not another. Or, you may have a dog who reacts to random other dogs, but you can't pinpoint the type of dog who sets him off. If this is the case, just write down "random dogs." It is better to be general with your list than to overlook a trigger altogether.

Once you have your list, match each trigger with details on what aspect of the trigger causes a reaction in your dog. Also, at what farthest distance does the trigger have to be before your dog reacts? For example, does he only react when a person is near enough to touch him or when he sees someone blocks away? Here is a sample list:

| Trigger | Details | Distance |
|---|---|---|
| Boys on skateboards | Only when they are moving. | 1 block |
| People on bicycles | Only when they are moving. | 2 blocks |
| Motorcycles | When they are moving. When they make loud noises (revving, exhaust, etc.). | 3 blocks |

In creating this list, you may notice similarities you had not noticed in the course of just dealing with your dog's behavior. This will be helpful in determining a management and treatment plan.

*Sometimes, a fear reaction will be unmistakable.*

## Management

No matter what type of aggression your dog has, you will need a solid management program. This is a program that will help prevent your dog from experiencing his triggers, so that he doesn't have aggressive episodes. The more he practices, the better he will get at it, and the stronger a habit it will become.

**Goal:** To prevent your dog from experiencing a trigger for his aggression or from hurting a person or other animal.

**What you'll need:**

### Crate

If your dog is aggressive when you have guests over, toward other dogs in the household, or if he resource guards his food, a crate can be a safe place to confine him to prevent him from hurting someone.

Train your dog to enjoy confinement in the crate—it should not be used as punishment. You can use the "Settle" foundation behavior training to get him used to his crate.

If your dog resource guards his food, feed him his meals in his crate. Shut the door securely until he is done, then release him from the crate and retrieve his food bowl. This will give him a quiet place to eat his meals and prevent other animals and people from risking a bite.

If your dog does not resource guard food or toys, give him a food-stuffed toy as a reward for extended periods of confinement. For example, if your dog is aggressive toward other people and you are having guests over, confine him in his crate with a food-stuffed toy for entertainment until they leave.

## Baby Gates

For confinement that is less secure than a crate, use baby gates. These can be handy if your dog is fearful of guests in your home, but he opts to run away rather than engage and try to bite. Put your dog behind a baby gate within view of your guests and give him a safe place from which to observe.

You can also use baby gates for dogs who have succeeded with behavior modification enough to transition from a crate to being behind a baby gate (perhaps while wearing a muzzle).

Baby gates are useful for backup protection when keeping dogs apart who don't get along in your household. Just in case one dog slips through a door, the baby gate offers added security. You can also use them as backup security if your dog dashes out the front door or as a barrier to prevent your dog from looking out the window or door at a potential aggressive trigger.

## Front-Clip Harness

A harness that allows the leash to clip in the front will give you more control over your dog's forward movement. It also prevents your dog from choking since you won't be pulling back on his collar. Most dogs readily acclimatize to a front-clip harness. This tool is especially helpful when dealing with leash aggression or when trying to control a dog who lunges and barks at people or dogs. For people who have difficulty physically controlling their aggressive dogs and have concerns the dog may pull hard enough to get loose, a front-clip harness can be extremely helpful.

## Head Halter

For dogs requiring more control than a front-clip harness can provide, a head halter is a useful tool. Head halters are especially good when gradually introducing dogs who are aggressive toward other dogs or people because they enable you to quickly and humanely redirect the dog's head if necessary. If you control a dog's head, you control the dog. The head is where the teeth are; so, by controlling the dog's head, you are increasing the safety of the people and dogs around him. When using a head halter, it is best to

*A head halter offers more control than a collar or a harness.*

A basket muzzle is the recommended type of muzzle for training.

desensitize your dog to wearing it rather than just putting it on him and starting training. Some dogs find the nose loop annoying, so getting them used to the head halter gradually will help them acclimatize.

## Muzzle

Muzzles are excellent tools that can help keep people and other animals safe. There is a stigma associated with muzzles, which is unfortunate because they can prevent people and animals from getting hurt. When a dog is wearing a muzzle, the tension around him is eased because people feel more secure knowing the dog cannot bite them. It also prevents a dog from practicing bite behavior.

Muzzles are useful for most aggressive dogs, even those who only show aggression at the veterinarian's office. For example, get a muzzle and train your dog to comfortably wear it at home, then wear it to the vet's office. This is less scary than if your veterinarian has to muzzle your dog with no preparatory desensitization.

There are different types of muzzles. The recommended type is a basket muzzle. This will allow your dog to breathe easily, drink water, and take treats.

## Household Items

You may have items around your house that can help you prevent your dog from reacting to his triggers. Doors can confine your dog to a specific room. Blinds and drapes can block his view of the outdoors. You can also purchase contact paper that you affix to your windows to diffuse the view so your dog won't be able to focus on a trigger. You may be able to tether a dog by looping his leash around a sturdy piece of furniture. You may be able to bolt a hook into your baseboard to serve as an anchor for a tether. Be creative. What can you use in your household to prevent your dog from practicing aggression?

## Medication

Your veterinarian or veterinary behaviorist may recommend that your dog take prescription medication. There are many medications now available to help dogs with aggression (and fear) issues. You may be worried that the drugs are tranquilizers, and your dog will just be sleepy. Or that they will change your dog's personality. That's not how these drugs work. Proper medication for aggression helps balance the blood chemistry in your dog's brain. You can try behavior modification all you want, but if your dog has a chemical imbalance preventing him from learning, you will not see progress.

On the other hand, a drug alone will not stop your dog from being aggressive. Medication is not magic. You will need a behavioral modification plan working in conjunction with medication in order to be successful.

It may take more than one drug trial to find the drug that works for your dog's issue. It may take trials at different doses. This is not unusual. Monitor your dog carefully and record his reactions to see if they are improving or getting worse, so you can work with your veterinarian as a team to help your dog. You should always address any concerns you have about medication to your veterinarian. Not every aggressive dog will need medication, but those who do can make tremendous strides with its proper use.

## Foundation Behaviors

### "Come"
For calling your dog to you, away from an aggressive trigger.

### "Leave it!"
To avoid the trigger. If you are diligent in observing your environment, and you see your dog target a person, dog, or item, cuing, "Leave it" may prevent him from reacting aggressively in the first place.

### "Settle" or "Stay"
To get your dog into a "safe place" away from a trigger, such as when company comes over.

### "Wait"
To prevent your dog from bolting out the door without you first checking the environment for triggers.

## Counterconditioning
Counterconditioning involves pairing a stimulus that causes a response with another stimulus that causes the opposite. The first stimulus then starts triggering the second response. In the case of aggression, you pair something your dog really loves with the thing he is aggressive toward. In time, he starts associating the trigger with the item he loves, which changes his response from an aggressive one to a neutral or happier one. Counterconditioning is often used in conjunction with desensitization. You will get better results if you incorporate both into your training sessions.

This technique is especially useful for aggression based in fear, whether that is dog–dog aggression, dog–human aggression, or leash aggression. You teach your dog to have a positive association with a person, animal, or item that he finds scary. It's also used for resource guarding. You teach your dog to have a positive association with someone approaching his food bowl, toy, or other item he is guarding.

**Goal:** Your dog will associate an object he finds scary with something better, thus transferring the pleasant association to the object.

**What you'll need:** Really delicious treats, leash, an object toward which your dog is aggressive. The leash is to prevent your dog from going after the trigger, not for correction.

1. Determine how far away your dog needs to be from the scary object so that he is not stressed or reacting aggressively.
2. Wait for him to notice the scary object. The second he does, feed him a treat. If the object moves, such as a passerby or a car driving by, feed your dog the entire time that the object is in view. Note with just counterconditioning, you are not moving. You and your dog should stay in place. Do not move toward the trigger.
3. When the item is out of view, stop feeding treats. The treats should only be fed when the trigger is in view.

NOTE: Try to stay at a distance at which your dog will not react. This can be challenging if the object is moving and you have no control over it, as, for example, if you are working to get your dog not to react toward a child on a bicycle. (If you can, get a friend to ride the bike!) Even if your dog does growl slightly or starts to react, keep feeding him. You may feel like you are rewarding the reaction, but you are trying to change his association with the object. If he refuses to take the treats, then they are not enticing enough, or you are too close to the trigger. Move farther back and try again.

## Desensitization

Desensitization is the process of increasing an animal's tolerance to a stimulus by gradually increasing the presence of the stimulus. In the case of an aggressive dog who reacts toward a person, animal, or object, desensitization helps you to get your dog used to the trigger so that he no longer reacts aggressively toward it. Desensitization is often used in conjunction with counterconditioning.

This technique is useful for aggression based in fear (whether it's dog–dog or dog–human aggression), leash aggression, and territorial aggression. In these situations, you keep the dog far enough from the trigger so that he doesn't react, then gradually move closer. Desensitization is also used to help get over the problem of resource guarding. In this situation, you start with a lower value item that the dog is not as likely to guard and then gradually work up to higher value items.

**Goal:** To gradually get your dog more comfortable in the presence of an aggression trigger, thus causing a reduction or elimination of reactivity.

**What you'll need:** Treats, leash, object toward which your dog is aggressive. The leash is to prevent your dog from going after the trigger, not for correction. You must *not* use the leash to make your dog approach the scary object! You use it simply to ensure your dog's safety and that of anyone around you.

1. The key to desensitization is to stay below the threshold at which point your dog exhibits fearful behaviors and stress signals. (Remember, much aggression is based in fear.) Determine how far away your dog needs to be from the scary object so that he is not stressed or reacting aggressively.

*Desensitizing your dog to things that upset him can be time-consuming, but such training is well worth the effort it takes.*

Depending on how fearful he is of the object, this could be several feet, yards, or even blocks away. This is the point where you start.

2. Take one step closer to the scary object. Wait and determine if your dog is stressed. If he is not, then take another step closer. Repeat, taking enough time as necessary in between steps to determine if your dog is not stressed. If he is, stop. Do not go closer to the object. It is OK if, for the rest of your training session, you simply stand there and let your dog get used to things. This is still progress! Your goal is to end the training session *before* your dog gets stressed. Total training time should be about 10–15 minutes.

3. In between training sessions, try to avoid the trigger as much as possible.

NOTE: Done properly, a desensitization session should look fairly boring to an outsider! Your goal is for your dog to be comfortable throughout the session, not to get stressed or react aggressively. This may take many sessions, depending on your dog and how reactive he is to the object. The biggest challenge people have with this exercise is being patient and not pushing the dog into having a reaction. It will just set you back if you do!

## Counterconditioning and Desensitization Combined

As mentioned, counterconditioning and desensitization are often used together for more effective results.

### Resource Guarding

Here is an example of how you can use both counterconditioning and desensitization with a dog who resource guards his food bowl. Again, if your dog is having strong reactions over his food bowl—and especially if he has already bitten—work in conjunction with a qualified, reward-based professional. If you don't, you could make the problem worse or you could get hurt.

**Goal:** Your dog will look forward to you approaching his food bowl and not react aggressively.

**What you'll need:** Food bowl, regular kibble, extra delicious treats.

1. Place the empty food bowl in front of your dog. Stand facing him, from about four to five feet away. Check to ensure that he has a loose body and is not already displaying any signs of stress or aggression. If he is, stop the exercise and consult a professional. If he isn't, approach him, drop a few pieces of kibble in his bowl, and then take several steps backward. You will just be approaching the bowl, casually dropping in a few kibble pieces, then casually backing off.

2. Wait for him to eat the food. If he doesn't eat the food—if he freezes over it, gives you a hard stare, or growls, stop the exercise and consult a professional. If he eats it and looks at you, with loose body and no signs of agitation, repeat Step 1.

*Dropping kibble into your dog's bowl is an essential step in eliminating resource guarding.*

3. Repeat for each of your dog's meals. If you have a young puppy 6 months or younger, do this three times a day. For dogs older than 6 months, do this twice a day.

4. When your dog is starting to look forward to your approach—he has a loose body, low tail wag, relaxed or happy expression—move to this next step. Repeat Step 1, except give him a handful of kibble. Then, *while your dog is eating his kibble*, approach him again and drop a couple of delicious treats in his bowl, then leave. Wait for him to finish all of the food in his bowl. Look for signs that he is getting agitated. This can include a high tail, freezing, eating faster, or body blocking you from the bowl (sometimes he will just cover the bowl with his head). If you see these signs, go back to a previously successful step and work at it for a few days before trying this step again.

5. Repeat Step 4 until your dog starts to look forward to your approach while he is eating.

6. Repeat Step 4, except now you will wait until your dog looks at you, with a loose body and happy expression, before you give him the tasty treats. You will place the empty food bowl down and leave, then approach and put a handful of kibble in the bowl, then leave. Wait for your dog to finish the kibble and look at you expectantly. Walk over to the bowl and give him several treats and more kibble. Repeat for all meals.

NOTE: The desensitization part of this exercise is that you work "under threshold," at a point where your dog will not react aggressively. You start with an empty bowl, then add kibble, then add treats. The counterconditioning part of this exercise is that you associate your approach with *bringing* food, rather than with taking food away. Your dog resource guards because he doesn't have a good association with your approach. He is concerned that you will take his food away. This teaches him that when you approach, you bring him food instead.

### Dog–Human Aggression

Here is an example of desensitization combined with counterconditioning for a dog who is aggressive toward people. In this example, it is assumed that the dog is friendly toward his handler, but not strangers.

**Goal:** Your dog will reduce or eliminate his reactivity toward other people and begin to look forward to their approach.

**What you'll need:** Leash, treats, another person. Your dog should be in a head halter or front-clip harness.

**Preparation:** If your dog has any bite history, then muzzle training should be done first. In this exercise, as outlined, *do not get close enough to the other person for your dog to ever make contact*. As a safety backup, however, he should be muzzled. Remember, having an aggressive dog takes a tremendous amount of management. Always have backup plans in place before beginning any training session. What if my dog gets loose? What if the leash breaks? What if… ? Have one or two backup plans in place and ready to implement to help prevent serious failures. For example, you should not get close enough to the other person for your dog to make contact. But if something happens and your dog does get close enough, he will not be able to bite the person while wearing a muzzle. So don't start the training session until he is muzzled.

1. Start at the distance at which point your dog will not react to the sight of the person. He should have a loose body and be relaxed. If he looks stiff or has any stress signals, you are too close. Move back farther.

2. The person should come into view and walk across your dog's line of vision. Not toward you and your dog—just horizontally across your dog's line of sight, keeping the same distance throughout. As soon as your dog shows he is becoming alert to the person, feed him treats. When the person disappears from view, stop the treats.

3. Take one small step closer. Repeat Step 2. Only proceed as far as your dog will not react. He should have a calm, relaxed body with no stress signals. *Do not get any closer than 15 feet from the person without the assistance of a professional.*

NOTE: The desensitization part of this exercise is staying back far enough from the trigger so that your dog does not react. The counterconditioning part is the association of the trigger—a stranger—with treats. Your dog should start to turn to you when he sees the other person, anticipating his treats. When he starts doing this, you are making progress!

Again, in order for this to be a successful training session, it should look really boring! If your dog reacts and blusters, you have pushed him too far and should immediately stop. Wait and try again another day, at a greater distance.

## Muzzle Training

Muzzle training is a technique that is useful for any level of aggression when there is a risk the dog may bite.

**Goal:** To get your dog to enjoy wearing his muzzle.

**What you'll need:** Muzzle, treats, peanut butter (or cream cheese).

1. Smear peanut butter in the tip of the muzzle, where the tip of your dog's nose will go. Hold the muzzle at the same height as your dog's head. Encourage him to reach in and lick the treat. When he does, praise him! After he has had some of the peanut butter, remove the muzzle and be quiet. During the training session, you will give him lots of attention when his head is in the muzzle and be quiet when the muzzle is off. Do not buckle the muzzle on yet, just hold it for your dog. Repeat two more times. Practice this several times each day, over several days.

2. When your dog is eagerly pushing his nose into the muzzle, it's time for the next step. Smear the inside of the muzzle with peanut butter as before. Encourage your dog to stick his head in the muzzle. When he does, quickly buckle the muzzle and immediately give your dog three treats through the muzzle, one after the other, praising him the entire time. Quickly remove the muzzle and be quiet. Repeat two more times. Practice this several times each day, over several days.

3. When your dog is successful with Step 2, it's time to put on the muzzle for longer periods of time. You no longer have to smear the inside tip of the muzzle with peanut butter. Offer your dog the muzzle, and, when he puts his head in it, praise him! Buckle it, give him five treats, one after the other, praising him the entire time. Remove the muzzle and be quiet. Repeat two more times. Practice this several times each day, over several days. Gradually space out the time in between treats.

4. Continue making wearing the muzzle a positive experience for your dog. You can gradually fade out treats, but always praise him when you put it on him.

NOTE: After muzzle training, if your dog needs to wear a muzzle at the veterinarian's office, put the muzzle on your dog at home first. Let him wear it to the office and during his visit, then on the way home. Take it off when you get back home. After all your hard work getting your dog used to his muzzle, you don't want him to only associate it with vet visits!

## Trade

Teaching your dog to trade items can be useful if he is a resource guarder.

**Goal:** To teach your dog to willingly give up items.

**What you'll need:** A list of items your dog finds valuable, from lowest value to highest value. For example, if your dog does not guard a specific toy, that would be first on the list. If he starts to tense when you take away a tennis ball, that would be second. If he growls or snaps over a rawhide chew, that would be even higher. Start this exercise with the first two items on the list.

*Teach your dog from puppyhood to "Drop It" on your cue.*

1. Offer your dog Item 1, the lowest value item. Let him settle with it.

2. Show your dog Item 2. Since it is a higher value, he will likely drop Item 1. When he does, praise him! Toss Item 2 a couple feet away so you can easily pick up Item 1.

3. Offer your dog Item 1. When he drops Item 2, praise him! Toss Item 1 a couple feet away so you can easily pick up Item 2.

4. Repeat, gradually working your way through the list. If at any time your dog begins to tense or show signs of guarding, stop and call a professional.

*Getting a dog to turn away from a trigger when you want him to can help prevent an aggressive episode.*

## Emergency U-Turn

You can have the best of intentions. You can work hard at training your reactive dog and always practice good management techniques. But all those best-laid plans can go up in flames when you go out in public because you can't control the environment. All it takes is one neighbor letting his dog off leash and having that dog rush up to your dog. Or you're walking your dog at 5 a.m. to ensure that things will be quiet, and the neighborhood paper boy comes zooming along on his bicycle, throwing newspapers and sending your dog into a barking fit. In your own home, you can control many things. Outside, you can't. This is where an emergency U-turn comes in handy.

You will use the turn when you are out walking and you see a potential trigger up ahead. You do an emergency U-turn and head in the opposite direction, thus avoiding the trigger.

**Goal:** Your dog will immediately turn with you on cue and walk in the opposite direction.

**What you'll need:** Leash, clicker (or verbal marker), treats.

1. Teach this at home, in your yard if possible, where your dog can learn the behavior first without experiencing a reactive trigger.
2. Walk forward. Stop and turn smoothly around, facing the way you came. This is easier to do if you turn away from your dog, so your sudden turn won't make you collide with him. So, if you choose to walk with your dog on the left, turn right. If you walk with your dog on your right, turn left. As you turn, encourage your dog to keep up with you. Pat your leg and verbally encourage him to keep up. Don't just yank him around with you!
3. Start walking forward, now in the opposite direction from which you started.
4. Repeat, gradually working to where you can walk at a brisk pace and your dog will turn with you immediately when you turn.

NOTE: Your act of turning should serve as a cue to your dog. If you want to add a verbal cue, you can. First, get the behavior to the point at which it is reliable. Then, just before you turn, cue "U-turn!" or whatever cue you have chosen. Say it once in a friendly voice. With practice, your dog can also learn to associate the verbal cue with the action.

# 4

# Barking

**M**urray has things to say. Since this Miniature Schnauzer/Poodle mix was a puppy, he would bark when someone came to the door, but the problem seems to have grown worse over the years. Now 5 years old, Murray barks when he wants something, especially food or for someone to throw his squeaky hedgehog. His owners yell at him to stop, but it doesn't work. Murray just barks more. It's easier just to give Murray what he wants so he'll be quiet.

Although Murray gets along OK with the other dogs in his family, he can be snippy with dogs outside his circle of friends. So, when he's out for a walk, he'll bark at other dogs he sees. He always barks in the car, whether he sees another dog or not. It gets worse when the car comes to a stop. One day, when his mom was pulling into a parking space, Murray erupted into a frenzy of barking and scared the heck out of a poor senior lady trying to get into her car in the spot next to them. Some days it seems as though the only time Murray is quiet is when he's sleeping.

Murray is barking for a variety of reasons. He barks to get what he wants—and it pays off for him, so the behavior gets stronger. He could be barking out of fear of other dogs, since he does not have a history of liking dogs outside his family. The car barking is likely alarm barking, sparked off by things Murray sees along his travels.

## Symptoms

Barking! Some dogs will bark at specific things or in specific situations.

## Why It Happens

There are many reasons why dogs bark, and some dogs will bark at specific things or in particular situations:

**Barking is rewarding.** Dogs can find barking to be great fun. They also get paid for barking. The laws of learning state that behavior that is rewarded increases in frequency. If your dog barks at the delivery man and the delivery man leaves, your dog may think he was successful in chasing the delivery man off. The next time the delivery man visits, your dog barks again.

If your dog barks at you because he wants you to throw the ball and you do, you're paying him for barking. If your dog barks at you while you prepare his dinner and you feed him, you're paying

*Some dogs have more to say than others!*

him for barking. Barking also pays off in attention. Negative attention is still attention to your dog.

**Some breeds have a tendency to bark.** Herding breeds, especially, were bred to move livestock. In this task, barking can be an effective tool. Just because you don't have goats or sheep doesn't mean your herding breed loses his inherited trait to make noise. You may find the barking accelerates when your dog is chasing something or if he sees a person or dog moving quickly.

**He could be protecting his territory.** This is called territorial barking. Your dog could consider his territory to be your house, yard, or your car. He might also bark when others come near his crate.

*Some dog breeds are born to herd, which can make them more prone to barking in potential herding situations.*

*Some dogs bark because they are simply happy to see you!*

**He could be happy to see people.** Some dogs bark in greeting. If your dog is happy and excited to see visitors, he is welcoming their arrival.

**He might be bored.** Dogs who don't have enough physical exercise or mental stimulation may engage in barking to alleviate their boredom. Barking is fun!

**He could be raising the alarm.** If your dog barks at any little noise he hears, he could be an alarm barker. This dog doesn't necessarily confine his barking to his territory: he can alarm bark in other locations as well. Your dog's body language will be stiff, and he may give other signs of stress. It can be a symptom of a nervous dog. He's insecure, so he barks.

**Dogs like to join a party.** If other dogs bark, it can inspire your dog to bark, too. This can cause quite a racket if you have a multiple-dog household. Once one starts, the rest chime in! Note that this can also happen when you yell at your dog. To your dog, you're simply chiming in! Yelling at your dog to stop barking is usually ineffective and can make the problem worse.

**He could be frustrated.** If the tennis ball rolls under the couch and your dog can't reach it, he could start barking out of frustration. This type of barking can also be confused with territorial barking. Some dogs are not actually barking to protect their territory; they are barking out of frustration because they want to get to a dog or person passing by to say hello.

**It could be compulsive.** If your dog runs back and forth while he barks, or spins in circles, this could be compulsive behavior. This is often tied to stress and anxiety.

**He could be anxious.** Dogs who suffer from separation anxiety might bark when you leave. Barking can be a sign of stress.

## The Training Program

Helping your dog learn to be quiet will partially depend on why he's barking. Here are some techniques that can be useful. You may not need every exercise for every barking issue.

## Research

**Goal:** To determine your dog's barking triggers.

**What you'll need:** A list of barking triggers. Before you choose a training exercise, you need a list of what makes your dog bark. It's OK to admit you might be on the list!

## Management

No matter what kind of barker your dog is, a good management program can help.

**Goal:** To prevent your dog from experiencing triggers for barking.

**What you'll need:**

**Blinds, drapes, doors, window film.** Use these to block your dog's view of items that trigger his barking. Some people hesitate to lower the blinds or otherwise block views, but remember, the

Some dogs bark to say "Notice me!"

more your dog practices barking at triggers he sees outside, the better he will get at the behavior. If you only work on training sometimes but let him go ahead and bark at other times, the behavior will not improve.

**Also implement as part of your management program:**

### Exercise

Many dogs have plenty of energy to bark because they are not getting enough physical exercise. This is especially true of adolescent dogs, and it can lead to boredom barking. Just being outside in a fenced backyard is not exercise. Play games with your dog, play fetch, have other dogs over for playdates, and engage in other cardiovascular activities with your dog. A tired dog doesn't have as much energy to bark.

## Foundation Behaviors
### "Down," "Settle"

Some dogs find it harder to bark when they are lying down. For others, it's not a hindrance.

## Hush

Teaching your dog to be quiet on cue can be extremely useful. This exercise will not be as helpful if your dog is barking because he is anxious or afraid, such as with alarm or territorial barking. Imagine being afraid of something and wanting to tell someone you love that you are frightened, but that person keeps telling you to hush up. It won't make you feel better—you're still afraid. If your dog is a greeting or attention barker, this exercise can help.

*You can use a visual as well as a verbal cue to train your dog to stop unwanted barking.*

**Goal:** Your dog will stop barking when you cue him.

**What you'll need:** Clicker, treats.

1. Do something that is likely to get your dog barking. This sounds odd, but if you don't get your dog barking, you can't teach him the opposite!

2. When your dog is barking, wait for him to be quiet. Even if it's just for a second. As soon as it happens, click and then treat. Repeat. You will find your dog stays quiet for longer periods of time because that is what is being marked and rewarded.

3. When your dog starts to quiet on a regular basis, start cueing "Hush" just before you think he will be quiet. Say it once and don't yell it. As soon as your dog quiets, click and treat.

## Desensitization and Counterconditioning

If your dog is barking because he is afraid of his triggers, then desensitization and counterconditioning can help. They will help teach your dog that scary objects are not as frightening as he thinks they are, so he won't feel a need to bark at them. See the Aggression chapter for more details on desensitization and counterconditioning.

*Frustration can also cause barking. The dog here is barking because his tennis ball is getting away from him.*

**Goal:** To teach your dog to not be afraid of a trigger.

**What you'll need:** Leash, treats, trigger. This example uses a vacuum cleaner. The leash is simply to prevent your dog from wandering. You will not use it for correction or to drag your dog closer to the vacuum cleaner.

1. Place the vacuum cleaner at a distance far enough away that your dog will not bark at it. Keep it turned off. Have your dog on leash. Your dog should have a loose, relaxed body and not show signs of stress. When your dog notices the vacuum cleaner, feed him several treats.

2. Take one step toward the vacuum cleaner. Check your dog for signs of stress. As long as he is still calm and not barking, feed him some treats. If he starts barking, end the exercise. Later, try it at a farther distance.

3. Repeat Step 2 until you can get to the vacuum cleaner without your dog barking.

4. When you can repeat this exercise successfully several times, it's time to turn the vacuum cleaner on.

5. Start at a distance far enough away so your dog will not bark at the vacuum cleaner when it is turned on. Please note you may have to start farther away than you did originally. It just depends on if the combined visual and auditory trigger will make your dog want to bark. At this point, the vacuum cleaner is just stationary. Feed your dog several treats.

6. Take one step closer to the vacuum cleaner. Check your dog for signs of stress. As long as he is still calm and not barking, feed him some more treats.

7. Repeat Step 2 until you can reach the vacuum cleaner without your dog barking.

8. When you can repeat this several times successfully, then you can start getting another person to move the vacuum cleaner while it's turned on. At first, the person will just move it back and forth a foot or so.

9. Feed your dog treats when the vacuum cleaner moves. Only proceed as far as your dog can succeed. If he barks, stop the exercise and try again later, at a farther distance.

**10.** Take one step closer to the moving vacuum cleaner. Check your dog for signs of stress. If he is still calm and is not barking, feed him more treats.

**11.** Gradually work up to where the person can vacuum the room without your dog barking.

NOTE: The desensitization part of this exercise is the distance between the vacuum cleaner and the dog. You only move closer when your dog has acclimatized to one spot. The counterconditioning part is associating the vacuum cleaner with treats. Your dog should start to look to you when he sees the vacuum cleaner, waiting for his treat. When he does this, you're making progress!

## Substitute a Quiet Behavior

This exercise is just as much about training you as it is your dog. If your dog is demand barking and you are paying him for it, then you are rewarding the behavior. It will continue and likely get worse. It's time to train you! If you don't change your habits, your dog will never change his.

Understand that problem behavior gets worse before it gets better. This is normal. So once you stop paying your dog for barking, he is very likely to bark worse. This is because your dog is confused—you just changed the rules on him, and he doesn't understand. His barking always got him what he wanted before, why isn't it working now? He'll try barking louder to get what he wants. If this happens, just be aware that it's normal and you can work through it. If you go back to what you were doing before, you will just make the problem more cemented and so harder to fix.

**Goal:** To teach your dog that his barking does not result in a desired reward.

**What you'll need:** Items your dog find rewarding, for which he usually barks to get; clicker. You'll also need resolve, to stop paying your dog for barking. If you stick with your plan sometimes, but give in other times, then the barking will get worse. It may be hard, but you can do it!

**Preparation:** Teach "Sit" and/or "Down" first.

**1.** When your dog starts to bark for something, such as his food bowl, your attention, for you to throw his ball, or whatever, wait. Wait for him to be quiet, even if just for a second.

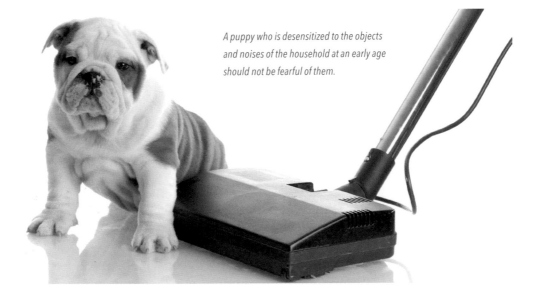

*A puppy who is desensitized to the objects and noises of the household at an early age should not be fearful of them.*

*Playing tug with your dog can distract him from barking.*

2. The second he is quiet, cue him to do something else, such as "Sit" or "Down." If he keeps barking, wait and try again when he is quiet. If he complies but still barks, cue him to do something else. The goal is to cue him to do another behavior that you can reward him for. It doesn't really matter what it is, but it should be done without barking.

3. When he performs the behavior you've requested, and he's quiet, click. Then give him what he wants, if it's appropriate. For example, if he's barking for you to throw the ball and you don't mind throwing the ball, throw the ball once he's quiet and sitting. If he's barking for you to give him a potato chip, you don't have to give him the chip! Give him a more appropriate reward.

NOTE. You may wonder why you don't just immediately give your dog what he wants when he is quiet. With demand barking, it can be easy to accidentally chain the behavior. Here's the chain: the dog barks to get a valued item, he is quiet and then immediately gets the valued item. What he learns is that he still needs to bark to get what he wants. This is why we insert a different behavior in between. It's better for him to learn to be quiet and sit or lie down in order to earn his reward.

## Non-Treat Alternatives: Chomp on This

Some dogs find it harder to bark with something in their mouths. Some still manage barking just fine, but at least it's muffled! If your dog likes to play fetch, consider using a ball or other toy as a reward during your training session. You may also want to try a game of tug. It's harder to bark with your mouth full!

# 5

# Begging

When her family sits down to meals, Sally, a 4-year-old Goldendoodle, is right in there with them. She sits inches from her mom, staring intently at every bite her mom eats. If she ignores her, Sally can be pushy. Sometimes she even nudges her mom's hand with her nose. If her mom yells at her to go away, she will, but she returns minutes later. Or, she'll walk over to another family member at the table and start begging there.

If she's ignored, Sally will start dramatic sighing and whining. It also doesn't seem to matter what the family is eating. Sally is happy to beg for pizza just as much as she is for steak. It's really annoying. It's hard to enjoy your dinner when you have eyes boring into you!

Sally has learned to beg at the table. Some dogs learn to beg for food no matter where or what you are eating.

## Symptoms

Dogs who beg will stare at you while you are eating. If they don't get rewarded with your food, they may escalate their behavior. This can include pawing you, pushing at you with a nose, or jumping up on you. Some dogs will jump up on the table, even on top of the table. They may whine or bark.

## Why It Happens

Dogs beg because it is rewarding. It can start if you feed your dog while you're eating. That's a slippery slope. You can't reward your dog for being near you while you're eating sometimes and then expect him to leave you alone at other times. How is he supposed to know the difference? Your dog also doesn't understand that it's OK when you feed him from the table, but that he should leave your dinner guests alone.

Sometimes your dog can develop a begging habit even if you've never fed him directly while you were eating. If your dog finds crumbs under the table, or if a family member is a sloppy eater and leaves a mess, dogs learn that people eating at the table are a good source of tasty surprises. Other times, kids are a source of the rewards, slipping your dog treats under the table, especially if they don't want to eat what's on their plates.

*Giving in to a begging dog even once can encourage an ongoing behavior problem.*

# The Training Program
## Management
If your dog is getting rewarded at the table, the first thing you need to do is set your meals up so that the rewards stop. Otherwise, he'll continue to beg. You can implement other training exercises, but without stopping the rewards, you won't stop the begging.

Goal: To prevent your dog from access to where you are eating.

What you'll need: Area for confinement, food-stuffed toy, or long-lasting chew.

1. Make sure you and your family members are not feeding him at the table.
2. If you have messy eaters and your dog is getting rewarded with crumbs, then put your dog in a different room while you eat. Crate him if he can't be trusted unsupervised in another room yet. Be sure to give him a food-stuffed toy or a long-lasting chew toy as a reward for his confinement. Clean up the dining area before letting your dog back in there.

## Foundation Behaviors
### "Down," "Settle," or "Stay"
To give your dog a designated, acceptable place to stay while you're eating.

### "Leave It!"
If you drop something while eating, "Leave it!" can prevent your dog from getting it and therefore being rewarded for scavenging.

*Some dogs will even jump up in search of tasty tidbits. The golden rule is never to feed a dog from the table.*

## "Settle" in a Crate/on a Bed

**Goal:** To teach your dog an alternative behavior to begging, namely, settling away from where you eat into a bed or in a crate.

**What you'll need:** A bed, crate, or tether. You'll also need a food-stuffed toy and some treats. If your dog will not stay confined on a bed at first, then use a crate or a tether. Then, transition to a bed once you establish the new habit.

**Preparation:** Teach "Settle" first.

1. Place a bed (or crate) away from where you normally eat, but where your dog can still see you. You need to be able to supervise your dog to ensure he remains in his bed. Put the treats near the dog bed, but out of your dog's reach. Do not have them with you at the table.

2. During meals, cue your dog to "Settle." Give him a food-stuffed toy that will keep him busy while you eat. If he

*Giving your dog a special bone to chew can keep him busy while you are eating.*

leaves the toy and starts to beg, then the toy is not high value enough. Be sure you stuff it with really tasty treats.

**3.** Occasionally, throughout the meal, get up and give your dog a treat while he's in his bed.

NOTE: If your dog breaks position, immediately put him back. Yes, this means that it may take you a while to finish your meal at first! With consistency and practice, he will learn to stay put. Stick to the training program. Also note that if you stuff the toy and freeze it, the contents will last longer and be more challenging for your dog to eat. This can occupy him for a longer time.

## Non-Treat Alternatives: Chew Bones

Depending on how strong your dog's begging habit is, you may be able to use a special chew bone to keep him occupied in his bed while you eat. There are a variety of safe, synthetic or natural chews you can find in any pet food supply store or online. Just know that some of them are not as enticing as the meal you have ready at the table. Try deer or elk antlers, which are long-lasting, don't splinter, and don't stain your carpet. Avoid small cooked bones, especially chicken bones, which can be dangerous to dogs. They can splinter and get caught in the throat, in which case a dog can choke.

Save the chew treat only for meal time, to keep it special. Cue your dog to "Settle" and reward him with the chew. You may need to try a variety of long-term rewards before you find one that keeps your dog interested during meal times.

# 6

# Carsickness

Penny the Pit Bull puppy loves to be at the park, out for hikes with her family, and at the pet supply store to pick out her own toys. She even loves visiting the veterinarian's office. She'll prance right into the lobby, wagging her entire body for the veterinary staff to give her attention. What Penny doesn't like is traveling to those places. Penny gets carsick.

As soon as the car starts moving, Penny starts drooling. If she's in the car for more than 10 minutes, she vomits. Her family loves for Penny to join them on their outings, but they're getting awfully tired of cleaning up after her. They also feel badly for her, since Penny looks miserable when she's carsick. Lately, Penny has started not wanting to get into the car at all. When they try to get her in, she tucks her tail and puts on the brakes. The family has to pick her up just to get her in the car.

## Symptoms

Your dog may start showing signs of uneasiness as you approach the car. He may hesitate to get in or downright refuse. This is because he has associated the car with feeling bad and getting sick. You may see signs of stress, including yawning, lip licking, and whining. When in the car, your dog could be lethargic or cower. Or, he may try to pace. Other symptoms include drooling and vomiting. He may throw up food or just bile, depending on what's in his stomach at the time.

## Why It Happens

Some dogs can get nauseous in the car just like people can. It can happen more often in puppies and young dogs than in adults. This is because the ear structure in puppies isn't as developed as when dogs get older. You may find your dog outgrows it around age 1. Sometimes dogs don't, however.

If a dog has an ear infection or other problem with his ear, it could also cause him to be nauseous enough in the car to vomit.

If a dog doesn't travel in the car much, but only goes to a place that causes him anxiety, such as the veterinarian's office, this can cause him to be stressed enough in the car to get sick. Some dogs can also get sick in the car due to medication.

*Puppies often suffer more frequently from carsickness than do older dogs.*

# The Training Program
## Management

First of all, try not feeding your dog for several hours before his car ride. It may help reduce nausea if there's no food in his stomach.

**Goal:** To set up your dog's car environment to reduce the chances he will get carsick.

**What you'll need:**

**A crate or a seatbelt.** Dogs need to be confined in the car for safety reasons, just as people should wear seatbelts. A dog who gets anxious in a car might pace or try to jump into your lap while you are driving. This could be dangerous. Plus, if you are in a car accident, you want to make sure your dog is safely confined. What if you are injured in the accident, and your dog gets loose? Don't take a chance. Safely confine your dog in the car.

If you want to use a crate, be sure to crate train your dog first, so he doesn't associate anxiety in the car with the confinement of a crate. Properly trained, a crate can be a safe haven for your dog. From a practical standpoint, confining your dog will also confine his drool and vomit and make it easier to clean up!

**Medication.** Talk to your veterinarian about medication to help your dog combat nausea. Just realize that drugs can treat nausea, but they won't fix your dog's anxiety. If he is getting sick because he is stressed, you will need to work on behavior modification to help your dog as well.

## Foundation Behaviors
### "Settle"
To help teach your dog to enjoy confinement in a crate.

## Desensitization to the Car
Depending on the level of your dog's anxiety about car rides, this could take several or many sessions. Only continue each session for as long as your dog remains comfortable and relaxed.

**Goal:** To get your dog used to car rides so he no longer gets sick.

**What you'll need:** A car, leash. The leash is not for dragging your dog to the car. It's for keeping your dog in the training area and safely preventing him from bolting in an unfenced area. If your car is in a closed garage, and you are approaching it from inside the house, you may not need the leash.

1. Find the distance at which point your dog can see the car but does not show signs of stress. This is the distance at which you start.

*Just like us, dogs need to be secured while traveling in a car for their own, as well as your, safety. This dog is wearing a special safety harness.*

2. Take one step toward the car. Relax. Let your dog get used to being nearer to the car. Once he relaxes and does not show signs of stress, take one step closer. Repeat, one step at a time, until you can get to the car.

3. Go to the car. Put your dog in the car and set him up where he would normally travel, such as in his crate or seatbelt. Give him lots of praise, then remove him and give him some distance from the car. The distance will be a reward to your dog as well, since the car is stressful to him. Repeat until he is relaxed in place.

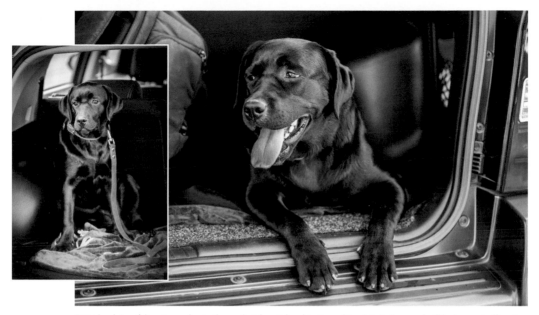

*Use a leash to safely get your dog to the car, but do not drag him toward it or into it. Your goal will be to eventually get your dog comfortably and securely settled in the car.*

4. Put your dog in the car, in his place. Get in the driver's seat and start the car. After a few seconds, turn off the engine and remove your dog from the car, giving him some distance from the car. Repeat until he is relaxed in place.

5. Put your dog in the car, in his place. Get in the driver's seat, start the car, and drive down the driveway. Immediately drive back up it, stop the car, and remove your dog, giving him some distance from the car. Repeat until he remains relaxed while the car is moving in the driveway.

6. Gradually increase the time your dog is in the car while it is moving. Only drive as far as your dog can remain calm without getting anxious. It is normal for this to take several sessions. Don't rush the process.

## Non-Treat Alternatives: When Food Isn't a Good Idea

Desensitization and counterconditioning are often used together. In the case of carsickness, though, counterconditioning using treats can work against you. Your dog can throw them up!

If your dog enjoys playing tug with a toy, physical affection, or other non-food rewards, you can combine the desensitization program with counterconditioning. Just ensure that the reward is of high value enough to counter your dog's anxiety of the car. You don't want to accidentally teach him that the presence of tugging, for example, means that a car ride is coming.

# 7 Chasing/ Herding

The Terrence family wanted a dog for their children. They don't have a big yard, so they decided to get a medium-sized dog. They fell in love with the expressive face of the Shetland Sheepdog, so they brought home an 8-week-old Sheltie puppy and named him Brodie.

Brodie was a good companion for the children at first. He was bright and loved to play. As he got older, though, he started to chase them exuberantly. Sometimes, he would knock the youngest one down, although the family never believed it was out of meanness. The children would scold Brodie and wave their arms at him to shoo him away, which just made Brodie worse. He began leaping and nipping at their hands. After a while, the children didn't think it was fun to play with Brodie anymore.

Brodie is a Shetland Sheepdog—a herding breed. Chasing is in his genetic makeup. This can be a challenging combination with young children who love to run. A dog who chases can be annoying or a menace. Some dogs just want to chase, but sometimes this behavior can tip over into hurting the one being chased.

## Symptoms

Your dog chases something. It could be another animal or a person. Some dogs will chase cars, people on bicycles, skateboarders, a broom, a vacuum cleaner, or another moving object. It could escalate into nipping, especially at a person's heels. Sometimes, if the person being chased stops moving, the dog will continue to nip at him or her. Some dogs will bark while chasing, while others are quiet.

Some dogs also develop obsessive chasing behaviors, such as chasing their own tails, lights, and reflections. If this just happens once in a while, it's usually not a cause for concern. If your dog is so obsessed with chasing his tail or lights that he will not listen to you, and if he doesn't seem to be able to easily stop himself, this is a more serious problem.

## Why It Happens

Chasing is a natural dog behavior. In some breeds, the trait has been accentuated on purpose. For example, herding breeds were deliberately developed to move livestock. It doesn't do a farmer much good if his Border

Collie won't round up sheep, or his Australian Cattle Dog won't herd cattle. Terriers have been bred to persistently pursue vermin. If a terrier didn't earn his keep chasing and killing rats, he didn't last long.

You may not have livestock. Hopefully, you don't have unwanted vermin! That doesn't mean your dog's DNA stops giving him instructions to chase. But just because the instinct to chase is inherent in your dog's breed (or breed mix), that doesn't mean you have to put up with a dog chasing your children. You can channel that energy into other types of behavior.

Your dog doesn't necessarily have to have herding or terrier genes in order to find chasing fun. Many dogs love to chase. The chase instinct can be very strong. This is why some dogs are fine with cats and other small animals when those animals are still, but the minute the animals run, the dog gives chase.

*A dog chasing his own tail can be a sign of obsessive chasing behavior.*

For a dog who obsessively chases his tail, even to the point of hurting himself, this can be the result of an obsessive-compulsive disorder. Some dogs develop an obsession with chasing lights as well. Some dogs can chase a laser light or a flashlight and not develop a problem. Others will start to chase all light reflections and shadows and do not find it easy to stop. This can also be an obsessive-compulsive disorder.

# The Training Program

Until you can train your dog to stop chasing, it's important you manage his behavior to prevent him from chasing. The more he practices the behavior, the better he will get at it. Your dog also finds chasing rewarding. The more he chases, the more fun he has. This means the behavior will just get stronger.

## Management

As a first step, do not allow your dog access to items he wants to chase. For example, if he enjoys chasing the children, don't let him loose in the yard when the kids are running free there.

**Goal:** To prevent your dog accessing triggers for his chasing behavior.

**What you'll need:**

**Blinds, drapes, doors, window film.** If your dog is leaping at windows, eager to chase wildlife, cats, or other triggers outside, block his view.

**Baby gates, doors, leash.** If your dog chases other animals in the house, do not ever leave them alone together. Keep them apart in different rooms if you cannot supervise them. If your dog chases a cat, use a baby gate to block the dog but give the cat a barrier he can leap over to safety if necessary. If needed, you can also let your dog drag a leash in the house so you can interrupt him from chasing. Always supervise your dog closely if he is dragging a leash to prevent him from getting tangled up in something and getting hurt.

**Medication.** If your dog has an obsessive disorder that manifests itself in chasing his tail or lights, he may need medication prescribed by your veterinarian or a veterinary behaviorist. Medication often works best in combination with a behavior modification plan.

Also implement as part of your management program:

### Exercise
Increase the amount of exercise your dog gets. He needs a preferred outlet for his chasing energy.

## Foundation Behaviors
### "Leave it!"
This behavior is for when your dog is headed toward something and you want to prevent him from engaging with it. If your dog has a strong chase instinct or has had the chance to develop the behavior over time, you will need to teach him very solid "Leave it!" behavior in order for it to work and stop him from chasing.

### "Come"
To call your dog away from an object he wants to chase.

### "Sit," "Down"
Your dog can't chase if he is sitting or lying down. Again, if your dog has a strong chase instinct, you will really need to teach these behaviors to fluency.

## "Leave It!": Advanced Steps
Before you can work up to deal with the temptation of chasing, you will need to transition this behavior to more challenging items than we covered in the Foundation Behaviors chapter. In this exercise, you will teach your dog to leave increasingly tempting things alone.

**What you'll need:** Treats. You'll also need other items your dog considers to be high value, such as socks, hats, any item your dog may already like to steal or would find tempting.

**Preparation:** Teach "Leave it!" first.

1. Have treats in both hands. Cue "Leave it!" Drop a treat on the floor from about an inch off the ground. The bouncing of the treat is an enticement for your dog. Keep your hand near to cover the treat if your dog goes for it.

*Giving your dog more exercise will help to use up his surplus energy.*

2. If your dog goes after the treat, just cover it. Don't say anything. Wait for him to move away. The second he moves away, cue "Take it!" and toss a treat in the opposite direction from your other hand.

*Getting your dog to leave a treat alone until you cue him to take it is a crucial step in teaching advanced "Leave it!" behavior.*

3. Right before you drop the treat, cue "Leave it!" Gradually work up to dropping the treat from higher distances. This will create some nice bouncing temptations for your dog. There will come a point at which you can't cover the treat any more with your hand. Just cover it with your foot. Take care not to accidentally kick your dog! The second your dog looks away from the dropped treat, cue "Take it!" and toss a treat in the opposite direction from your other hand.

4. Practice in different areas of your home and various places outdoors.

5. When your dog can successfully leave treats alone no matter how high you drop them from, it's time to move onto other high-value items.

6. Cue "Leave it!" Place a sock, hat, or other high-value item on the ground. Cover it with your hand or foot if necessary. The second your dog turns away from the item, cue "Take it!" and toss a treat in the opposite direction from your other hand.

7. Cue "Leave it!" Gradually work to where you are dropping the item from different heights, just as you did the treats. When your dog moves away, cue "Take it!" and toss a treat in the opposite direction from your other hand.

8. Repeat the exercise, working with different high-value items.

NOTE: If your dog has already developed an obsession with an object, then you'll need to be sure to use a reward that has the same or greater value to your dog. If you pay him with the same reward you use for all his other training exercises, it may not be a match for what you're asking him to leave alone. You can also increase the value of a reward by giving your dog a repeated, extended reward. For example, if your dog is obsessed with socks and he successfully leaves a sock alone, you cue "Take it!" and praise him the entire time while you dole out three successive treats. This extends the reward. For most dogs, if you were to just hand them three treats they would swallow them just as fast as if it were one.

## Desensitization and "Leave It!"

Once your dog has established reliable "Leave it!" behavior, it's time to take it to the next level. For a strong chaser, you will have greater success if you combine desensitization with an advanced "Leave it!" You will need the distance of a desensitization program in order for your dog to be able to concentrate enough to leave a trigger alone.

**What you'll need:** Really high-value treats, a leash, and an object for your dog to chase, such as a child running or on a bike. Ideally, use a trigger you can control. This could be a child who will follow your instructions and ride his or her bike where you direct, when you direct. In a pinch, go to a public place and use environmental triggers, but you will need to be very careful to keep your dog under threshold so it doesn't trigger him to chase. You don't want him to continue practicing this behavior! If you find the new location is challenging for your dog, bring back the clicker as well. The clicker is for building behavior, so you may need to build this behavior in a new, challenging location.

**Preparation:** Teach "Leave It!": Advanced Steps first.

1. Have your dog on leash. The leash is not for correcting your dog. It's to ensure your dog doesn't bolt.

2. Set yourself up in a location where the trigger—say, the child riding the bike—will only be visible from one direction. It will be too much at first for your dog to handle triggers from multiple directions. Find the distance at which your dog will not chase and can respond to your cue. You want a distance at which your dog is not anxious or showing signs of stress.

3. Cue your trigger to pass by. Cue "Leave it!" Say the cue once, in a friendly voice. This is not a threat. It is instruction.

4. The second your dog turns away from the trigger, click and treat. Or, if he will respond without the clicker at this point, praise and treat.

5. If your dog successfully performs the behavior, take one step closer to the trigger. If he doesn't respond and is agitated to chase, you are too close. Move farther away from the trigger.

6. Repeat Steps 3–5. Only proceed as far as your dog successfully leaves the trigger alone.

NOTE: This can take several sessions or many, so please don't get discouraged. Keep your sessions very short, about 15 minutes at the maximum. The goal of your training session is to end it in a better place than where you began. Let's say you have to start a session two blocks away from the trigger. After one session, you're at a block and a half away from the trigger. This is progress! You might be tempted to push it, but resist. End the session on a successful note.

When you start your next training session, begin in a location that is a bit farther than where you left off the last one. For example, if you ended your last session one and a half blocks from the trigger, then start this session at about one and three-quarters of a block from the trigger. This will give you a good cushion to start

*Getting a friend to ride a bike under your direction can help you teach your dog not to chase.*

your session on a successful note, and it will also give you some extra room in case your dog has regressed.

As with any training session, you will have good ones and some that may not go so well. This is normal! Don't get angry with your dog. Try to determine what went wrong and work to avoid the problem during your next session. Chasing can be a strong, instinctual behavior. Be patient.

## Non-Treat Alternatives: The Flirt Pole

Since chasing is a natural dog behavior, it can be hard to extinguish entirely, especially with a dog who really is born to chase things. You don't have to completely extinguish this behavior: just give your dog an appropriate outlet for his chasing.

Use the other exercises to teach your dog what you *don't* want him to chase. They will also help you give your dog acceptable alternate behaviors to chasing. With this exercise, you teach your dog what you *do* want him to chase. The flirt pole is also an excellent exercise outlet for your dog. You can use it indoors with limited space. You can use it even in smaller yards as well.

**What you'll need:** Flirt pole. This is a long stick that has a cord attached. At the end of the cord is a toy, usually a stuffed animal.

1. Hold the flirt pole behind your back. Cue "Sit." When your dog sits, bring out the flirt pole. Flick it and encourage your dog to chase the toy.
2. When your dog chases the toy, praise him!
3. Occasionally stop the game. Repeat from Step 1.

NOTE: By asking your dog to sit before you start the game, you're also teaching your dog good self-control.

*Most dogs are willing pupils provided they are not pushed too hard and too fast. You need to be patient even if it seems that things are not going as well as they could.*

# 8

# Chewing

"You're the reason we can't have nice things!" is a common exclamation in the Johnson household. The statement is always directed with a glare at Oscar, their 24-week-old Weimaraner. Even at this tender age, Oscar has managed to chew up an ottoman, the legs of three kitchen chairs, the lever on a recliner, three pairs of reading glasses, four beloved stuffed animals, half a dozen shoes, five socks, the corners of the kitchen cabinets, and an Adirondack chair. His family has bought him a ton of toys, so they are getting frustrated. Why doesn't Oscar chew those, instead? They're afraid he's just getting started. They're right!

Dogs can be extremely destructive with their chewing, especially as puppies. Some dogs outgrow it, but not all of them do. This can be extremely frustrating, especially when your dog chews something expensive or with sentimental value.

## Symptoms

All dogs chew. It becomes a problem behavior—destructive chewing—when your dog chews something you don't want him to chew. This can be furniture, rugs, shoes, your belongings, and more. Some dogs have even been known to chew holes in walls.

If it is related to separation anxiety, the chewing will be focused on doorways or other exit points. Some people mistake this for destructive chewing, but the location of the destruction will often indicate it's really a separation anxiety-related problem.

Some dogs will even chew on themselves, causing self-injury.

## Why It Happens

Dogs do not chew out of spite or because they are mad at you. There are many other and more practical reasons for why dogs chew.

Puppies start to lose their baby teeth at about 4 months of age. This is when you will see an acceleration in chewing behavior. Chewing feels good to a puppy's sore gums. You may find baby teeth on the floor or stuck in a toy. Chewing may slow down after the puppy teeth fall out, but it will soon kick in again. At about 7 months, a dog's back molars will come in, so dogs will start chewing again to soothe their gums.

Dogs also chew because it's fun. They can chew when they are bored. They can also chew to relieve stress. If your dog is frightened of thunderstorms and there is a storm while you are at work, you may come home to a dog who has chewed his way through the house. Chewing helps a dog relieve his stress.

If a dog has separation anxiety, he will do just about anything to escape confinement. This can mean chewing through a crate or even a door. You may also notice destruction around windows or other exit routes.

Dogs can chew on themselves for several reasons. They may have parasites, such as fleas or ticks. For some dogs, it takes just one flea bite to send them into a frenzy. Some dogs are allergic to flea bites, so the resulting itch and irritation can be very frustrating for them. This also occurs with dogs who have other skin irritations due to allergies or illnesses. These dogs can chew on themselves enough to cause damage.

*Dogs chew destructively for all kinds of reasons, including boredom, stress, and, in teething puppies, to relieve the pain of sore gums.*

## The Training Program

It's easy to get frustrated and angry with your dog for chewing something important to you … but always remember that your dog is more important, and irreplaceable, than any possession.

### Management

Goal: To prevent your dog chewing things he shouldn't.

What you'll need:

Crate, exercise pen, or other confinement. If your dog is chewing destructively and it's not related to true separation anxiety, confinement can help preserve your belongings. More importantly, it will keep your dog safe. Dogs can easily chew things that will harm them. If something gets stuck in a dog's digestive tract, it may require major surgery to remove it. He could eat something that is

### Small-Dog Options: Don't Let the Tiny Ones Fool You

When you think of a dog described as a "power chewer," do you think Pit Bull? Rottweiler? Labrador? Think again. Some "power chewers" come in little, tiny packages.

Some small dogs are just as capable of chewing a destructive wake through your house as their larger cousins. Toys you may have purchased to last a lifetime can be destroyed in minutes. Little dogs have teeth, and some of them are really good at using them! So don't let the size fool you. Always determine the durability of your dog's toys based on his ability and predilection for chewing. You may find your teeny dog needs a wolf-sized chew toy.

*A baby gate can be used to keep a destructive chewer confined when you are not available to supervise his behavior.*

poisonous. To keep your belongings and your dog safe, confine him when you cannot supervise him closely.

Always train your dog to enjoy confinement before putting him in a crate or an exercise pen. See the "Settle" section in the Foundation Behavior chapter on how to crate train your dog.

**Flea/tick preventive, other medication, different food.** If your dog is chewing due to fleas or ticks, consult with your veterinarian on an appropriate flea or tick preventive. There may also be some natural remedies that can help prevent those nasty blood-suckers from taking hold. If your dog is chewing on himself due to allergies or other issues and he is causing himself damage, definitely make a trip to the veterinarian. Your veterinarian can help get to the root of the problem and recommend something, such as a different food, medication, medicated shampoos, or injections, to help give your itchy dog some relief.

Also implement as part of your management program:

## Supervision

The more your dog practices destructive chewing, the better he will get at it. Close supervision is critical, especially when your dog is a puppy and going through his chewing phases. You will be shocked at how quickly a young puppy can completely destroy something in the time it took you to check a text message. You really do have to pay attention to what your dog is doing, or he will get hold of something he shouldn't in a flash! If you are not watching your dog, then he will likely get into trouble. It's not his fault—he hasn't learned what you expect yet, and chewing is natural to him. You need to keep really close watch on him to effectively prevent further destruction.

*One reason a dog may chew at himself is to relieve an itch caused by mites or fleas.*

*If your dog is a compulsive chewer, nothing will stop him if he is left on his own and given the chance to enjoy his passion.*

## Exercise

If your dog is chewing on inappropriate items due to boredom, he may not be getting the exercise he needs. Puppies and adolescent dogs need a great amount of exercise—far more than the average city or suburban dog gets. Exercise will give your dog a better outlet for his energy.

## Foundation Behaviors
### "Leave it!"/"Take it"

If your dog is headed for something inappropriate, use the "Leave it!" behavior to deter him. Use "Take it!" to indicate to your dog what he is allowed to chew.

### "Come"

To call your dog to you, away from an inappropriate item.

## Appropriate Toy Play

Dogs are not born understanding what you want them to chew. To a dog, the world is one big chew toy! You need to teach him what is safe for chewing and what is not.

**Goal:** To teach your dog to play with appropriate toys.

**What you'll need:** Safe toys your dog will enjoy chewing. Toys should be larger than your dog's mouth. If a toy starts out the correct size, but your dog chews pieces of it away so that it ends up fitting entirely in his mouth, throw it away. He could swallow it. Not everything will pass through him—if it doesn't, he may require surgery to remove the obstruction.

Every dog is different in what types of toys he will enjoy. You will likely have to try a variety before you find your dog's favorites. Just avoid toys that your dog will shred or ingest. For example, if your dog will destroy a plush toy and eat the stuffing, that's not the toy for your dog! Some dogs are also obsessed with surgically dissecting the squeaker out of a toy. This might be OK as long as your dog does not swallow

*Puppies in particular need lots of exercise. Otherwise, they may get bored and start chewing.*

the squeaker or any of the stuffing he removes to get to his prize.

1. Present a toy to your dog. Make it enticing. Tease your dog a little with it. Pretend it's the best toy in the world. Your interest in the toy will increase your dog's interest in the toy.

2. Give the toy to your dog. When he takes it, praise him!

NOTE: It helps to rotate toys. Have several sets of toys that you alternate frequently. This will make them seem new to your dog.

Giving your dog special toys to chew on can help redirect his behavior.

## "Drop It!"

If your dog already has hold of an item, getting him to let go of it on cue is a very handy behavior. It also could save his life should he get hold of something that can hurt him.

What you'll need: An item your dog is likely to take in his mouth, such as one of his toys; clicker, treats.

1. Give the item to your dog. Let him settle with it.

2. Hold a treat in front of your dog's nose. He is likely to spit out the item in order to get the treat. The second he spits out the item, click and give him the treat.

3. Repeat two times.

4. Give the item to your dog. Let him settle with it.

5. Hold your hand the same way as if you had a treat in it, in front of your dog's nose. This is not to fool your dog. He can smell there is not a treat in your hand. You are actually teaching him a hand signal. By losing the treat in your hand quickly, you are helping prevent you and your dog from getting dependent on treats. Otherwise, you will end up with a dog who only spits out items for bribes and not paychecks. When your dog drops the item, click. Then give him a treat.

6. Repeat Step 5 nine more times. When your dog is performing the behavior reliably, it's time to add a cue.

7. Give your dog the item. Cue "Drop It!" and then give your hand signal. When your dog spits out the item, click and give him a treat. Repeat nine times.

NOTE: Practice this in a variety of locations, with a variety of items.

## Redirection

Sometimes, you're just not fast enough. Your dog will get hold of something he shouldn't. Or, you see that telltale gleam in his eye as he's headed for contraband. This is when you should redirect his behavior.

**Goal:** To stop your dog from chewing on something inappropriate and to redirect him to something more appropriate.

**What you'll need:** Safe toys your dog will enjoy chewing.

## Non-Treat Alternatives: Not Your Stuff

Don't make the mistake of giving your dog something to chew that really isn't a dog toy. For example, tying a sock into a knot and giving it to your dog could teach him to chew socks. Letting him chew on an old towel could teach him to chew any towel. An old shoe? Tastes just as good as new shoes. Don't accidentally teach your dog to chew on things you don't want him to have!

**Preparation:** Teach "Leave it!" and "Drop it!" first.

1. Any time your dog is headed for something he shouldn't chew on, cue "Leave it!" Remember, "Leave it!" means leave something alone entirely. Your dog should never touch it. If your dog already has hold of the item, cue "Drop it!"

2. Immediately give your dog an appropriate toy. It helps to give him the toy a bit away from where he was chewing on the contraband item. This will help put some space between him and temptation.

3. When he takes the toy you've offered, praise him! Really make a big deal of him chewing on the right item. Many folks know to give their dog an alternative item to chew, but they forget to praise the dog for chewing on the preferred item. Your dog needs to understand that you really love it when he chews on his toys. Your praise is an additional reward.

NOTE: If you have a puppy, you will have to repeat these steps a lot! Puppies have no attention spans. You will need to give them frequent reminders of what you want them to chew on. This is normal.

*Praising a dog for putting into practice what you've been teaching him is a welcome reward for improved behavior.*

# 9

# Digging

nnie the Cairn Terrier is on a mission. Her family isn't sure exactly what mission Annie has in mind, but they figure it must have something to do with digging her way to another continent. Annie is a digger. She has excavated huge holes in the backyard. Sometimes it's at the base of a tree, but other times it's out in the middle of the yard. The family suspects she may be going after moles because they have had a problem with moles burrowing in their yard.

Annie is a small terrier, but she can dig gaping holes in next to no time. One day, her mom looked out the window and the only thing she could see above ground was Annie's stubby little tail!

Her mom gets furious, but Annie just looks back at her happily, with her pert face all covered in mud. Annie ends up in the bathtub a lot.

If you have a digger, you are probably frustrated, especially if you are a gardener. There's nothing like pouring the power of your green thumb into a beautiful landscape, only to have your dog destroy your artistic vision by digging holes throughout it.

## Symptoms

Your dog digs. It could be anywhere in the yard, but digging behavior is not always confined to the outdoors. Some dogs will dig in the cushions of your sofa or dig into blankets. Some dogs will dig for a while, circle a few times, then lie down in the holes they have dug. Others will carry on digging until interrupted or distracted.

## Why It Happens

Your dog is not deliberately trying to destroy your landscape. Digging is another natural dog behavior. This is why you sometimes see the behavior in unlikely places, such as on your couch. A dog will go through digging motions even if he isn't really excavating anything, such as on a firm sofa cushion. Some breeds are especially born to it, such as terriers or Dachshunds. For example, Dachshunds were bred to go after badgers in their dens and kill them. Your dog may not need to hunt badgers for you, but the instinct is still there. Dogs can dig to pursue vermin or other critters. If you have moles, voles, lizards, or other critters in your yard, your dog may pursue them, digging if necessary to catch his prey.

Dogs are built for digging well. Even dogs missing one front leg have been known to dig deep pits in a yard! Dogs dig because it's fun, especially when they are bored. Dogs can also dig to create cool or warm spots to lie in.

# The Training Program

An effective way to stop digging is to prevent your dog from having access to dig in the first place by keeping him indoors. If you are worried about damage inside the home, see the Chewing chapter for information on how to protect your house from a dog who chews destructively; and also the Potty Problems chapter for help on housetraining your dog.

## Management

Goal: To help prevent your dog from digging.

What you'll need:

Confinement. If you will not be out in the yard to supervise your dog, consider confining your dog in

*Digging comes naturally to dogs, but it is behavior that ought to be discouraged.*

the house. Your dog may prefer the outdoors, but you can also teach him to enjoy being indoors. You may be leaving your dog out for exercise, but just being loose in the yard is not exercise to an active dog. Also, if your dog is outdoors and you come home every day angry at him for digging, this is not a successful strategy.

Is your dog outdoors when you are not there because you can't trust him in the house? Is he destructive or perhaps not housetrained? Teach him to enjoy appropriate confinement. A dog who is confined in a crate or exercise pen cannot destroy your belongings.

Environmental comfort. If your dog is digging to stay warm or cool, set up his environment to make him more comfortable and less likely to resort to digging pits in your yard.

If you suspect that your dog is too cold, he needs to be provided with a warm, dry resting place, such as a dog house or access to a porch. For warmth, a dog house should be just big enough so that your dog can stretch out, stand up, and turn around in it. Anything larger will be harder for your dog's body heat to keep warm. Use blankets or towels for added warmth and comfort.

If you think your dog is too hot, he needs access to shade, a regular supply of drinking water, or maybe a baby pool full of water or a water misting system. You can also freeze ice blocks for your dog, using a bucket.

Once you set up a warming or cooling station, encourage your dog to settle there.

Environmental enrichment. Get your dog some fun chew toys. Know that it's not enough just to present your dog with the toys. After a while, he will grow bored with them so they will be less likely to distract him from digging. Have a variety of toys and rotate them on a daily basis. This will keep them fresh for your dog and help maintain his interest.

*A doghouse can provide warmth in cool weather and shade in warm weather so your dog will be comfortable and won't feel the need to dig during time spent outdoors.*

Interactive toys are preferable because they are more engaging, but because they require you to put food in them, be careful they don't attract ants or other bugs. Whenever you see your dog playing with his toys rather than digging, praise that behavior.

**Also implement as part of your management program:**

### Supervision

You can't interrupt a problem behavior if you are not around to see it happening. If you give your dog free rein of your yard without supervision, it is likely he will continue to dig. Remember, practice makes perfect. It will be much harder to teach your dog not to dig if you allow it to happen sometimes but not others. If you are outside with your dog, watch him carefully so you can prevent digging before it starts.

### Exercise

A dog who has energy to dig holes is likely one that is not getting enough exercise. Exercise is not simply turning your dog loose in your yard. Engage with him. Play fetch. Use a flirt pole. Play training games to engage his body and his mind. Aim for at least 30 straight minutes of activity. If your dog is tired, he is less likely to have the energy to dig holes.

## Foundation Behaviors
### "Come"

To call your dog away from an area where you believe he wants to start digging.

### "Leave it!"

To leave something alone, such as a critter in your yard he may dig after.

### "Settle"

To get your dog used to and comfortable with a new warmth or cooling station.

## Redirection

**Goal:** To deflect your dog from digging and redirect him into more appropriate behavior.

**What you'll need:** Toys and/or a dig pit. For dogs who are natural diggers, giving them a place where they are allowed to dig can be a healthy option. For the dig pit, use a baby pool and fill it with sand. Or, get some landscape timbers or plastic fencing and block off a small section of your yard. Leave an opening for your dog to enter and exit, then fill the area with sand. You want a defined area so that your dog can easily differentiate between dig pit and lawn. When you build the dig pit, half bury some toys in it. Rotate these toys frequently to keep them feeling new to your dog to hold his interest.

1. For toys: When you see your dog start to dig, use your voice to interrupt him. Immediately give him a toy and encourage him to play with it. When he takes the toy, praise him! Really make it clear you

are very happy when he has the toy. Repeat.

2. For a dig pit: When you see your dog start to dig in the yard, use your voice to interrupt him. Encourage him to run with you over to the dig pit. (Running will be more exciting for your dog and make him likely to chase you. If you can't run, however, then just move as quickly as you can, encouraging your dog the entire way.) Enter the dig pit and start digging! Encourage your dog to join you. When he does, praise him! Really let him know you are thrilled he's digging in his dig pit. Repeat every time you see your dog start to dig in an inappropriate place.

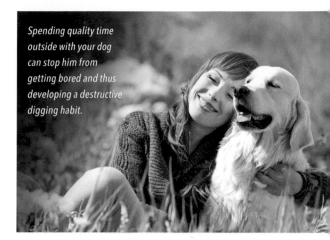

*Spending quality time outside with your dog can stop him from getting bored and thus developing a destructive digging habit.*

**NOTE:** As with most training, this will take repetition. It is unrealistic to think that you will redirect your dog twice and he will never dig in your yard again, especially if it is now a long-time habit. Be patient. Redirect him every time. If you allow him to dig sometimes but then redirect him at other times, he will not learn what you want. Consistency is important.

## Outdoor Dog Options: It's an Inside Job

Some dogs do great in the outdoors unattended. Some do very well left outdoors during the day and brought into the house at night. Other dogs don't! Some dogs will dig pits in the yard. Others will chew your lawn furniture, hoses, deck, outdoor appliances, and more. Some will develop bad barking habits or scratch your doors. If your dog is exhibiting these problem behaviors, continuing to leave him outdoors on his own will not help. The problems will continue and likely get worse.

Another challenge with dogs who spend a lot of time outdoors unattended is that they are not as invested in their people in comparison to dogs who spend most of their time indoors with their families. This is not a judgment! It's simply canine nature. Dogs will naturally bond with whomever they spend the most positive time with—or, whatever animal they spend the most quality time with. This is why, if you have more than one dog and they spend all day together outside without you, you may find the dogs pay more attention to each other than to you. Or, if your child spends a lot of time with your outdoor dog, your dog may actually listen to your child more than you.

Dogs who share everyday life with their families bond more closely to them. So if you have an outdoor dog and your family spends lots of time outdoors with him, it will definitely help you in your training. If your dog spends a lot of time outdoors without you, however, you will face a harder challenge in getting your dog to listen to you and care about doing what you want. You will need to have extra patience and work harder to achieve results, but you can do it! If you want to transition your dog to spend more time indoors with your family, this book can help you tackle some of the problem behaviors that may be barriers to him becoming a good indoor family companion.

# 10 Escaping

When the Edwards family brought home a fluffy Siberian Husky puppy, they named him Riley. Now that Riley is an adolescent, they're thinking they should have named him Houdini. Riley is an escape artist.

Riley can jump the fence. Riley can dig out from under the fence. Riley will bolt out the door before anyone can catch him and run down the street. And once he's out, Riley thinks it's a wonderful game when the family chases him! He'll stay just out of reach, sometimes for hours, while family members coax, threaten, and beg him to come back. When they finally get Riley back to the house, dog and family are exhausted.

Sometimes it takes a while for the family to notice Riley is gone. Luckily, Riley wears a collar with an ID tag and is also microchipped. Neighbors will call if they spot him, and twice now animal control has picked him up. This has incurred some fines for the Edwards, which they are not thrilled about. Most importantly, the family is terrified Riley will someday get out and get hurt. What if another dog attacks him? What if a person hurts him? Riley is friendly, but he's a big, exuberant dog and someone could mistake his approach for a threat. Riley also doesn't seem to understand much about traffic—the Edwards have seen him run right out into the street. What if he gets hit by a passing car or truck?

Roaming dogs are a serious problem. They can ruin neighbor relations. If your dog is getting loose and peeing and pooping in your neighbors' yards, this is going to upset them. Or maybe your dog rummages in their trash cans or digs up their flower beds. This is not going to make you popular at your neighborhood block party.

Not all dogs who roam are friendly, which can cause extremely serious problems. If someone is walking his dog on leash and your loose dog attacks them, this is dangerous. People and animals can be hurt, and you will be liable. Roaming dogs who are intact can find mates, creating unwanted litters of puppies. The typical suburban or city environment is also just not safe for loose dogs. Other animals, people, and traffic can hurt or even kill them.

*This is how a dog should be behaving in the street, not out roaming on his own.*

## Symptoms

Your dog escapes your house or your yard. When escaping the house, it is usually when someone opens the door and is not able to block the dog from bolting outside. Some dogs will dig under fences, while others will jump or even climb over fences. Some dogs even learn how to undo latches.

In extreme cases, some dogs will work to escape the house by destroying your property or even hurting themselves. This is usually the result of a dog having a panic attack during a storm or suffering from severe separation anxiety. Please see the Phobia and Separation Anxiety chapters for information on helping such dogs.

## Why It Happens

Many people are hurt when their dogs escape. Doesn't your dog love you? Are you not providing enough for your dog? Please be assured that your dog does care about you, and you are in all likelihood a great caregiver. The simple reason that dogs escape is because it is rewarding to them.

The first time your dog escaped, he probably saw, heard, or smelled something he wanted to investigate. If it was a rewarding experience, he wanted to repeat it. Remember that the laws of

*Some dogs will even manage to climb fences to escape from their yards.*

learning state that behavior that is rewarded increases in frequency. The more fun your dog has outside your property, the more likely it is that he will go in search of that fun again. It's paying off for him.

Exploring is fantastic to a dog. Your neighborhood's smells and sights are entertainment. Maybe he discovered a trash can that delighted him with leftover pot roast. Maybe he found another dog, made friends, and they enjoyed a grand play date together. Maybe he went swimming in a nearby pond. While you're home worrying, your dog is on a wonderful walkabout. If the adventure was more interesting than your yard, it will make it very hard to contain him in the future.

Another reason that dogs escape is because you chase them when they do. This is fun! These dogs have not been taught that coming to you is more fun than being chased. Sometimes, they've been taught the opposite—that when you finally catch them, they will be punished. If this is the case, it's in your dog's best interests to stay away longer. You have accidentally taught your dog to avoid you.

Hormones will also make dogs roam. If your dog is intact, he or she may go wandering looking for a mate. The call to breed is not romantic—it's more like a compulsion. Male dogs have been known to run right out into traffic while pursuing the scent of a female in heat. A male dog can smell a female in heat from miles away. And the boys aren't the only ones likely to roam. Your girl in heat may decide to go in search of a baby daddy, too.

*Dogs are curious creatures, and most, if given the chance, will take the opportunity to become natural explorers.*

*This roaming dog is lost, hungry, and probably scared.*

Some dogs are born runners, such as Siberian Huskies, Malamutes, and many sporting breeds. These dogs were purposely bred to cover great distances. If your dog is not getting enough exercise for his breed (or breed mix) and age, then he may escape your yard to expend some bottled-up energy.

Some dogs escape their yards due to fear. If your dog is afraid of fireworks and is outside during a nearby fireworks event, he may escape the yard to get away from what is scaring him. Thunderstorms also cause dogs to panic and leave their yards. Separation anxiety can cause escape as well. When a dog is in a blind panic and running, he could easily run out into traffic and get hit by a vehicle. He may also calm down miles away, only to realize he can't find his way back home.

# The Training Program
## Management

If your dog is roaming because he or she is seeking a mate, talk to your veterinarian about the best time to spay or neuter your dog. The timing of such surgery can be a controversial subject among pet owners, as well as veterinarians, dog trainers, breeders, and other pet professionals. You may prefer to keep your dog intact until he or she is fully grown. Or, you may be ready for your dog to have the surgery next week. It's a personal decision. Talk to your veterinarian and make the decision you are most comfortable with and what will be best for your dog. A dog who is not following his hormones is more likely to stay at home. If your dog is escaping because he is terrified of fireworks, storms, or other loud noises, try to anticipate when these events will occur and keep your dog indoors during those times. Sometimes that can be unpredictable, so forecasting may not be completely accurate. See the Phobia chapter for more help. If your dog suffers from separation anxiety, please see the Separation Anxiety chapter for more tips. A

*Even if your dog has never roamed before, it's a wise precaution to have him microchipped just in case he gets lost, loses his collar, and cannot find his way back home.*

comprehensive management program can help prevent your dog from escaping and also teach him that it is more rewarding to be at home.

**Goal:** To prevent your dog from escaping the yard or house.

**What you'll need:**

**Confinement.** If you will not be present in the yard to supervise your dog, consider confining your dog in the house. This is a much safer alternative than leaving him unattended if he has a consistent habit of escaping. Even if he only has escaped a few times, do you want to take the risk?

Is your dog outdoors when you are not there because you can't trust him in the house? Is he destructive or perhaps not housetrained? Teach him to enjoy appropriate confinement. A dog who is confined in a crate or exercise pen cannot destroy your belongings. See the Chewing chapter for information on how to protect your house from a dog who chews destructively. Also see the Potty Problems chapter for help on housetraining your dog.

**Fencing.** If your dog digs under fences, reinforce your fence to prevent him from getting out. Real fences, as opposed to "invisible" electronic fences, are preferable. Make sure your fence is secure all the way around. Carefully check to see if there are any gaps in the corners or spots where the ground rises and might make it easier for your dog to use as a launching point for going over the fence.

If you bury chicken wire at the base of your fence (be careful that sharp ends cannot hurt him if he digs), bury it several feet deep. You might have success with putting a couple feet of wire fencing down flat along the ground inside your fence line, anchoring it down with rocks. Your dog will not be able to dig through it close to the fence line in order to get out. Or, try burying large rocks or cinder blocks along your fence line. You might also try partially burying landscape timbers.

If your dog climbs or jumps over your fence, there are things you can do to strengthen the fence. Fences with flat boards do not have as many toe holds as chain link. Try fixing flat boards, plywood, or reed fencing to your existing fence to stop him climbing. You can also rig the top of the fence so your dog can't gain enough purchase to vault over it. Extend the height of your fence, tilting the top inward at a 45-degree angle. You can also use "coyote rollers"; these are hollow bars suspended at the top of a fence that spin so your dog can't get a grip. You can purchase them or use PVC pipe.

At the risk of sounding like you need to build Fort Knox, you might also consider double fencing or a kennel within your fence. If your dog absolutely has to be outside without supervision, this may be what it takes to keep an extreme escapist on his home turf. Even if he escapes one fence, he'll have to tackle another before finally making it to freedom. Such precautions can discourage some dogs from trying.

If you suspect someone is actually leaving your fence gate open for your dog to escape, install locks. There are people out there who will steal dogs from yards, and sometimes neighborhood children think it's fun to release your dog and play with him while you're not home. Installing locks may not keep your dog in the yard if he's good at escaping, but they can definitely help keep people out.

**Indoor barriers.** If your dog bolts out the door, use barriers to keep him from having access until you can train him. Shut him in a room before you answer the door. Keep him behind a baby gate. Put up an exercise pen as a barrier (an exercise pen has multiple panels that you can stretch out, as well as use to form an enclosure).

## Outdoor Dog Options: Real Fences

Real fences are much preferred to electric containment systems (underground fences). While some dogs do fine in an electric containment system, the fences have several serious drawbacks:

- Dogs can and do escape them. If the motivation is strong enough, a dog will risk the shock to go past the barrier. This dog may then be hesitant to risk the shock to return home.

- They don't keep other dogs and people out.

- They can cause behavioral problems, such as fear and aggression. A dog who gets zapped while approaching a child in front of his yard may associate the punishment with the child. This is why some dogs develop fear and aggression issues toward children on skateboards or bicycles, strollers, other dogs, and more. Also, if someone comes into your yard and goes to pet your dog, if your dog does not want to be petted and he's trapped between the person and the electric boundary, he may defend himself. Some dogs develop a fear of the lawn, not understanding the specific cause of the electric shock. These dogs often start eliminating in the house because they are too afraid to go outdoors.

Electric containment systems should not be used for any dog with an existing fear or aggression problem because this and other punishment-based training and experiences can make those issues worse. They should also not be used with young puppies, especially during their critical socialization periods, because they could cause them to develop fear or aggression issues. Whenever possible, please use real fencing.

**Environmental enrichment.** Get your dog some fun chew toys. Rotate them on a daily basis so they feel new to your dog and keep his interest. Interactive toys are preferable as they are more engaging, but because they require you to put food in them, be careful they don't attract ants or other bugs if you use them outside. Encourage your dog to play with his toys and praise him heavily when he does. You need to make your yard more exciting than the great big world out there.

Also implement as part of your management program:

## Supervision

If you are in the yard with your dog and he is known to be an escape artist, supervise him carefully. It's easy to get caught up in your barbeque or gardening and not notice your dog hitting the road, but the more he practices this behavior, the more it's paying off for him. Keep an eye on your dog so that you can prevent him from taking off in the first place.

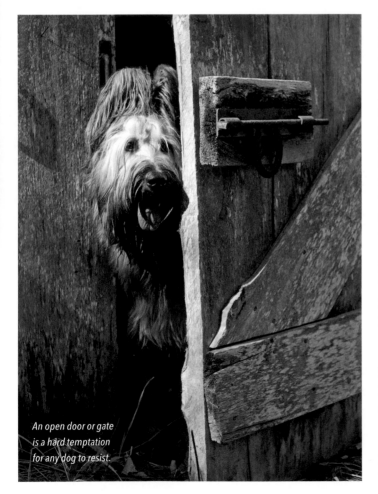

*An open door or gate is a hard temptation for any dog to resist.*

## Exercise

Increase your dog's daily exercise. A dog who is bored is more likely to wander in search of fun. Play fetch. Use a flirt pole. Arrange for play dates with dogs of comparable size and play styles. Play training games to engage his body and his mind. Aim for at least 30 straight minutes of activity. Some dogs may need more. Consider a quality doggie daycare if necessary. If you have questions or concerns about exercising your dog, please consult your veterinarian.

## Foundation Behaviors
### "Come"

For calling your dog to come to you if he has escaped.

### "Leave it!"

If you see your dog approaching the fence line and you believe he is about to jump or start digging to escape.

### "Wait"

For waiting at doorways so your dog doesn't bolt out the door.

## "Come": Advanced Steps

This behavior will not prevent your dog from escaping, but a solid recall will help you get your dog to return to you once he has escaped.

**Preparation:** Teach "Come" first.

**What you'll need:** Clicker, treats, regular leash, long line (or retractable leash). The retractable leash is good for getting distance from your dog while still maintaining contact. Just be careful you don't drop it because it could startle your dog if he runs and it "chases" him. Also be careful that the line does not retract while touching you or you could sustain a friction burn. You'll also need items to use for distractions, such as people, toys, and whatever you think your dog would find tempting to go investigate.

1. Put your dog on a long line and walk with him outside. Allow him to get distracted. Cue "Come" one time, in a friendly voice. Start running backward (still facing your dog). Be careful you don't trip or run into something and hurt yourself. Dogs love to chase, so your dog is likely to run after you.

2. When your dog reaches you, click and treat. If you have already incorporated "Sit" into this behavior, then click and treat after your dog sits.

3. Repeat nine times.

4. Add one distraction to your environment. Repeat Steps 1–3. If your dog goes to the distraction instead of you, then remove the distraction from the environment and repeat Steps 1–3 until your dog is more reliable.

5. Gradually add more distractions to the environment. Repeat Steps 1–3 nine more times.

When your dog is very good at ignoring distractions in your home environment, it's time to take this training out onto the road.

1. Put your dog on his regular leash. Warm up with a few recalls in your yard. Then, take your dog for a walk in your neighborhood.

2. After you've gone a few blocks, cue "Come" once, in a friendly voice. Start running backward (be careful!). When your dog comes to you, click and treat.

3. Repeat randomly throughout your walk.

## Non-Treat Alternatives: When Games Trump Treats

If your dog is too distracted by the environment to come to you, you will need to use a greater reward. For a dog who has built up a habit of escaping to go on adventures, the world is an exciting place. So your regular treats, or even really delicious ones he normally would flip over, may not be able to compete.

Try using a game as a reward. Does your dog love tug? Play tug! Does he love balls? Bounce a ball for him to catch. Do not use these as bribes. Use them as rewards only after your dog performs the desired behavior. If your dog simply won't respond in spite of the games, back up your training to the last successful step and practice that for several more sessions before trying this phase again.

*Dogs find a busy environment very distracting. Your aim should be to get him to pay attention to you when you need him to do so.*

4. When your dog performs reliably, switch him to a long line and repeat Steps 6–8. Be careful with your dog on a long line in the neighborhood—make sure you manage him so that he doesn't approach other dogs or people or get into trouble or tangled along your walk.

5. Start reducing the amount of times you run backward and see if your dog still recalls quickly. If you ever see him lagging, then try jogging backward again to entice him to chase you.

## "Wait": Advanced Steps

This is an excellent behavior for dogs who bolt out the door. Some of them can be ingenious at wriggling between you and the door just to get outside.

**Goal:** To teach your dog to wait at the doorway, even if you leave the house.

**What you'll need:** Clicker, treats, leash.

**Preparation:** Teach "Wait" first.

1. Have your dog on leash. Stand at the doorway. Cue "Wait" one time, in a friendly voice.

2. Open the door. Shut the door. As long as your dog remains behind the threshold, click and toss the treat behind him, inside. This will make your dog retreat from the doorway to get his reward. Repeat nine times.

3. Cue "Wait." Open the door. Take one small step outside while your dog remains at the threshold. Quickly come back inside, shut the door, click, and toss the treat behind your dog, inside. If your dog tries to go outside with you, don't yell at him or tell him "No." Just position your body so he can't get past you and start over, except this time, just move one foot out the door and back in. You

might feel a bit silly, but you will gradually work up to one step! Once you can take one step outside and return successfully, repeat nine more times.

4. Cue "Wait." Open the door. Take one step outside while your dog remains at the threshold. Quickly come back to the threshold, just outside the door. Leave the door open. Click and toss the treat behind your dog. This is now making the behavior more challenging because the door will be open. (This is also why your dog is on leash.) As long as your dog is successful, repeat nine more times.

5. Repeat Step 4, except take two steps outside. Return to the doorway threshold, leaving the door open. Click and toss the treat behind your dog. Work up to where you can go a leash length away from your dog with him staying at the threshold. Only proceed as fast as your dog succeeds with the behavior. Repeat each stage for a total of 10 times.

6. Cue "Wait." Open the door and go as far as a leash length away outside. Return, click, and toss the treat behind your dog. Casually drop the leash, so that your dog now drags it. Repeat nine more times with your dog simply dragging the leash.

7. Repeat Step 6 for at least 10 total training sessions. You want your dog to learn the new habit of waiting at the door even though you go outside.

NOTE: This may take several sessions, which is normal. Just remember where you left off. Then, when you start your next training session, review the previous step, overlapping a bit to refresh your dog. Continue from there.

## Settling on a Bed when the Doorbell Rings

Some dogs don't just rush out the door when you are trying to leave the house. Some will bolt when you open the door to greet guests. This behavior will teach your dog to go settle on his bed instead of rushing out the door.

**Goal:** To teach your dog to go settle on his bed, away from the door, when guests arrive.

**What You'll Need:** A bed, clicker, treats, leash. You will also need another person to be the "guest."

**Preparation:** Teach "Settle" first. It will also be more effective if you teach "Wait": Advanced Steps first because your dog will then have a foundation of remaining behind the door.

## Pay Attention to Your Body Language: Practice What You Train

If you have been working on this exercise and your dog does manage to escape, remember to perform the exercise the way you trained it. Do the same actions you did during the training sessions, and you are much more likely to communicate to your dog what you mean. If you yell at him or start running after him, this is not what you practiced!

Dogs are very specific. For example, if you bend down every time you cue "Come" and that's how your dog learns the behavior, you might throw him off kilter if you cue "Come" without bending over. Your dog takes note of your body language very carefully. You want to be sure you're giving him consistent communication.

*Training your dog to wait for you rather than trying to run off takes time, patience, and a lot of treats!*

1.  Have your dog on leash. Place a bed away at a far distance from the door, but within sight of it.
2.  Standing next to the bed, cue "Settle" one time, in a friendly voice. When your dog lies down on his bed, click, and feed him a treat while he's on the bed. Repeat nine times.
3.  Standing one step away from the bed, cue "Settle." When your dog lies down on his bed, go to the bed, click, and feed him a treat. Repeat nine times.
4.  Standing two steps away from the bed, repeat Step 3.
5.  Gradually work up to the distance from the door to the bed so that you are standing at the door, cueing your dog to "Settle" and he will go all the way to his bed and lie down. At a certain distance you may need to drop the leash. Keep it on for safety, just in case you need to stop your dog from running. Ideally, you will only proceed as far as your dog can succeed. The leash is just for extra safety.
6.  Standing at the doorway, cue "Settle." When your dog lies down on his bed, open the door, immediately shut it, then go to your dog, click, and give him a treat. Repeat nine times.
7.  Repeat Step 6, gradually working up to keeping the door open for longer. Aim for 10 seconds.

8. When your dog is reliably lying on his bed even with the door open for 10 seconds, it's time to add another person to the picture. Your "guest" should be outside. He should not knock or ring the doorbell at this point. Cue "Settle." When your dog lies down on his bed, open the door to reveal your "guest." Exchange hellos, but keep an eye on your dog. If he gets up, immediately shut the door (your "guest" will understand!), walk your dog back to his bed, and cue "Settle" again. Do not yell at your dog or tell him "No"; just set him up to try again. If he does not get up, shut the door (again, you have a very understanding "guest"), go to your dog, click, and give him a treat. When you are successful at this level, repeat for a total of 10 times.

9. Your friend should knock lightly on the door. Cue "Settle." When your dog lies down on his bed, open the door, and exchange pleasantries with your friend, inviting him in. Once he is in, shut the door. If your dog has remained on his bed, go to him, click, and treat. Your "guest" can go to pet your dog (as long as your dog already likes him or her) but only on his bed. If your dog should break position and run to your "guest," your "guest" should completely ignore him. All rewards should come on the bed, which is where you want your dog to be. If at any point your dog breaks position, stop the exercise and set him up again. When you are successful, repeat for a total of 10 times.

10. Repeat Step 9, except this time your friend should ring your doorbell.

NOTE: A knock at the door and the sound of a doorbell are highly arousing things to your dog. They are to you, as well: every time you hear it, you leap up and go to see who is at the door! So this part of the training may be extra challenging for your dog. Just be patient and work through it. Remember the three strikes rule—three strikes and you are out. If your dog fails the exercise three times, you are pushing him too fast. Back up your training to where he was successful and repeat the lesson there until he learns it better.

*Getting your dog to settle on his bed rather than rushing to the door when guests arrive is a behavior that may take some time to achieve.*

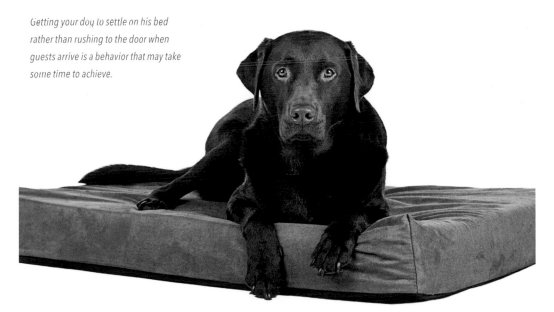

# 11 Food Stealing

Richard's shouting was heard throughout the house, "Stellaaaaaaaaaaaaaaaaaaa!" As Mary came rushing out of the laundry room, she was almost bowled over by the Stella in question, all 70 pounds of Golden Retriever exuberance. Stella did not move fast enough, however, to hide the fact she had a loaf of bread in her mouth. Apparently, Mary's husband had been making a sandwich. When he turned away from the counter to get some mayonnaise from the fridge, Stella pounced. Now Richard was screaming her name and chasing her through the house. Before he and Mary could catch up with her, Stella had bolted down half the loaf. As they scolded her, she lowered her head, ears flattened. She looked crestfallen, but still licked the crumbs from her fuzzy lips. The thief!

Stella loves food. If she could break into a 25-pound bag of dog food, she would wolf down the whole bag. Although that has not happened yet, Stella still has quite a criminal record when it comes to food stealing. Mary still tears up thinking of the time she cooked her very first Thanksgiving meal for their combined families. She was so nervous about getting everything just right. The table had looked picture-perfect when they went to greet their guests. When they returned, there was a delighted Stella with paws up on the dining room table and the beautiful roasted turkey a shredded disaster. Mary was so upset she threatened to rehome the dog, but took it all back when Stella got violently ill from the turkey and had to be rushed to the emergency veterinarian.

Stella is not picky about her thieving territory. She steals food from TV trays, countertops, tables, or even right out of your hand if you aren't watching. Whenever she is caught, she looks appropriately guilty, but she doesn't stop stealing. Stella is a happy-go-lucky committed food felon.

Food stealing is an annoying problem behavior. It can also be a dangerous one if your dog gets hold of food that can hurt him or if he has food allergies and eats something not on his approved diet.

## Symptoms

Your dog steals food, whether it's on the table, countertop, or even by sneaking into your pantry. Some dogs are bold enough to snatch food right off your plate. Dogs have been known to jump completely on top of tables in order to grab a tempting food item.

# Why It Happens

Dogs are natural scavengers and can be natural opportunists. If they find food tempting, they may try to get it if it is within reach. Once they do, it rewards them, so the behavior is repeated. You may wonder why your dog persists in doing this if you punish him for it. The laws of learning state that, in order for punishment to actually be punishment, it must decrease behavior. So your punishment is not enough.

This is not to say you need to be harsher with your dog! To your dog, the reward is worth the crime. That bite of your bacon cheeseburger was worth getting yelled at. Your dog may also enjoy the chase—he's the center of attention! So it's not just the food that is a reward, but all the attention he gets for stealing it. You need to try other, more effective ways of dealing with the problem.

Some dogs have physical reasons for why they steal food. If a dog appears ravenous most or all of the time, and he always wants to eat, this is called *polyphagia*. It can be caused by psychological reasons or by diseases. Symptoms of polyphagia include obesity, increased thirst, increased urination,

*Dogs are natural scavengers. If food is left around, they will more than likely try to steal it.*

increased appetite, weight gain or weight loss, and an inability to properly absorb food. One psychological reason that your dog may develop polyphagia is age. Sometimes, dogs experience an increase in hunger in their senior years. Physical reasons for polyphagia include diabetes or problems in the gastrointestinal tract.

Medication can also increase your dog's hunger. Prednisone, for example, is a steroid that dogs are prescribed for a variety of reasons, ranging from skin conditions to intestinal upsets. Prednisone can dramatically increase your dog's hunger. You may find that your dog who has never stolen food before suddenly becomes a hungry thief.

## Dangerous Foods for Dogs

Some foods are very dangerous for dogs. This includes grapes, raisins, onions, and chocolate. Sugar-free candies and gums that contain xylitol are also dangerous. Very fatty foods, such as turkey skin, can cause pancreatitis, a condition in which the pancreas becomes inflamed.

If you suspect that your dog has eaten something toxic, call your veterinarian immediately. If it is after hours, call your local emergency veterinary clinic. You can also call the American Society for the Prevention and Cruelty to Animals (ASPCA) Poison Control Center at 888-426-4435. (Please note that there is a charge for this service.) The ASPCA also has a free mobile app for Apple and Android smartphones that you can download and that contains great information on potentially dangerous substances and access to its hotline number. Look for "APCC by ASPCA" in your download store.

If your dog is obese and always hungry, he may be suffering from a condition called polyphagia. If you suspect this, get your dog checked over by a veterinarian.

If your dog has been diagnosed and is on medication for hypothyroidism, he is likely on medication to increase his thyroid hormones. You need to have his thyroid hormone levels checked by your veterinarian. Too much thyroid hormone can cause an increase in appetite, so his medication may need adjustment. Hyperthyroidism, a condition in which the thyroid produces too much hormone, is rare in dogs, but it can occur with high doses of thyroid hormone medication or cancer of the thyroid.

Before you treat any problem behavior with behavior modification and training, rule out any physical causes. This is especially necessary if your dog has suddenly developed a new food stealing habit. Check with your veterinarian to rule out any physical problems or to see if your dog's current medication could be at the heart of his food stealing. If you don't address the physical problem, you will not be able to train the problem away.

# The Training Program
## Management

Take your dog to the veterinarian, if necessary, to make sure there isn't a physical problem behind your dog's hunger. Also, do not leave food where your dog can easily get to it. It will be too much of a temptation during your training. If your dog is a committed food thief, this would be like leaving cake and cookies out for someone on a diet.

**Goal:** To prevent your dog from access to where you are eating.

**What You'll Need:** Area for confinement, food-stuffed toy or long-lasting chew.

If your dog is getting rewarded at the table, you need to set your meals up so that the rewards stop. You need to teach him that it is more rewarding to be away from the table.

Make sure you and your family members are not feeding him at the table. If you give him tidbits from your meals but then yell at him later for taking his own, this is conflicting communication. All feeding from the table, or wherever you are preparing meals, must stop.

If you have messy eaters and your dog is getting rewarded with crumbs, then put your dog in a different room while you eat. You can crate him if he can't be trusted yet unsupervised in another room. Be sure to give him a food-stuffed toy or a long-lasting chew toy as a reward for his confinement. Clean up the dining area before letting your dog back there. Make sure you've put away all food before giving your dog access.

## Foundation Behaviors
### "Down," "Settle," "Stay"
To give your dog a designated, acceptable place to be while you're eating.

### "Leave it!"
To prevent your dog from getting food.

### "Come"
To call your dog away from food and come to you. Also, if your dog has already gotten hold of the food, to call him to come to you. This is preferable to chasing your dog. Just keep in mind that if you call your dog to come to you and he does, you should *not* punish him! You will be punishing him for coming to you, which could damage your recall. Just calmly take the food away from him.

## Settle in a Crate/on a Bed
**Goal:** To teach your dog an alternative behavior than being near the table while you are eating, namely, settling away from where you eat onto a bed or in a crate.

*If you want to stop your dog from stealing food, you must stop offering him food from your plate.*

**What you'll need:** A bed, crate, or tether. You'll also need a food-stuffed toy and treats. If your dog will not stay confined in a bed at first, then use a crate or a tether. Then, transition to a bed once you have established the new habit.

**Preparation:** Teach "Settle" first.

1. Place a bed (or crate) away from where you normally eat, but where your dog can still see you. You need to be able to supervise your dog to ensure he remains in his bed. Put the treats near the dog bed, but out of your dog's reach. Do not have them with you at the table.

2. During meals, cue "Settle." Give him a food-stuffed toy that will occupy him while you eat. If he leaves the toy to beg, then the toy is not high value enough. Be sure you stuff it with really tasty treats.

3. Occasionally, throughout the meal, get up and deliver a treat to your dog while he's in his bed.

NOTE: If your dog breaks position, put him back immediately, even if this means taking extra time to finish your meal! With consistency and practice, he will learn to stay put. Stick to the training program.

## Redirection

Right now, your dog has learned to look up for his food rewards—up on counters, up on tables, up on TV trays, and the like. This exercise will teach your dog to focus his attention downward.

1. Randomly, throughout the day, grab a small handful of your dog's kibble (or treats, if you don't feed kibble) and toss it on the kitchen floor. Your dog will scramble to get all the treats. Do this at least twice a day. This will start focusing your dog's attention on the floor, rather than on the countertops.

NOTE: If you are watching your dog's weight, reserve a portion of his regular meal for this training.

2. Prepare some food-stuffed rubber chew toys. Keep them in the freezer. At times when you think your dog would normally go counter surfing, place one or two of the toys on the kitchen floor. Do this *before* he starts counter surfing. For example, if you fix a sandwich in the kitchen, when you put all your sandwich materials away, get a food-stuffed rubber chew toy out of the freezer and place it on the floor. Then leave the kitchen. Your dog should go right to

*Getting your dog to ignore even the tastiest-looking hamburger is proof that your patient training is succeeding.*

the food-stuffed toy. This is also teaching him to focus his attention downward, with a nice reward for doing so. You can place two toys there in case your dog is the type to go back later and check the counter again.

## "Leave It!": Advanced Steps

**What you'll need:** Treats. You'll also need food items your dog finds tempting. What has your dog stolen in the past? Use that.

**Preparation:** Teach "Leave it!" first.

1. **Have treats in both hands.** Cue "Leave it!" Drop a treat on the floor from about an inch off the ground. The bouncing of the treat is an enticement for your dog. Keep your hand ready to cover the treat if your dog goes for it.

2. If your dog goes after the treat, just cover it. Don't say anything. Wait for him to move away. The second he moves away, cue "Take it!" and toss a treat in the opposite direction from your other hand.

3. Right before you drop the treat, cue "Leave it!" Gradually work up to dropping the treat from higher distances. This will create some nice bouncing temptations for your dog. There will come a point at which you can't cover the treat any more with your hand. Just cover it with your foot instead. Take care not to kick your dog accidentally! The second your dog looks away from the dropped treat, cue "Take it!" and toss a treat in the opposite direction from your other hand.

4. Practice in different areas of your home, especially where your dog has a habit of stealing food.

When your dog can successfully leave treats alone no matter how high you drop them from, it's time to move onto a higher value food item. You will practice this in a location where your dog has stolen food, with a food item your dog has stolen. For example, practice in the kitchen with a hamburger.

5. Cue "Leave it!" Place the hamburger on the kitchen counter. Keep your hand near it in case you need to hold onto it. The second your dog turns away from the item, cue "Take it!" and toss a treat in the opposite direction from your other hand. Repeat nine times.

NOTE: If your dog is really obsessed with the food item you are working with, start with a lesser value item. You may also have to pay him with an item of greater value. The same treats you use for your regular training may not be as rewarding as the food item he wants to steal. For example, when working to teach him to avoid stealing a hamburger, reward him with bits of hamburger. This will teach him that he gets a tasty reward for leaving something alone.

6. Take one step away from the counter. Cue "Leave it!" and place the hamburger on the counter. When your dog moves away, cue "Take it!" and toss a treat in the opposite direction from your other hand. Repeat nine times.

7. Gradually take steps farther from the counter. Be prepared to move back in closer if necessary. Repeat Step 6. For each level, repeat a total of 10 times.

8. Repeat the exercise, going back to Step 5, with different food items. When your dog is reliably leaving food items alone when you are several feet away, go back to Step 5 and practice in other locations where your dog likes to steal food. For example, start with Step 5 at the dining room table.

# 12 Humping/ Mounting

The Campbell family refuses to have guests over. It's not that they don't like people, it's just that their Cockapoo, Monty, likes people too much. Way too much. When Monty sees a guest, he goes bonkers with delight. He rushes over to greet them, gives them kisses, and wants to be petted. Then he starts humping their legs. The Campbells are mortified. Several of their friends just laugh it off, but some look really uncomfortable with Monty's behavior.

Monty doesn't limit his humping to guests. He has a "special toy" that he is very fond of—a giant stuffed bone. Mrs. Campbell has caught Monty humping that a couple of times. It's very perplexing. The Campbells had Monty neutered when he was 6 months old. He's 3 years old now—why all the humping?

While some people do find it funny, if your dog is a humper, it can be a particularly embarrassing problem behavior. If your dog humps people, you may be hesitant to have guests over. If he humps other dogs, you may find he sparks off fights. Not every dog appreciates it when another dog mounts him, and they can react defensively as a result.

## Symptoms
Your dog will hump or mount a person, animal, or object. You may or may not be able to easily interrupt him. Male and female dogs can both exhibit this behavior. It doesn't matter whether or not the dog is neutered or spayed.

## Why It Happens
Humping and mounting certainly can be sexual in nature, especially in young dogs who have not been spayed or neutered. It's not always sexual in nature, however. Dogs hump other dogs when they are playing. You may see one dog hump another, and then they switch. It can be a common play gesture. Problems arise when the other dog doesn't want to be played with like that. Not every dog has good social skills with other dogs, so if your dog doesn't recognize that his intended hump victim is not amused, your dog could trigger a fight.

Dogs can also hump when they are overly excited. They haven't learned to exhibit that excitement otherwise. So, in the excitement of meeting a new person, your dog might hump your guest. Or, he may hump a toy, piece of furniture, or other object. You may see it when you drop your dog off at doggie daycare. He might be so excited to see the other dogs he starts trying to hump them. Humping can also occur when a dog is stressed. Just as with excitement, the dog doesn't know how to express his stress otherwise.

*Dogs can hump for sexual reasons, because they are stressed or excited, or because they are simply playing.*

As with all problem behaviors, humping will become worse if you reward it. If you think it's adorable that your small puppy Rottweiler humps his toys, and you laugh and pay him lots of attention when he does, you will likely face a very large Rottweiler humping his toys when he's full grown. So what may have started out as a sexual or play behavior in a young puppy now has become an ingrained habit in an adult dog. This will be harder to fix, since your dog now has had a lot of time to practice the behavior.

*Dog humping is not funny and should not be rewarded. Otherwise, it can become an ingrained habit.*

# The Training Program
## Management

As a healthy outlet for his excess energy, engage your dog's mind and teach him tricks, such as the Foundation Behaviors in this book. It will also build his confidence if he is a nervous dog, and teach him behaviors you prefer.

**Goal:** To prevent your dog from having access to people, animals, and objects he may hump.

**What you'll need:** A confinement area, food-stuffed chew toy, and leash.

**Preparation:** If he is not used to confinement, teach "Settle" first.

**Confinement.** If your dog likes to hump your guests, simply don't let him come near them. Confine him in his crate or another room. You can also keep him on leash, or let him trail a leash. If you believe he is about to start humping, simply lead him in another direction. The leash is not for administering a correction. It's just to give you control over his movement. If your dog is trailing a leash, keep a close eye on him to prevent him from getting tangled around something and hurting himself.

If your dog typically humps one toy, and you would be embarrassed if guests saw this behavior, simply remove the toy from the area before your guests arrive.

*Letting your dog trail a leash means you can get him under control quickly if he looks like he may begin humping.*

Also implement as part of your management program:

### Exercise

This can be helpful if your dog's humping behavior is due to overexcitement or stress. By increasing the amount he exercises, you are providing him with a healthier outlet for his excess energy and stress.

## Foundation Behaviors
### "Leave it!"

To stop your dog from getting to the object or person he wants to hump.

*If your dog starts to hump another dog, even if it looks like play, put a stop to the behavior quickly.*

### "Come"
To call your dog to come to you, away from the object or person he wants to hump.

### "Settle"
To give your dog an alternate behavior you prefer. If he is settling on his bed, he is not humping. (This does assume he doesn't hump his bed!)

## Redirection

**Goal:** To stop your dog from humping and to redirect him to an alternate behavior.

**What you'll need:** It will depend on the situation, but could include interactive toys and a leash.

1. If your dog is humping you, calmly and quietly interrupt the behavior and redirect your dog to an interactive toy. Don't make a big deal over the humping because that gives it attention. Repeat every time your dog humps you, as soon as he starts. Be sure to praise your dog for performing the alternate activity. You want him to be rewarded for doing that instead of humping.

2. If your dog is humping another person and if it's not a family member who is also working with your dog, perform Step 1. Be sure your guest doesn't pay your dog any attention for the humping behavior.

   NOTE: If your dog keeps returning to the person to hump him or her, remove the dog from the area.

3. If your dog is humping another dog, immediately interrupt the behavior. You may have to clap your hands sharply or use "No!" if your dog is so highly excited that he doesn't respond. If necessary, leash your dog and give him a time out, or remove him from the area.

# 13 Ignoring Cues/ Forgetting Training

"Roxie, come here! Come! Come! COME! COME HERE RIGHT NOW!" Roxie the Bulldog wasn't even looking at her dad as he repeatedly commanded, scolded, and begged her to come inside the house. She was staring at the kids playing across the street. "Stubborn dog," he muttered.

Roxie's dad, Joe, was getting increasingly frustrated with Roxie's lack of attention. Did she have attention deficit disorder (ADD)? At 1½ years old, Roxie certainly seemed to suffer from ADD at times. Joe had thought she might be deaf, but disproved that theory when Roxie came running from across the house at the sound of the measuring cup scooping her kibble. If she could hear that sound across the house, she could certainly hear him yelling at her to do something.

Roxie and Joe had attended puppy kindergarten and basic obedience classes. They had done OK in class, but Joe admittedly didn't practice much now that the classes were over. Still, shouldn't Roxie remember what he had taught her? The other day, she was pestering him with her tennis ball while he was trying to play a video game, so he cued her to lie down. She just looked at him as though he was speaking alien. Joe was beginning to think that although his girl was very sweet, she might just be dumb.

It can be very frustrating for pet parents when their dogs don't respond to their cues or when they are ignored. It can also make them angry. It's especially a concern when the dog is doing something potentially harmful. For example, if your dog slips his collar and runs out into the street, but doesn't respond to your "Come" cue, this is very dangerous.

## Symptoms

Your dog will not respond to your cues or pay any attention to you. He may act as though he has forgotten any training you have given him. This can happen even if he has previously responded well in the past. It often happens when a dog reaches adolescence, but can happen at other times as well.

## Why It Happens

There are many reasons why a dog may not respond to your cues. One reason that does not top the list, however, is stubbornness. Dogs are not inherently stubborn. And yes, this includes some breeds that may have previously been accused of it! Stubbornness is defined as having or showing determination not to change one's attitude or position on something, especially in spite of good arguments or reasons to do so. Someone who is stubborn believes he is right despite evidence to the contrary. This does not describe a dog so much as the word "persistence." Have you ever heard of "dogged determination"? Dogs can be extremely persistent, which is determinedly continuing a course of action despite any hurdles in their way. Some breeds of dogs have even been bred to enhance this trait.

Think of your average terrier, originally bred to hunt and kill vermin. If the vermin were wily and hard to capture, or if they fought back, did the terriers just give up? Not at all! They pursued the vermin until they caught them, or at least they kept trying. This is why some dogs will persist in digging under your couch if their tennis balls roll under it. Or why your dog will sit under a tree, gazing up where the squirrel disappeared, waiting for the squirrel to return. The squirrel may be in another county at this point, but your dog will steadfastly wait,

*If your dog starts ignoring your cues, you need to figure out why and then start retraining him.*

not giving up! There is a big difference between being stubborn and being persistent. If you think your dog is being stubborn or defiant, it can make you angry. This would be incorrect, and it also won't help you solve the behavior problem of a dog who doesn't listen to you.

In Part I, we covered the main reasons why problem behaviors occur. All of these reasons are especially applicable to dogs who ignore you or forget their training. For example, if you have never taught your dog a behavior to fluency—in a variety of different environments with a variety of distractions—then your dog is not likely to perform consistently. This is normal. Another example is inconsistent communication

## Adolescent Dog Issues: Selective Hearing

As a dog enters adolescence, it is very common for him to seem to forget any training you have given him. This is a dog who is now in full possession of his senses, so he faces a lot of distractions. If your dog is still intact, he or she has a lot of hormones raging throughout his or her system, competing for attention. In short, your dog is a teenager.

Do you remember what it was like for you at that age? Your parents may have felt like you'd forgotten everything they ever taught you, too. This is a phase, although you should address the problem behavior now so it doesn't become an ingrained habit. Be patient, and work to regain your dog's attention. This teenage phase won't last forever!

in training—using different cues for the same action or the same cues for different actions. This will just confuse your dog. If you have unrealistic expectations, you may think your dog should follow your cues when normally he would not.

Physical problems, such as pain or deafness, can also cause a dog to ignore you. For example, a dog who lies down on a walk, refusing to continue, might have orthopedic problems. A dog who is losing his hearing may not hear you when you call him to come inside.

## The Training Program
### Management

**What you'll need:** This will vary depending on what cues your dog is ignoring. Include the following as part of your management program:

**Control the environment.** If your dog is not responding to you, it's time to get back to training. In the meantime, you need to manage your dog so that he doesn't have the opportunity to ignore you. Treat him as though he was a young puppy. If you continue to give him opportunities to ignore you, then this will become habit.

If your dog is not coming when you call him, you will need a leash. The leash is not for corrections; it's just to keep your dog close to you. Another example is if your dog is not responding when you give the "Leave it!" cue. If that's the case, you'll need to manage his environment so he doesn't have access to things you don't want him to have. If your dog is stealing your shoes off the bedroom floor even though you have cued him to "Leave it!" put the shoes away safely in a closet until you have retrained him.

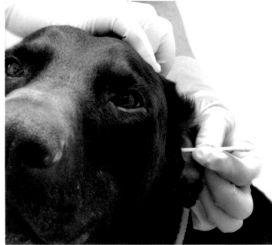

*If your dog is obviously not listening to you, it's always worth getting his ears checked out by a veterinarian. It could be something as simple as a wax blockage that's causing the problem.*

**Veterinary check-up.** If your dog suddenly stops listening to you, it's time for a veterinary check-up. Any sudden change in behavior could indicate a physical problem. Look for signs of stress when you ask your dog to perform a behavior. For example, if you cue him to jump into the car, does he start licking his lips? Does he whine? He could be trying to tell you something's wrong. If your dog's training response has been inconsistent all along, then it's probably not a physical problem.

## General Training

This will vary depending on what cues your dog is ignoring.

**What you'll need:** Clicker, treats.

**Determine which behavior is an issue.** Is your dog ignoring the "Settle" cue? Is he not coming when called? Is it everything? Make a list.

**Go back to the foundation behaviors.** If you have taught these earlier, it should not take your dog as long to learn them again. You should be able to make progress faster than you did in the beginning. Even if you can't, it's OK. It never hurts to review the basics with your dog.

*Rewarding your dog for paying attention to you is all part and parcel of a disobedient dog's retraining.*

**Be consistent.** Are you using different cues for different actions? Are you using the same cue each time for each action? Is your body language the same each time? If you are not consistent, your dog will not respond consistently.

**Don't repeat your cues.** If you repeat your cues in training, your dog will not learn to respond the first time you cue him.

**Click the second the dog performs the behavior.** Always follow a click with a treat.

**Keep your training sessions short,** just a few minutes at a time.

**Practice just one behavior per session.** For example, if you practice "Sit" and "Down" in the same session, your dog may start getting them confused. Then you'll end up with a dog who first sits, then drops into lying down. Have fun!

You may be frustrated that your dog is not responding to you, but please remember that it's all about communication. If you are angry and frustrated, then your dog will feel that as well. No student wants to learn when his teacher is grumpy. If you make training a chore, your dog will not want to work for you any more enthusiastically. Training your dog should be a fun experience. You are learning to work together, better.

**Practice the behavior in different locations.** Every time you start in a new location, back your training up a couple steps and gradually progress from there. Where do you want your dog to listen to you? In the back yard? Practice there. At the park? Practice there. When you visit friends' homes? Practice there.

Gradually add distractions to your training. Start with low-level distractions and gradually make them harder.

# 14 Leash Pulling

Cooper is always in a hurry. A 3-year-old, 90-pound retriever mix, Cooper is more than happy for his people to be in a hurry with him. Cooper's family thinks that if they could just bottle his energy, they'd be rich. They love his boisterous nature but hate taking him for walks. Cooper simply drags them everywhere.

If Cooper sees other people on a walk, he pulls to get to them. If he sees other dogs, he pulls to get to them. Cooper's a social guy! He just loves people and other dogs so much he wants to meet them … RIGHT NOW! His enthusiastic approach has frightened a few neighbors. It's a little disconcerting to see a large dog barreling down the street right at you, with his owner in tow, barely hanging on to the leash.

Last week, Cooper's mom was walking him and things started out OK. They hadn't been out long when a squirrel ran right in front of them. Cooper bolted in hot pursuit. He yanked so hard that his poor mom went sprawling, sustaining some serious scrapes and bruises. She was lucky she didn't have the leash wrapped around her wrist or it surely would have broken. When the squirrel ran up a tree, Cooper bounced back to his mom, still lying stunned on the ground. He kissed her face and looked utterly puzzled as to why she was lying there.

Pulling on leash is an extremely common problem behavior. It may be one of the most frequent reasons that people call professional dog trainers or why they take group dog training classes. It can be extremely frustrating. It can be dangerous if your dog pulls so hard that you get injured. It also has negative consequences for the dog. Dogs who pull are no fun to take places, so they often don't get enough exercise. When their owners finally do take them out, the dogs have so much pent-up energy that they pull on leash even harder than before. So their owners take them out even less. It's a cycle that isn't healthy for the dog and is extremely frustrating for his family.

## Symptoms

Your dog pulls while on leash. He may even pull hard enough so that he chokes or gasps. This may or may not deter him. Some dogs are incredibly strong and will pull even though they sound like they are about to

*Being dragged along by a disobedient dog is no fun. It is one of the most common dog behavior problems.*

pass out! Your dog may pull steadily, the entire time he is on leash, or only when he sees something he wants to investigate or chase.

## Why It Happens

Pulling is a natural dog behavior. Dogs like to cover ground quickly. Your dog wants to explore, to follow scent, to learn about his environment. If he didn't have you attached to him, he could do this very quickly, and he could go where he wanted. Your dog doesn't understand that you want him to walk with you. You'll need to teach him.

Dogs also pull because you accidentally reward them for it. If you let your dog drag you on leash to someone and that person pets and praises your dog, your dog just got a paycheck for pulling. If you drop a treat while training and let your dog pull you so that he can eat the treat, your dog just got a paycheck for pulling. Behavior that is rewarded increases in frequency.

### Brachycephalic Dog Options: Harnesses Are Better

If you have a brachycephalic (flat-faced) dog who likes to pull on leash, this is harmful to him. These dogs have limited capacity to breathe due to the shape of their noses. It's just harder for them to intake oxygen. So if they're pulling on leash so badly it's constricting their airways, they are in danger of respiratory distress. If you live in a hot climate, it can make your dog's ability to breathe even more limited.

Always use a harness with these dogs to avoid additional pressure on their necks that can limit airways. They should still wear collars with ID just in case they get away from you, but a harness is a safer option for walking and training.

*It's a natural instinct for dogs to pull. What you must not do is fall into the trap of rewarding them for doing it.*

You may be surprised that your dog continues to pull even when it seems like he is choking. Some dogs will gasp and wheeze, but still continue pulling you down the street. This is simply because the reward of pulling is greater than your dog's discomfort. Some dogs are also incredibly strong, with thick neck muscles. For example, the average Labrador Retriever or Rottweiler can handle a lot of discomfort. So it's easy for them to just keep pulling because the joys of pulling are worth it.

# The Training Program
## Management

Be careful not to reward your dog for pulling. Keep in mind that rewards are in the eye of the beholder. So if your dog continues to get paid for pulling, it will be harder for you to change this behavior. A harness or halter will help making walking your dog easier. They will not train your dog to walk nicely on leash, but they are excellent management aids to help you in the process. Both of these tools need to be properly fitted. Get a sales associate or professional dog trainer to assist you.

**Goal:** To prevent your dog from pulling on leash.

**What you'll need:**

**Front-clip harness**. Most dogs do not need additional training to get used to a front-clip harness. Use the harness for walking and training. Do not leave it on your dog unattended. Dogs have been known to chew through their harnesses. Plus, your dog could rub up against something and get caught while wearing his harness, which means he could panic or hurt himself.

**Head halter.** If your dog is extremely strong or you have concerns about your safety, consider a head halter. Head halters should not be left on all the time—they are for training and walking. It is best to acclimatize your dog to a head halter. The nose loop can be annoying to some dogs at first. In order to do this, you will also need treats.

## Foundation Behaviors
### "Sit"

A nice behavior to have as an option. You can add it when you stop walking, so that

*If your dog is a persistent puller, using a head halter while walking him can be helpful.*

## Getting Your Dog Used to a Head Halter

1. Have 10 treats. Hold the head halter with the nose loop open, at your dog's nose level. Hold a treat on your side of the nose loop so your dog pushes his nose through the loop in order to get the treat. Do not fasten the head halter at this point, but just give your dog the treat. Repeat at least three times a day for several days, until your dog is eagerly pushing his nose through the loop to get the treat.

2. Hold the head halter with the nose loop open, at your dog's nose level. Hold a treat on your side of the nose loop so your dog pushes his nose through the loop in order to get the treat. Quickly clasp the head halter, and immediately feed three treats to your dog, one after the other, praising him the entire time. Immediately remove the head halter.

   If your dog does well with this and doesn't get upset at the halter, repeat two more times. While your dog is wearing the head halter, praise him and talk sweetly to him. When you remove it, be quiet. Your goal is to shower your dog with attention while he is wearing the halter. Repeat for several days until your dog is comfortable wearing the head halter during each session.

3. Repeat Step 2, gradually increasing the amount of time your dog wears the head halter. Also, before each meal, put the head halter on your dog, feed him his meal, and then remove the head halter. Meal time is especially reinforcing to your dog, so this will help him associate the head halter with his meals.

Always supervise your dog while he is wearing the halter. You don't want him to rub up against something and get it caught. Do not allow him to paw the nose loop off.

## Non-Treat Alternatives: When the Temptation Becomes the Reward

Sometimes, a high-value treat or even a game just won't cut it as a reward for a persistent problem behavior. For example, treats are working well as rewards for teaching your dog to walk politely on leash in your neighborhood. Your dog can nicely go by children, adults, and even other dogs. But he will lunge at the sight of a squirrel. This is a whopper of a temptation for some dogs. A fleeing squirrel is just too enticing for your dog to stay where he should be by your side. So you need to match temptation with reward—not as a bribe, but as a reward for your dog responding to you. Why not use chasing a squirrel?

When your dog bolts after the squirrel, hold your ground. Cue "Sit." Say it one time, in a friendly voice. And then just wait. Your dog will eventually come to his senses when you don't go anywhere. The second he sits, click and then go quickly with him to where the squirrel was, so he can sniff the area. You don't need to follow the click with a treat—the reward is going after the squirrel. It may be at the foot of a tree, where he can look up at where the squirrel disappeared. Of course, you don't want to release him so he catches and hurts the squirrel, but if you are attached to him it's not likely to happen. (Besides, the squirrel is likely long gone.) So let him go sniff.

You will find that if you allow your dog to get what he wanted, but on your terms in that he has to do something for you first, he will begin responding more quickly to you. This is called the *Premack principle*—more probable behaviors (your dog will chase squirrels) will reinforce less probable behaviors (your dog sits even while a squirrel is distracting him). It is especially hard for your dog to sit when he wants to chase a squirrel, but if he then gets to chase the squirrel, he will learn to sit more promptly. This can be a powerful principle that you can use to teach challenging behaviors.

every time you stop, your dog sits. Do not add it until your dog completes the steps for walking nicely on leash first.

## Walking Nicely on Leash

**What you'll need:** Treats, clicker, leash.

1. Choose which side of your body you want your dog to walk on. You will get progress faster if you consistently walk your dog on one side. If you walk your dog on one side one time and then your other side another time, you will be training your dog to just go back and forth while you walk. This could cause you to trip.

   Have your dog on leash. Have a handful of treats in your hand. Take two steps. Stop, click, and feed your dog a treat. When you give him the treat, hold the treat at your side, where you want his head to be while he's walking. If you feed him in front of you, he will push forward to get the treat. This is teaching him to continue pulling ahead of you.

   Do not lure your dog with the treats—don't hold the treat in front of your dog's nose so he's walking to follow the treat. You want him to learn to focus on your body and his position in relation to it, not just blindly follow a treat.

Repeat for a total of 10 clicks and treats. Take a break. Repeat this step until your dog is walking nicely at your side for this distance.

2. Take two steps. Stop, click, and treat. Repeat twice. Take three steps. Stop, click, and treat. Continue taking three steps in between clicks and treats for a total of 10 repetitions. Repeat this step until your dog is walking nicely at your side for this distance.

3. Take three steps. Stop, click, and treat. Repeat twice. Take four steps. Stop, click, and treat. Continue taking four steps between clicks and treats for a total of 10 repetitions. Repeat this step until your dog is walking nicely at your side for this distance.

4. Gradually work up to increasing your steps in between clicks and treats. Always start at the last step to warm your dog up for the exercise.

NOTE: This can be a challenging behavior to fix, especially if your dog has been pulling you for a long time. Be patient. You can do this! Find a way to comfortably hold the leash, treats, and clicker. It may feel awkward at first, but remember that you are learning something new, too. For example, try holding the handful of treats in the hand closest to your dog. Hold the leash across your body, with the clicker in that same hand. Or, try something completely different. There is no right or wrong way, just do whatever is comfortable for you and allows you to perform the training properly.

Practice this in an area with very few distractions, inside if possible. When you first start this training, he will not be ready to learn this in your neighborhood. It's too distracting for him out there. As your dog learns the new behavior, gradually move to areas with more distractions. Start easy and work to make things harder as your dog progresses.

*It can take time and patience to train a pulling dog to walk nicely on the leash, but it is well worth making the effort.*

# 15 Jumping Up

Sammy is a super-friendly English Springer Spaniel. When he was a little puppy, his owners would let him jump up on them, giving him kisses and showering him with attention. Now that Sammy is a teenager, however, they don't think his jumping is fun anymore. He's gotten big! They've tried yelling at him and pushing him off, but Sammy seems to love that. It just makes him jump on them more.

A neighbor told them they should knee Sammy in the chest when he jumps on them. His dad tried that once and regretted it. His knee was sore for a week, but Sammy was still jumping. Someone else told them to try turning their backs on Sammy, but he just got really excited and started mouthing at their arms and legs. Sammy has turned into a bouncy menace.

Sammy's problem behavior is not an unusual one. It's another reason why people call in professional dog trainers. Depending on their size, dogs who jump up on people can easily hurt someone or even knock a person down.

## Symptoms

Your dog will jump up on someone. He may reach to kiss a person's face, or he may paw at the person. If he escalates his behavior, he may start nipping. Your dog may also jump up on furniture.

## Why It Happens

Dogs mainly jump up to get attention and affection. If you have ever rewarded this behavior, it has made the behavior stronger. Remember, attention is attention! Even if you yelled at your dog or pushed him off you, those are still paychecks. You gave him attention. Some dogs may interpret you pushing them as exuberant petting. This is why it can make the behavior worse.

If you've ever been sitting down and your dog put his paws up in your lap, and you petted and praised him, you've paid him for jumping up on you. Your dog will not understand why it's OK to put his paws on you sometimes but not others.

Maybe your dog doesn't jump up on people so much as he does furniture. If you've ever let your dog up on the furniture, he probably enjoyed it. So he won't understand when you don't appreciate him leaping up there whenever he feels like it. Even dogs who have never been permitted on the furniture may discover the joys of couch lounging sooner or later. It's a natural part of exploration. Plus, you sit up there. They want to join you!

## The Training Program
### Management

Do not give your dog paychecks for jumping. Remember that payment is in the eyes of the receiver. So, if your dog loves it when you push him off you or when you give him verbal attention, stop doing it. You may not be able to just ignore him, however, especially if he's the type of dog to get overly excited and mouth you. Just remove yourself from the area as quickly as possible, or give him a timeout for about 10 minutes until he can calm down if necessary. If you continue to reward your dog for jumping, then you will not be able to fix the behavior.

**What you'll need:** Leash, front-clip harness, or head halter to manage your

*Jumping up like this is not to be encouraged. Even if a big dog has the best intentions, he could easily knock someone over.*

dog while you train him. For example, if your dog likes to jump on guests to your house, and you allow him to greet your guests off leash, you are allowing him to jump on people. You are setting him up to practice the behavior you don't like. Instead, when you have guests over, always have your dog on leash. The leash is not for corrections. It's just to control your dog's movement. A front-clip harness can help you better control your dog's forward movement. If you have a really bad jumper, consider a head halter. If you control your dog's head, you control the dog. If you do choose a head halter, see the chapter on Leash Pulling to find out how to get your dog used to it.

## Small-Dog Options: Little Jumping Beans

Some people don't mind their little dogs jumping on them. They don't weigh much, and it can make it easier to reach them to pet them. If this is not a problem behavior for you, then you don't have to work to change it. Just be sure you are not allowing your dog to jump on you sometimes and then reprimanding him at other times. For example, you encourage him to jump up on you when you're wearing jeans, but get mad at him when you're dressed for church. Be sure to be consistent in your communications.

## Foundation Behaviors

### "Sit"

If a dog is sitting, he's not airborne.

### "Down"

If a dog is lying down, he can't jump on people.

### "Settle"

To have your dog settle in a bed or other desired place, rather than your furniture if you don't want him up there.

### "Leave it!"

If your dog is headed toward someone, and you just know he's about to jump on them, "Leave it!" can prevent him from reaching him or her.

*Be consistent if you want to discourage your dog from jumping up on the couch. Allowing it at some times but not others will only confuse the dog.*

## Automatic "Sit" for Greeting

Right now, your dog greets people by jumping on them. This exercise gives your dog a lovely alternative behavior that you will enjoy much better. When someone approaches your dog, your dog will automatically sit. A dog who is sitting cannot jump on someone at the same time. Do not ask your dog to sit if he is afraid or shy of the person approaching him. It is not fair to ask a fearful dog to hold still while a "monster" approaches. He could react by snapping or biting, trying to defend himself. If you have a shy dog, only practice this behavior with people he already loves.

**What you'll need:** Leash, treats, clicker, another person (or people).

**Preparation:** Teach "Sit" first.

1. Have your dog on leash. The leash is not for correction. It is for preventing your dog from jumping on the approaching person. You and your dog will remain in place—the person should approach you from a couple feet away. The person should approach quietly and casually at first, but not attempt to pet your dog.

2. When your dog notices the person, cue "Sit." When your dog sits, click, and toss the treat to set your dog up so you can practice again. As soon as you click, the person should withdraw. If your dog goes to jump on the person, don't say "No" or scold him. Just hold the leash taut so your dog can't reach the person, and the person should immediately withdraw several feet. Wait a few seconds and try again. Your dog will soon understand that he's not going to get a click and treat by jumping on the approaching person.

3. Repeat Steps 1–2 nine times.

4. The person should approach your dog, still being quiet and not attempting to pet him. When the person reaches you, he or she should just stand and wait. See if your dog automatically sits. Give your dog several seconds to see if he does. Just be patient. If after 30 seconds your dog does not sit,

repeat Steps 1–2 for a total of 10 times. If your dog does sit, click and toss a treat. Repeat for a total of 10 successful repetitions.

Work until your dog is automatically sitting when the person approaches. Then you are ready for the person to start petting your dog.

5. The person should approach your dog, still being quiet. If your dog automatically sits, the person should reach out with a hand under the dog's chin, allowing your dog to sniff, and then pet your dog under the chin and then up behind an ear. After just a few seconds, click and treat. When you click, the person should withdraw. If your dog gets up, the person should withdraw, wait a few seconds, and try again. Repeat for a total of 10 successful repetitions.

NOTE: Many dogs do not like being petted on top of the head. Dogs can see this as overly assertive. This is why the person should reach under your dog's chin.

When your dog can successfully sit for one full minute while being petted, it's time to add a greater distraction.

6. Repeat Step 5, except this time the person should approach more animatedly. Up until now, the person has been approaching quietly. This is not how most people will greet your dog. Typically, people will squeal and exclaim, "Helloooooo, puppy! Helloooooo! Are you a good puppy? Yes you are! You ARE a good puppy!" and other gibberish we fall into when we see a cute dog. This makes it much harder for your dog to resist jumping up because it's very exciting.

The person should approach gradually, keeping his or her level of enthusiasm under control. If the enthusiasm is too much for your dog, ask your friend to tone it down so that your dog can succeed in sustaining his sit during petting. Repeat for a total of 10 successful repetitions.

7. Repeat Step 5, gradually increasing the amount of time and greeting enthusiasm your dog can handle while holding a sit.

Training a dog to sit automatically to greet guests rather than jumping up at them takes time and effort, but it is well worth it.

## Non-Treat Alternatives: Petting

Dogs generally jump up to get attention, so when you teach the automatic sit for petting, you are teaching your dog that he only gets rewarded with attention when he is sitting. For social dogs, petting can be a great reward.

It can be harder to train other people than it is to train your dog. Be sure your friends and others who interact with your dog only pet him while he is sitting. Just explain that you are training your dog not to jump up, and they can help by only petting your dog when his rear is planted on the ground. You may find you have to repeat that cue with your friends!

# 16 Mouthing/ Nipping

asha is an adorable puppy. A 17-week-old German Shepherd, her ears are having difficulty deciding what they want to be when they grow up. One day, one ear's up while the other flops, the next day they've reversed. Sasha is also wicked smart. She already knows "Sit," "Down," "Shake," "Roll over," and is doing great with her potty training. She gets along great with people and other dogs, too. Her family thinks she's practically perfect in every way … except for the fact that Sasha is also a shark on four paws.

Sasha nips at everyone's hands. Her little teeth hurt! She nips so badly that she's caused bruises on family members' hands and arms. Caroline, the family's teenage daughter, just wants to cuddle with her puppy, but she can't pet Sasha for 15 seconds without becoming a pin cushion. Sasha simply latches onto her hands or wrist and chomps down over and over. She's not aggressive. The family understands Sasha isn't attacking them, but her teeth are definitely a hazard.

At 17 weeks of age, Sasha is teething. While this age is a prime one for mouthing and nipping, there are other reasons why these are common problem behaviors.

## Symptoms

Your dog mouths and nips at you, especially at your hands, but often at your arms and sometimes even your clothing. He may use his entire mouth, clamp down on you, and then press and release slightly several times without letting go. Dogs will also sometimes strike out, close their jaws or front teeth onto your skin and let go, especially when they are overaroused. He may cause bruising or break the skin, depending on how firmly he latches onto you.

If your dog still has his baby teeth, this behavior can be extremely painful for you. Even when the adult teeth come in, it still hurts.

## Why It Happens

When your dog mouths you, he is not trying to dominate you or assert himself as an alpha. He also is not being aggressive. Mouthing and nipping are very different from aggressive biting.

Puppies mouth when they are teething. Baby teeth normally start falling out at about 16 weeks, when the adult teeth are pushing through the gums. This can be painful, so puppies chew and mouth on things to relieve pain. Chewing on you is soft and probably feels good to those sore gums. A puppy's large back molars come in at about 7 months of age, so mouthing is also common at that time.

Dogs also mouth you to engage you. They mouth and nip at each other in play, and your dog wants to play with you. He doesn't understand that you don't want him to do this until you teach him.

Dogs mouth, too, when they are rewarded for the behavior. If you play wrestle games with your dog and let him chew on you during those games, you are teaching him it's OK to mouth and chew on people. He will not easily understand that he shouldn't play those games with everyone.

*Mouthing and nipping might seem cute in a young puppy, but these behaviors can quickly get out of control.*

## The Training Program
### Management

Mouthing and nipping are common canine behaviors. There are definitely ways of fixing them, but there are also things you can do that will make them worse. Do not:

- Forcibly close your dog's mouth
- Pinch his muzzle
- Push your fingers down his throat
- "Pop" your dog under his chin
- Flip your dog upside down in an "alpha roll"
- Use any kind of physical punishment to "correct" your dog

## Pay Attention to Your Dog's Body Language: When Nipping Isn't Playing

Sometimes, nipping isn't play or engagement behavior. If your dog is growling, his fur is raised on his hackles, he freezes, or gives you a whale eye, these are signs of stress and aggression.

What is going on at the time? Are you trying to pick up your dog? He may be telling you he doesn't want to be picked up. Are you trying to take something away from him? He may be resource guarding. If you suspect your dog is not mouthing, but actually trying to bite you, then consider calling in a professional for an assessment. See the Aggression chapter for more details.

*Encouraging a puppy to mouth and nip at you is never a good idea. You may regret it if it becomes established as acceptable behavior.*

Any or all of these can make mouthing and nipping worse. Some dogs will come back at you harder. Or, you may frighten your dog and he will stop mouthing you, but this will not teach him to stop mouthing everyone.

**What you'll need:** Safe chew toys, interactive toys.

**Appropriate chew objects.** Get a variety of toys for your dog to chew on, especially when he is teething. Know that it is not enough simply to provide a lot of toys. You will need to rotate them frequently, maybe even daily, to keep your dog's interest. This is especially the case if you have a young puppy with no attention span. Interactive toys—toys that you load with food that your dog needs to work to dispense—will retain your dog's interest for a longer time. You may need to try a variety of toys to find the ones your dog enjoys the most.

**Also implement into your management program:**

## Confinement

Sometimes a young puppy will get a glazed look in his eyes and go on a mouthing or nipping spree. This is not unusual, although it can be alarming if you've never experienced it! The puppy is just overaroused and has not learned how to calm himself down yet. If this happens, just give him a timeout in his crate or other confinement area. Don't yell at him or scold him; just crate him and give him a chance to settle down. After 10 minutes, let him out and give him appropriate toys to play with instead.

## Appropriate people play

If your dog is extremely mouthy, do not play wrestle or roughhouse games with your dog. This will just encourage him to mouth more. You will also be teaching him that such behavior is appropriate. Do not allow family members or friends to play such games with him either.

## Small-Dog Options: Mouthing Is Still Off Limits

Just because your small dog has small teeth doesn't mean you should let him mouth or nip at you. Even tiny teeth can be painful. Also, young children and senior citizens have fragile skin, and a small dog's mouthing can cause bruising or puncture wounds. So teach your small dog that his pointy teeth are for toys, not people.

## Foundation Behaviors
### "Leave it!"

If your dog is headed for a person you think he will mouth, "Leave it!" can help deter him before he starts.

## Redirection

**What you'll need:** Appropriate toys.

1. When your dog mouths you, give a pathetic, sad little whine. This will indicate to your dog that his mouthing hurts you. Your dog doesn't want to hurt you, he wants to play with you. Your whine should cause him to stop.

    When you whine, you really need to sound pathetic. If you give a sharp "OW!" then that will likely just rile your dog even more. Indicate to your dog that he has injured you. Most dogs will stop suddenly. Some will even apologize by kissing you.

2. The second your dog stops, give him an appropriate toy. Praise him for chewing on the toy.

NOTE: If you are working with a young puppy, you will have to repeat this exercise many times. Puppies have no attention spans. This is normal. Just be consistent and do it every time your puppy mouths you. If you try this a couple times and then try something else a couple times, the mouthing will likely persist. But if you're persistent and consistent, one day, the light bulb will go off for your dog and he will start to mouth you … then stop on his own. Now he's learned! Be sure you are ready for that moment so you can reward him generously.

*Getting your dog to chew on suitable toys is an effective way of discouraging him from further mouthing and nipping.*

# 17

# Phobias

**B**entley, a 7-year-old Corgi, was better at predicting storms than the local TV weathermen. About 20 minutes before a storm would hit, he would begin trembling. When the first peal of thunder echoed in the distance, he would start to pace, pant, and drool. Poor Bentley would get so worked up during a thunderstorm that he would get diarrhea. His mom, Natalie, felt so badly for him. She wished she could reassure him and tell him it was just a storm.

Unfortunately, in Bentley's area of the country, storms can last a long time. Natalie was worried he would give himself a heart attack, he would get so stressed. She tried giving him an antihistamine, thinking it would make him sleepy, but it didn't work. Bentley sometimes stopped pacing, but he'd still drool, whine, and look miserable. During especially bad storms, he would run into the bathroom and try to get into the tub or behind the toilet.

Some dogs are absolutely terrified of thunderstorms. Others are scared of fireworks or other loud noises. Some dogs develop phobias over odd things, like sewer drains or balloons. Some are scared of household appliances, such as vacuum cleaners or hair dryers. These dogs are not acting this way to try to get attention. They are truly afraid.

## Symptoms

A phobia is an extreme or irrational fear or aversion to something. Some dogs develop phobias to things, such as thunderstorms, fireworks, or even household appliances. In some cases, a phobia that starts with one specific thing can generalize to other things. For example, a dog who starts out afraid of fireworks then becomes afraid of a car backfiring or a motorcycle revving. When your dog is exposed to the trigger, he will exhibit symptoms of extreme fear.

If he is afraid of storms, he may start exhibiting symptoms before you can hear there is a storm coming. Dogs' senses of hearing and scent are stronger than ours, so they can often perceive storms before we can.

Symptoms include pacing, drooling, trembling, and whining. Your dog may be very clingy, or he may try to hide. If it is a trigger he can see, he may try to bolt, running in a panic in the opposite direction. Some dogs have been known to burst through windows trying to get away from something that terrifies them, even if they hurt themselves in the process. Your dog may bark. He may chew to escape, even through doors or drywall. Some dogs get diarrhea, or they may urinate. You may also notice wet paw prints on your floors. Dogs sweat through their paw pads, and this is a sign of fear. Your dog is truly terrified.

## Why It Happens

Sometimes it's easy to understand why a dog becomes phobic of something because you were there to witness what happened. For example, you accidentally caught your dog's tail in the vacuum cleaner, and from that point on, he's terrified of the vacuum cleaner. That is easy to understand. Other times, you may never know why your dog developed a phobia.

*Phobias can be triggered all too easily. One of the characteristic reactions is to run away and hide.*

Fear often doesn't make sense—why are we afraid of the things we are afraid of? If you're afraid of snakes, is it because you had a bad experience with a snake? Did one bite you? Maybe you've never even touched a snake, but they still terrify you. So why does one dog sleep through thunderstorms while another paces around in absolute terror? There are no current scientific explanations.

## Senior-Dog Options: Late-in-Life Fears

As dogs get older, they can develop fears or phobias. This can be confusing to you, especially if you've had your dog since he was a young puppy. He's gone years without a reaction to something, but now he suddenly has a problem with it. Why?

One reason may be that as dogs get older, they develop disabilities and illnesses that make them less tolerant. So a dog who never minded you cutting his nails is now afraid of the nail clippers. They can also grow more insecure. The dog who was fine not being in the same room with you while he was growing up is now practically your shadow. Dogs can lose their hearing, making them startle more when someone or another animal approaches them suddenly.

If your older dog is suddenly displaying fear behavior, take him to the veterinarian for a checkup to make sure he is physically OK. If all is well, then you can start to treat his phobias behaviorally. Even old dogs can learn new tricks. You'll just need to be extra patient with your companion as he becomes a little insecure on entering his golden years.

# The Training Program
## Management

Avoid or reduce the effect of triggers as much as possible. For example, if your dog is afraid of vacuum cleaners, keep him away when you are vacuuming until you can implement your training program. If your dog is afraid of thunderstorms, this can be challenging. Try giving your dog a "safe place," one where he already enjoys going. Try a room without windows (even if it's a closet), or cover the windows to help lessen the sight of lightning. Play some soothing music or leave the TV on.

**What you'll need:** These items may or may not help ease your dog's fear. It depends on the individual dog.

**Thundershirt™ or Anxiety Wrap®.** These are snug jackets that your dog can wear when he is afraid. They calm and soothe some dogs. The effect is supposed

*Senior dogs can develop new fears as they age, even becoming afraid of familiar parts of their usual routine, such as nail clipping or other grooming tasks.*

to be similar to swaddling an infant. There's no scientific explanation for why it works, but in some dogs, the snug wrap dramatically lessens anxiety. For other dogs, it may just "take the edge off" and allow them to cope better. On some dogs, though, it has no effect at all.

## No Ace Up Your Sleeve

It used to be that veterinarians would commonly prescribe a drug called acepromazine, or "Ace," for dogs with phobias. Today, veterinary behaviorists avoid the use of Ace for this treatment. Renowned veterinary behaviorist Karen L. Overall, MA, VMD, PhD, DACVB, CAAB, talked about this in an article published in DVM360:

"I know that the common 'treatment' for storm and noise phobias and veterinary office visits is acepromazine. In truth, I wish this medication would be placed at the far back of a top shelf and used only exceptionally. Acepromazine is a dissociative anesthetic meaning that it scrambles perceptions. Ask yourself if a scrambling of perceptions will make an anxious or uncertain dog worse or better. It's always worse, and we make many if not most dogs more sensitive to storms by using this drug. In part this is also because sensitivity to noise is heightened.

This is a recipe for disaster for these dogs, and, in fact, they learn to be more fearful and more reactive because of these associations. If what you need is sedation—acepromazine can be an acceptable adjuvant, but it makes most of my really fearful and really reactive patients worse, so all sorts of other drug combos can work better and do less harm than is done by the routine use of acepromazine."

**Calming cap.** This is a mesh cap that covers a dog's eyes. The dog can see through the mesh, but everything is muted. For some dogs, reducing their ability to see things that frighten them can have a soothing effect.

**Dog appeasing pheromone (DAP).** This chemical simulates the pheromones mothers release when they have nursing puppies. It comes in a collar, or as a spray or a diffuser. Kennels use it to calm dogs who are being boarded. For some dogs, it can be soothing. For others, it has no effect.

**Rescue Remedy.** This is a flower essence used for stress and anxiety. You can find it at many health food stores or online. Originally, people took Rescue Remedy to cope with their stress, including fear of flying or preparing for tests. They then began using it on their pets and noticed similar reductions in stress levels for some dogs.

**Medication.** If your dog is so afraid that he cannot think clearly or he is likely to hurt himself, he may need medication. You will not be able to reach him behaviorally if he is in a blind panic. Ideally, the drug will work to balance the chemicals in your dog's brain to help him better cope with his fear. This is not a tranquilizer. Some drugs do need to be given in advance of a storm, which is not always practical. Talk to your veterinarian or a veterinary behaviorist about medication to help your dog better cope with his phobias.

## Foundation Behaviors

Depending on the level of your dog's fear, you may be able to distract him by asking him to perform behaviors and rewarding him for them. The behavior itself can be something as simple as "Sit" or "Down" or even tricks. You just need to find something to distract your dog from whatever he fears. If this works for your dog, then try using training as a good distraction. Know, however, this may not work if your dog is terrified.

*Comforting a scared dog isn't rocket science. It's straightforward commonsense.*

If your dog ignores your cues, or performs them while exhibiting signs of stress, stop asking him to perform behaviors. It's too much for him to try to comply while he is afraid, and you are putting extra pressure on him. Too many times, a terrified dog will be asked to "Sit, Sit, Sit!" and it's just too much. You also could be associating training with the thing that scares him, which would not be good!

## Non-Treat Alternatives: Reassurance

For many years, many preached that you should not comfort a frightened dog because that would just reinforce a dog's fear and cause him or her to act afraid more often. Experts in canine behavior dispute this. Fear is an emotion, not a behavior. If your dog is afraid, and he turns to you for comfort, go ahead and offer it. If you pet your dog while he is afraid and he relaxes, then your comfort did not make him worse. If it doesn't work, and your dog is still acting in the same way, then your petting had no impact.

If a frightened toddler were to have a terrible nightmare and come to you for comfort, wouldn't you give it? A phobic dog is a terrified dog. If he turns to you for help, give it to him. Don't act in a panic yourself. Just be reassuring and loving. You'll make your dog feel better, and you won't be teaching him to "fake it" later for more attention.

## Desensitization to Noises

There are many factors involving fear to certain triggers, such as thunderstorms. Your dog may be afraid of the sound of thunder, but he also could be reacting to differences in barometric pressure or other aspects of a storm. If it is noise-related, work on desensitizing him to that noise. You'll know if your dog doesn't respond to the training. For example, some dogs will not react to a sound recording of a thunderstorm, only to a real one.

**What you'll need:** Sound effect CD of your dog's trigger.

1. Play the CD at the lowest possible setting. You want to find a setting at which your dog will not react. Remember, dogs can hear better than you can. So you may not be able to hear the CD, but he can.

2. Turn the CD up slightly. Watch your dog for signs of stress. Does he start panting? Pacing? You're going too fast. Turn the CD back down and keep it down for longer.

3. Gradually work up to playing the CD loudly. This may take many sessions, and that is normal.

## Desensitization and Counterconditioning

Desensitization and counterconditioning can help a dog learn to better cope with the things he fears.

**Goal:** To teach your dog to not be afraid of a trigger.

**What you'll need:** Leash, treats, trigger. In later steps, you will also need someone to help you. This example uses a hair dryer, but it could easily be any other household appliance your dog may fear, such as the dishwasher or the vacuum cleaner. The leash is simply to prevent your dog from wandering. You will not use it for corrections or to drag your dog to the trigger.

1. Place the hair dryer at a distance far enough away that your dog can see it but does not exhibit signs of stress. Watch him carefully. Is he whining? Does he look worried? Then you are too close. Back up until he appears comfortable and relaxed. Keep the hair dryer turned off. Have your dog on leash. When your dog notices the hair dryer, feed him several treats.

2. Take one step toward the hair dryer. Check your dog for signs of stress. As long as he is still calm and relaxed, feed him some treats again. Do not cover the hair dryer with treats or lure your dog to the hair dryer. This can backfire. Some dogs are so keen on eating treats that they will run up, eat all the treats, and retreat. They are still very stressed the entire time. The goal is to work slowly so that your dog approaches the trigger in a relaxed state.

3. Repeat Step 2 until you can reach the hair dryer without your dog showing signs of stress.

4. When you can repeat this exercise successfully several times, it's time to turn the hair dryer on.

5. Start a distance far enough away so that your dog will not show signs of stress at the hair dryer when it is turned on. Please note you may have to start farther away than you did originally. It depends on whether the combined visual and auditory trigger causes your dog to be afraid. At this point, the hair dryer is just stationary. You can lay it on the floor. Feed your dog several treats.

6. Take one step closer to the hair dryer. Check your dog for signs of stress. As long as he is still calm, feed him some more treats.

7. Repeat Step 2 until you can reach the hair dryer without your dog showing signs of stress.

8. When you can repeat this several times successfully, then you can start getting another person to move the hair dryer while it's turned on. The person should use the hair dryer normally. Some people make the mistake of using the "scary" item unusually, with jerking movements or thrusting it toward the dog. This is not natural, and it will not be helpful. The person should just use the hair dryer as he or she normally would to dry hair.

9. Feed your dog treats when the hair dryer moves. Only proceed as far as your dog can succeed. If he gets frightened, stop the exercise and try again later, at a farther distance.

10. Take one step closer to the moving hair dryer. Check your dog for signs of stress. As long as he is still calm, feed him some treats.

11. Gradually work up to where the person can use the hair dryer without your dog showing signs of stress.

NOTE: The desensitization part of this exercise is the distance between the hair dryer and the dog. You only move closer when your dog has acclimatized to one spot. The counterconditioning part is associating the hair dryer with treats. Your dog should start to look to you when he sees the hair dryer, waiting for his treat. When he does this, you're making progress!

*Many dogs develop fears of household appliances, but not this brave pup!*

# 18 Potty Problems

**P**rincess is living the good life. A tiny, 2-year-old Pomeranian, Princess has the best, most expensive toys. She has three different beds. She travels in a designer handbag carrier. She only eats the finest foods. Her leash and matching collar glimmer with rhinestones. And Princess poops and pees wherever she pleases.

Her mom adores her Princess, and cleaning up after her hasn't really been a problem. It's annoying sometimes, but she figures that all little dogs are unreliable in their housetraining. But mom has a new boyfriend, and he is none too pleased that Princess can't tell the living room from a bathroom. Mom's now under pressure to get Princess to poop and pee only outside.

Princess isn't eliminating wherever she wants out of spite or entitlement. She's just never been housetrained.

## Symptoms

Your dog eliminates in undesired locations. It may be infrequent, or it may be on a regular basis. It can be pee or poop, and sometimes it is both.

## Why It Happens

Elimination is a natural dog behavior. Your dog doesn't understand where you want him to eliminate unless you teach him in terms he can understand. The most common reason that your dog eliminates inappropriately is because of a lack of proper, thorough training. You may have thought you trained your dog to eliminate only in a certain spot, but if he's having housetraining issues, then he didn't learn the lessons you intended.

Your dog doesn't eliminate inappropriately out of spite or because he's trying to dominate you. Yes, this even means when he pees on your bed or in your shoe. That often happens because a dog is stressed. Housetraining accidents can be a symptom of canine stress. For example, you may find that you discover pee and poop in the house during a thunderstorm or fireworks display. When dogs are afraid, they sometimes seek comfort in places that smell most like you, like your bed, your shoes, or other articles of clothing.

Dogs also sometimes eliminate inappropriately due to illness. Certain diseases, such as diabetes, can cause a dog to drink excessive water, which means he needs to pee more frequently. Urinary tract infections can also cause your dog to experience increased urgency to urinate. Your dog may not be able to "hold it" until he makes it outside. If your dog has been reliable in his housetraining for months and suddenly starts eliminating inappropriately, consult your veterinarian. You need to rule out any physical causes before you try fixing the behavior with training.

Some medications, such as prednisone or other steroids, can also cause frequent urination. If your dog is on medication, ask your veterinarian about the side effects.

Illnesses that cause excessive or overly frequent elimination can be especially problematic for young puppies during their early learning periods. If you have a sick puppy who is often plagued with diarrhea or excessive urination, and you simply can't give him enough potty breaks outside of his crate before he makes a mess, he could learn that it's OK to soil his crate.

Similarly, if your dog came from a puppy mill or pet store, he may have housetraining issues just because of how he was raised. This is common. These dogs were raised in confined spaces with no chance to eliminate elsewhere, so eliminating in their "dens" is normal for them.

There is another urination issue that actually doesn't have anything to do with housetraining. If your dog only pees when he greets someone, this is called *submissive urination*. It often happens when someone reaches to pet your dog. Sometimes it only happens when men pet your dog, or tall people. Dogs can also submissively urinate when they greet other dogs.

*Simply scolding a dog for peeing indoors is counterproductive. He needs training to establish where he is allowed to eliminate.*

*Apart from the natural need to eliminate, one reason puppies and dogs urinate is to mark what they consider to be their territory.*

When a dog pees in greeting, it's a sign of overexcitement and respect. Dogs will urinate to indicate that they respect the other party. It can happen in young puppies. Some dogs outgrow it, but others will need a training program to help them stop.

## The Training Program

The best way to address a housetraining problem is to start from scratch in training your dog exactly where you want him to eliminate. It doesn't matter how old your dog is, whether he is a young puppy or an older dog. If your dog is older and has had a housetraining problem for a long time, it will be harder to address because it is an ingrained habit. But even older dogs can learn to be housetrained. What's the secret? Implement a solid, consistent management and training program.

Do not mix and match methods. For example, decide if you want your dog to eliminate indoors in a specific area (pee pads or a litter box) or if you want him to eliminate outside. Do not try both at the same time. You dog will find it too confusing.

If you want your dog to eliminate only outside, do not use pee pads indoors in your training program. Remember, pee pads are for where you want your dog to eliminate. For example, don't put pee pads in a dog's crate—you don't want him to eliminate in his crate. Also note that just because you put a pee pad somewhere doesn't mean your dog will eliminate on it. If you have a young puppy, he may choose to chew on it!

If you want him to eliminate inside, choose a specific place and set it up with pee pads or a litter box.

If you catch your dog eliminating in an inappropriate area, just interrupt him with a firm "No!" and then immediately take him to his designated area as per the training plan. Never use your hands for punishment. Do not roll up a newspaper and hit him. Elimination is a natural behavior, and you will not be teaching him to eliminate where you want him if you use physical punishment. You will be teaching him to be afraid of you or to go hide when he eliminates the next time around.

If you find a mess after the fact, and you did not catch your dog doing it, he's already moved on to other things. Do not punish him for the mess. Instead, just clean it up and remind yourself that you need to supervise him better.

## Puppy Mill/Pet Store Dog Options: Challenging Cases

If you got your dog from a puppy mill, then you may have a challenging housetraining case on your hands. If you got your dog from a pet store, he may be in the same boat, since most pet store dogs come from puppy mills.

In a puppy mill, mother dogs are kept in very small cages. This doesn't change when they have a litter of puppies. They are all kept in the same cage, all the time. A puppy's natural instinct is to eliminate away from its den. But what do you do if you can't ever leave your den? You still have to go. So puppies end up peeing and pooping right where they live. Since they are at a critical learning stage in their development, they learn that this is OK. It's fine to pee and poop all over themselves and just hang out in it. Once a puppy learns this, it's very, very hard to fix.

Another problem is that puppies are often taken from their mothers when they are way too young, so they can be shipped across the country while they are still small and cute and therefore easier to sell. A mother dog cleans her puppies after they eliminate. She does this for them until they get older and learn to do it for themselves. If pups are taken from their mothers too soon, one lesson they miss out on learning is how to clean after elimination. This is another reason why a puppy mill or pet store dog will simply eliminate in his crate and be quite content to sit in it for hours. It's all he knows.

If you have one of these dogs, then crate training is not recommended for housetraining. You can still teach your dog to enjoy being in a crate for other reasons–safety, health, to avoid destructive chewing–but for housetraining, it probably will not help to have your dog in a crate. He will likely just eliminate in the crate and be fine with it. Instead, set up a larger confinement area. For example, put his crate, with the door open or removed, inside a large exercise pen. Or try using a small bathroom or laundry room.

Incorporate extra potty breaks into your training schedule to give your dog many more opportunities to be rewarded for eliminating in his designated spot than for going indoors. Know that it may take longer for him to develop new habits because this was ingrained in him at a tender age.

It's not your dog's fault that he was raised in this manner. You may have adopted the dog not knowing about his background. Or, you may not have understood why getting a dog from a puppy mill or pet store is a bad idea. So now you're stuck with a very messy problem. This will take extra supervision and a ton of patience, but you can do it!

*Keeping a puppy confined to a specific area indoors during housetraining is a good idea.*

When you do clean up a pet mess, use an enzymatic cleaner. This will help to make it impossible for your dog to smell the odor. Remember that dogs can smell much better than you can. You don't want him to return to the spot again and again. An enzymatic cleaner can do a more thorough job of cleaning than vinegar or other household cleaners.

## Management

Management is important to any training program, but it's especially critical when it comes to housetraining. A dog left to his own devices will eliminate wherever and whenever he wants. He doesn't know anything else. In order to successfully train your dog to only eliminate where you want him to, you need to be a micro manager!

**What you'll need:**

### Crate

For the purposes of housetraining, the crate you use should be just big enough for your dog to stand up, turn around, and lie down comfortably. If you use a larger one, your dog will be able to eliminate in a corner and avoid it during his confinement.

Confinement is extremely important when housetraining your dog. If you cannot supervise your dog closely, then your dog needs to be confined to reduce the possibility of him eliminating anywhere he wants.

Dogs have a natural instinct to avoid soiling their dens. If that instinct has been nurtured from puppyhood, a crate can be an effective part of your housetraining plan. If your dog spent his formative puppyhood confined to a small cage, however, his natural instinct could have been extinguished. This can be the case, for example, with dogs from pet stores and puppy mills. If your dog didn't come from either of these sources, you can take advantage of his natural instinct to poop and pee in a place other than where he eats and sleeps.

*Instead of using newspapers for elimination, it's far better to train your dog to use pee pads or a litter box. You don't want him to learn to pee on a newspaper you haven't read.*

Before using a crate with your dog, you will need to crate train him. See the Foundation Behavior section to find out how to teach "Settle."

When using a crate for housetraining, your dog may be confined quite a bit, depending on how much you can supervise him during the day and night. It's important that you give your dog lots of exercise and affection outside of the crate.

## Leash

If you are training your dog to go outside, you'll need him to be on leash. Just putting your dog outside doesn't teach him that you want him to eliminate outside. You need to go with him so you can cue and reward him properly. If you are not attached to him, you are also allowing him to wander around the yard and get distracted by the various scents, sounds, and other temptations he'll find there. Keeping him attached to you helps keep your dog focused.

You can also use a leash to tether your dog to you. When you see him start to sniff in a circle or to hunch up, quickly take him to his elimination spot. Tethering gives your dog more freedom than a crate while still keeping him close to you so you can interrupt improper elimination and supervise him better. Some people wonder about installing a dog door. Will that teach your dog to eliminate outside? No. Not all dogs know to go outside to eliminate. Installing a dog door as a "train yourself" option is not a guarantee of success. What is better is to participate in the training and go outside with your dog.

## Supervision

You will need to supervise your dog extremely closely. If you are watching him, then you can interrupt any improper elimination and ensure that he is going to his designated elimination spot. Many people do not realize how much effort this task takes. Dogs can pee and poop quickly. If you take your eyes off your dog while you take a shower or answer a phone call, you are giving him the opportunity to eliminate somewhere inappropriate. You're setting him up to fail. When you are housetraining your dog, it really

Some dogs take readily to using a dog door to go outside and eliminate. Many do not. It's far better to train your dog to eliminate outside by going outdoors with him yourself.

does require major supervision. Yes, this can be trying. Fixing a problem like this is going to take some effort. You will be rewarded, however, with a dog who no longer uses your house as his bathroom.

## Scheduled Feedings

If your dog eats at set times each day, he will also eliminate around the same time each day, usually within an hour of eating. This helps you tremendously with housetraining. It will make your dog's elimination times more predictable so you can ensure he is in the right spot when it happens. It also enables you to better monitor your dog's food intake to help avoid obesity and to increase the appeal of food rewards when you are training. A dog who can graze food all day might be too full to think of a treat reward as very appealing.

For puppies 6 months and younger, feed three meals a day. Just put the food down; if anything's left after about 10 minutes, remove it. For puppies and dogs 6 months and older, feed two meals a day.

## Potty Schedule

In general, puppies need to eliminate when they wake up (either from a night's sleep or a nap), after they have been playing hard, after they eat, and after you give them a bath. If you have a very young puppy, he will not be able to hold it all night.

As a dog gets older, into adolescence and adulthood, he will not need as many potty breaks as a young puppy does. As a dog enters his senior years, he will need more potty breaks.

When estimating the amount of time a puppy can stay in a crate before needing to eliminate, a general rule is to take his age in months and add 1. So for a 4-month-old puppy, he can stay in the crate 4 +1 = 5 hours before needing a potty break. In general, puppies less than 6 months must have a mid-day potty break. They simply can't hold their bladder and bowels for longer. If you make them try, they can end up having accidents. This can teach them that it's OK to soil their crates, which is not a lesson you want them to learn!

Adolescent and adult dogs should not spend more than eight hours in a crate without a potty break. Ideally, every dog will graduate from confinement and be able to have more freedom, even if you are out of the house. This is not always realistic, depending on your dog. Sometimes, your dog will need to be crated if you are gone during the day. Consider hiring a petsitter or getting a trusted neighbor to come in the afternoons and give your dog a potty and exercise break. If you have to leave your dog crated for housetraining or his safety while you are away for a typical workday, then he will in all likelihood be just fine as long as you have properly crate trained him. Just be sure he gets plenty of exercise and affection outside the crate as soon as you get home and throughout the evening.

## Housetraining Log

"He pees all the time!" or "He poops everywhere!" Trainers hear these two complaints constantly. Sometimes this is accurate information, but sometimes it's actually just frustration. If you clean up two messes in one day, it's annoying. So it may feel as though all you do is clean up messes. Some days, it may feel as though your dog is nothing but a peeing and pooping machine. But is this an accurate description? You will best be able to address the problem if you accurately track it. A housetraining log is a perfect solution.

With a housetraining log, you'll chart when you feed your dog, when you take him for a potty break, and what elimination, if any, happened during the break. In this way, you can see where the training is falling short and where you are having success. For example, do you notice a trend of your dog having accidents in the mornings? This means you need an additional potty break in the morning, plus more supervision of your dog during that time. Do you notice your dog always has accidents on a specific day? What goes on during that day that is different from the rest? Perhaps you go to the gym after work or run errands and come home later. The log will show you that you need to find a way to better accommodate your dog on those days.

A housetraining log also is helpful when you have more than one person responsible for taking your dog out for potty breaks. It's easier for families to track who did what and when if things are written down. You can keep the housetraining log on the fridge for easy access.

While these are general guidelines, dogs are going to differ in what they need. Toy breeds, for example, seem to often need more frequent potty breaks. Your dog may need more or fewer potty breaks. With a housetraining log, you will be able to gauge what your specific dog needs in order to best learn.

## Putting It Together: Schedules and Housetraining Log

These sample schedules show you how to chart your dog's problem and progress. Your dog may differ in the number of breaks he needs and how many times he eliminates throughout the day. Some dogs need to pee and poop more often than others, and this is normal. A lot will depend on what you feed your dog, too. A food that is mostly fillers will go through a dog faster than one that has more quality nutrients in it.

Your schedule may also be different depending on what time you get up and if you are away from home during the day or evening. You may have to adjust your schedule or get people to help you while training, especially if you have a puppy.

See the sample schedule and housetraining log for a 16-week-old puppy on page 182.

In this example, you can see the mornings are going well. This puppy could not hold his bladder until his family came home from work, however. This means that, at this age, he may need someone to come home a little earlier to let him out. Alternatively, you could try making the lunch break a little later to spread the time out. Evening was also a problem when the puppy peed in the living room at 10:30 p.m. This usually indicates a lack of supervision. It's easy for someone to get caught up in a TV show or night-time chores and forget that he or she needs to watch the puppy. Since the puppy had already eliminated at 10:30 p.m., he didn't have to go again during his potty break at 10:45 p.m. If you take frequent potty breaks with your puppy, there will be times when he doesn't eliminate. This is normal, and you should chart it so you can better learn when he does have to eliminate.

| Sample schedule and housetraining log for a 16-week-old puppy | | |
|---|---|---|
| **Time** | **Activity** | **Results** |
| 7 a.m. | Potty break | Peed |
| 7:15 a.m. | Fed breakfast | |
| 7:30 a.m. | Potty break | Pooped |
| 12 p.m. | Potty break | Peed, pooped |
| 12:15 p.m. | Fed lunch | |
| 12:30 p.m. | Potty break | Peed, pooped |
| 5:30 p.m. | | Came home from work, puppy had peed in crate while gone. |
| 5:35 p.m. | Potty break | Peed |
| 7 p.m. | Fed dinner | |
| 7:15 p.m. | Potty break | Peed, pooped |
| 10:30 p.m. | | Peed in living room |
| 10:45 p.m. | Potty break | Nothing |

See the sample schedule and housetraining log for a 3-year-old dog opposite.

In this example, it looks as though the dog can't hold his bladder overnight. His last potty break is at 7:15 p.m., and he doesn't get another one until more than 12 hours later, at 7 a.m. This dog needs another potty break later in the late evening. The family should also consider confinement overnight so the dog doesn't continue to learn to eliminate in the bedroom.

## Outdoor Elimination Training

**What you'll need:** Treats, leash.

1. Have treats. During a scheduled potty break or when you think your dog needs to eliminate, take him to his outdoor elimination spot on leash.
2. Just before he eliminates, give a cue. You can use one cue to mean elimination in general. Or, if you prefer, you can use one cue for peeing and one cue for pooping. Just be consistent. Give your cue "Go potty!" (or whatever you choose).
3. As soon as your dog is finished eliminating, give him a treat (or praise him). Make a big deal about it!
4. Let your dog sniff around the yard a couple minutes. Or, if he is in a fenced yard, take him off leash and let him explore and play a little. You don't want to take him right back inside, or he will learn that elimination removes him from the outdoors. Many dogs enjoy being outside and exploring, so he will hold it longer in order to stay outside longer.

| Sample schedule and housetraining log for a 3-year-old dog | | |
|---|---|---|
| **Time** | **Activity** | **Results** |
| 6:30 a.m. | | Dog peed in bedroom overnight |
| 7 a.m. | Potty break | Peed, pooped |
| 7:15 a.m. | Fed breakfast | |
| 5:30 p.m. | Potty break | Peed, pooped |
| 7 p.m. | Fed dinner | |
| 7:15 p.m. | Potty break | Peed |

NOTE: If you take your dog out and he does not eliminate within 10 minutes, bring him back inside and either confine him or supervise him closely. Otherwise, you will be teaching your dog that it's fine to take 20 minutes or more to find the perfect spot to eliminate on. If you have that kind of time, it's OK! It's up to you. If you ever need your dog to eliminate quickly, however, do not let him develop the habit of taking a long time to find the right spot. You can teach your dog to eliminate as soon as he goes outside. You just have to train this behavior. This is also extremely helpful when traveling with your dog, when you don't have time to wander around a rest stop waiting for your dog to find an ideal spot.

When your dog is reliably eliminating outdoors when you take him out for potty breaks, and he has not had any accidents inside your house for two months, then you can begin to wean him off having you attached to him. If at any point things backslide—he stops eliminating when you take him out for potty breaks or he has accidents inside the house, go back several steps and wait longer before moving on to this method. It can be tempting to let your dog outside by himself too early in the process. Just remember that you need to be with him to reward him the instant he eliminates outside. If you wait to praise him or give him a treat when he comes back inside, you're not rewarding him for eliminating outdoors. You are rewarding him for coming inside. So stay close to him until he is progressing well in his housetraining.

1. First, let your dog drag his leash during potty breaks. You will trail behind your dog. Always supervise him carefully so the leash doesn't get caught on anything.
2. After several days, take him out off leash, but still trail after him.
3. After several days, take him out off leash, but wait and watch him outside, right at the door.
4. After several days, take him out off leash, and wait inside the door.

## Signaling

Some owners get frustrated that their dogs will not tell them when they need to go outside. While some dogs can be obvious about their need to go out, many others need to be trained to signal you. Your dog doesn't automatically know how to tell you he needs to go out. He could also be telling you, and you just don't understand his signals. For example, some dogs will stand by the door and just stare at you. If you're not looking at your dog, you'd have no idea he's trying to tell you anything.

*Even city dogs can learn to eliminate outside with proper training.*

This exercise will help you teach your dog to let you know he needs to go outside. You need to be careful about the method you choose. For example, if your dog starts barking at you to go outside or scratching at the door, is that what you really want? Instead of your dog choosing his method of communication, choose one that you will find pleasant.

**What you'll need:** Bell on a ribbon or a doggie doorbell system. There are a variety of pet doorbell systems on the market. This training lesson will cover any system that features a paw target—when your dog paws the bell or object, it will ring or trigger a chime. The ring or chime is your signal that the dog needs to go out.

First, you will teach your dog to paw a target.

1. Place the target on the ground near your dog. If your dog reaches out with a paw to touch the target, click, remove the target, and treat. This may not happen, though. Most dogs first explore new things with their noses. So, if your dog noses the target, that's OK. Click for the nose touch, remove the target, and treat. You remove your target so he won't touch it again before you are ready to click and treat him again.

   For dogs, nosing and pawing are closely connected behaviors. If your dog starts with his nose, don't worry. He will soon switch to pawing.

2. Repeat for a total of 10 repetitions. If your dog is reliably nosing the target, start withholding the click to see if he will switch to his paw. Give him several seconds to try before going back to a nose touch. If he is pawing the target, continue to the next step.

NOTE: Some dogs like to use their paws more than others and will pick this up quickly. Others take a while. So this may take just one session, or it may take several. This is normal. Just proceed as far as your dog can succeed. If you find your dog wants to pick up the target in his mouth, anchor it with your foot. You don't want him to learn to pick up the target.

When your dog is consistently pawing the target, it's time to move it around.

1. Start placing the target in different locations, but within a couple feet of your dog. Click and treat every time he touches a paw to the target.

2. Hold the target in the palm of your hand, against the ground. Click and treat for every correct response.

3. Gradually start moving the target a little higher, but still at a comfortable height for your specific dog. Click and treat for every correct response.

4. Repeat 10 times.

5. Gradually work to where the target is in its desired place. For example, a bell will be hanging from the door you use to go outside. Be sure to hang it at a height where your dog can paw it. A doggie door chime may be placed right next to the door.

When your dog is reliably going to the target and pawing it, it's time to associate the bell or chime with going outside. You will still remain close to the door at this point.

1. When it's time for a potty break, position yourself near the bell or chime. When your dog rings it, immediately clip on his leash and take him out for a potty break. Follow the outdoor elimination training instructions.

2. Repeat this every time you take your dog out for a potty break.

With consistency, eventually you will hear your dog ring the bell on his own when you are not positioned by the door. Immediately get your dog's leash and take him outside, even if you don't think he needs to eliminate. He is experimenting to see if the bell really means "go outside." You want to reinforce this. Because he will be on leash, you can control him outdoors. If he has not eliminated within his 10-minute allotted time, bring him right back in. If you always take your dog out on leash at this stage, it will teach him that if he doesn't eliminate, he has to come inside. If he rings the bell, it doesn't mean outdoor playtime. Just be consistent. This is actually a good sign that your dog has connected the bell with going outside.

## Puppy Options:
## When They Gotta Go, They Gotta Go

Young puppies often do not understand that they are about to eliminate until it's coming out of them. This is normal. You just need to act quickly! Also it's worth knowing that very young puppies, around 8–11 weeks of age, often have to go twice in one potty break. So you might take your puppy out, he pees and poops, and on the way back inside he pees and poops again. This is also normal. If you are housetraining a very young puppy, be sure to give him enough time to eliminate twice during each potty break, just in case.

## Indoor Elimination

You may prefer to teach your dog to eliminate indoors. This can be helpful if you have a small dog and live in a high-rise apartment. Just because you put out a pee pad or set up a litter box, though, it doesn't mean your dog will automatically understand he is supposed to eliminate there. You need to train him. This training is similar to outdoor elimination training.

**What you'll need:** Indoor elimination spot, with either pee pads or a canine litter box.

1. Have treats. During a scheduled potty break or when you think your dog needs to eliminate, take him to his indoor elimination spot.
2. Just before he eliminates, give a cue. You can use one cue to mean elimination in general. Or, if you prefer, you can use one cue for peeing and one cue for pooping. Just be consistent. As soon as he is finished eliminating, give him a treat (or praise him). Make a big deal about it!

When your dog is reliably eliminating in his designated spot, it's time for you to add distance between you and the elimination spot.

3. Take your dog to the elimination spot and stand one step away from it.
4. Cue your dog to potty and give him a treat when he eliminates.
5. Repeat Steps 4–5 for a total of 10 repetitions.
6. Take your dog to the elimination spot and stand two steps away from it.
7. Cue your dog to potty and give him a treat when he eliminates.
8. Repeat Steps 7–8 for a total of 10 repetitions.
9. Gradually work, one step at a time, until you can be across the room from the elimination spot, and your dog will still go to the spot and eliminate there. If at any time your dog misses the pee pads or litter box, back up your training and proceed at that level longer.

NOTE: Until your dog has not had an accident in the house for two months, do not leave him unattended when he eliminates on his designated spot. You want to be sure to be right there to reward him for proper elimination.

## Submissive Urination: Avoiding Messy Greetings

If your dog pees when greeting someone, you can train him to hold his bladder. Don't get mad and yell at your dog. Your dog is overly excited and being respectful, just not in a manner you appreciate! So yelling at him is likely to make him pee more.

**What you'll need:** Crate/confinement.

**Preparation:** Teach "Settle" in his crate first.

1. When training, it is best if your dog is confined when you are away from home so you can better control the environment upon your arrival. When you arrive home after having been away, ignore your dog for the first 10 minutes. Don't look him in the eye, don't speak to him, and don't let him out of his crate. Your arrival is very exciting to your dog. This will give him a chance to calm down.
2. Quietly and casually take him outside for a potty break. Do not give him any attention except to cue him to go outside and potty.
3. When he comes back inside, if he is calmer, you can greet him. First, sit down. You don't want to loom over him. Don't be enthusiastic. Just casually say hello. Offer him your hand below his chin. If he is still OK and hasn't peed, scratch him on the chest or behind an ear. Do not pet him on top of his head. This is an assertive gesture in canine language and could cause him to pee again.
4. In time, as your dog learns control, you will be able to greet him more enthusiastically. Just gauge it on his bladder. If he goes back to peeing when you greet him, tone it down again and practice at that level some more.

NOTE: You can still give your dog love and affection, and you should! You just need to adjust your delivery so you don't trigger your dog to pee. The more bubbly and enthusiastic you are, the more it will heighten your dog's excitement, and the more likely he is to pee.

When you have friends over, follow the same routine. They should ignore your dog for the first 10 minutes. Take your dog out for a potty break (even if he has recently gone), bring him back indoors, and let your guests casually greet him. If at any time your dog starts to pee, quietly remove him from the area and confine him a bit longer until he can calm down. With time and consistency, he will learn to do this himself. You just have to teach him how.

# 19 Separation Anxiety

Shadow is an Australian Shepherd who was adopted from a breed rescue group when he was 5 years old. His previous family said they gave him up because he was too energetic for them, but an energetic dog was exactly what the Garver family wanted. Shadow fitted right into the Garver family's active lifestyle.

The Garvers try to include Shadow whenever they can, but they are so busy that sometimes they have to leave Shadow at home by himself. This does not go well. At first, they would come home to find that it looked like Shadow had peed everywhere. On closer inspection, they realized it was drool. They tried leaving him some food-stuffed toys, but he would never eat them when he was left alone. One day, the family came home from a soccer game. When they walked in the door, they saw Shadow's head peering at them eagerly from down the hall. His head was in the hall, but his body was still in the laundry room, where they had left him. He had chewed a hole right through the door! When they untangled Shadow from the door, the Garvers saw the doorway was a disaster. It looked like Shadow had chewed and clawed all around the doorway before settling on chewing through the middle. Shadow has a classic case of separation anxiety.

Separation anxiety can be heartbreaking for pet parents. As well as being heartbreaking, it can be frustrating and very expensive. It can be one of the most challenging problem behaviors to treat, but there is hope.

## Symptoms

Symptoms of separation anxiety include:

- Destructive chewing or clawing around exits and entrances, such as doorways or windows.
- Whining, barking, howling, or other vocalizations when your dog is left alone.
- Signs of stress when dog sees that you are about to leave. For example, you start gathering your keys and purse, and your dog starts to get upset.
- Puddles of drool. This is a sign of extreme stress.
- Anorexia. The dog will not eat when you are not there.
- Elimination. The dog may pee or poop. You may find diarrhea, which in this case is another sign of stress.
- Self-injury. The dog will hurt himself in trying to escape. For example, he will rip up his gums chewing on doorways or trying to chew through his crate. He may injure his paws and legs clawing his way out of a crate. Some dogs will burst through windows or storm doors.

Most dogs with separation anxiety will exhibit several of these symptoms. If your dog has one or two, don't assume he has separation anxiety. For example, if your dog whines a bit when you leave the house, or barks at first and then settles down, then this is not true separation anxiety.

If your dog is destructively chewing, check the location. If he's chewing on many things all over the room or house, it's probably not separation anxiety. The damage needs to be specifically around an entrance or exit. (If your dog is destroying things by chewing in general, see the Chewing chapter.)

Also, just because a dog eliminates in the house while you are gone doesn't mean he has separation anxiety. He may just not be housetrained, or he could be sick. (See the Potty Problems chapter for help.)

# Why It Happens

There is no conclusive evidence to explain why a dog develops separation anxiety. Dogs who are adopted from shelters and rescue organizations seem to be more inclined to exhibit the behavior. This is not necessarily an indication that the dogs had the

*General destructiveness like this is normally not a sign of separation anxiety. Instead, look for destruction around entrances and exits.*

problem in the first place and that it led to their relinquishment. Instead, it may indicate that the loss of their families and homes triggered the stressful disorder.

Here are some situations that have been linked to dogs developing separation anxiety:

**Change of ownership.** Being relinquished to a shelter or rescue group, or even just given to a new family, can trigger separation anxiety.

**Loss of owner.** If a beloved family member passes away or leaves the household, this can be very stressful for a dog.

**Moving.** Going to a new home can be stressful enough for a dog to develop separation anxiety. This can include moving from the country to the city or from a house to an apartment.

**Change in schedule.** If you used to work from home, but then got a job requiring you to be gone all day, this can be confusing and stressful to your dog. Or, if you used to be home during the evening but worked during the day, and you changed shifts to work during the evening and you are now home during the day, your dog may also get confused and stressed.

You might also be contributing to your dog's anxiety. If you make a big fuss over your dog when you leave, you are making a big deal out of your departure. If you have never taught your dog to enjoy time without you, then it will be very difficult for him to cope. Do you allow your dog to sleep on the bed? The bed is a highly valued resting place to your dog, and it contains a strong dose of your scent. If your dog is already overly attached to you, this could be contributing to your dog's inability to live without you.

But don't you want your dog to love you and be your best friend? Of course you do. But there is friendship and there is an unhealthy relationship. If your dog is so attached to you that he will hurt himself, destroy property, and be terrified of being alone, this is not healthy for your dog. He needs to have the confidence to handle time alone.

*A dog suffering from separation anxiety may try to escape when left on his own.*

## The Training Program
### Management

You may be able to handle mild cases of separation anxiety with some management, desensitization, and counterconditioning exercises. For severe cases, please consult a veterinary behaviorist. Don't wait until your dog seriously injures himself or does serious damage to your house. Contact a veterinary behaviorist as soon as you see signs that your dog is suffering from this disorder.

While treating a serious separation anxiety case can be very challenging, it can be done. One of the hardest aspects is that, in order for the training to work, you will not be able to leave your dog alone past the point that he can handle. This is because the goal is to gradually get your dog used to being left alone. Leaving him alone for too long before he is ready will set back your training. Because the training will take several weeks or months, this sometimes is just not practical.

**What you'll need:**

**Confinement.** If your dog is a destructive chewer, not housetrained, or for any reason cannot be trusted to be loose in your house when you are gone, then you will need a safe confinement area for him. This should not

*Dogs find it hard to cope with loneliness, especially if they have been used to being the center of attention.*

be a crate if your dog already has a history of self-injury from escaping or has already gotten out of a crate.

**Food-stuffed chew toys.** These can help if your dog has a mild case of separation anxiety.

**Dog appeasing pheromone (DAP).** This chemical simulates the pheromones mothers release when they have nursing puppies. It comes in a collar, or as a spray or a diffuser. Some dogs find it very soothing. For others, it has little or no effect.

**Petsitters.** If possible, arrange for other people to be at your house, or consider a safe, quality doggie daycare or boarding situation so that your dog will not be left alone while you are working on fixing this issue.

**Medication.** If your dog has a severe case of separation anxiety, especially if he has injured himself or done extensive damage to your home, he may need medication from your veterinarian. The proper medication for this problem is not a tranquilizer. The goal is not to dope your dog up so that he sleeps while you are gone. Your veterinarian will prescribe a drug that helps balance the chemicals in your dog's brain so that he can cope with his distress better. For severe cases, please consult a veterinary behaviorist.

Medication will not work by itself. You must use it in conjunction with a behavior modification plan to get results.

Also implement as part of your management program:

## Change in your routines

If you have been making a huge fuss over your dog when you leave, you need to stop this because it is contributing to your dog's stress. If he is allowed on the bed, you should also stop this practice because he is currently overly dependent on you, and this can often contribute to the problem. Your dog needs to learn that he will be fine if he is apart from you. He can still sleep in your bedroom, but on his own bed or in a crate. (In some severe cases, a professional may recommend that he not sleep in your room at all. The professional should help you teach your dog to transition to another sleeping place.)

*Destroying furniture is likely a result of boredom rather than of separation anxiety.*

## Foundation Behaviors
### "Settle," "Stay"

To teach your dog to settle in his bed or a crate so that he is comfortable there.

**"Wait"**

To teach your dog that it's rewarding to wait at doorways, rather than bolting after you.

## Counterconditioning: Happy Goodbyes

If your dog has separation distress in which he doesn't display the symptoms of separation anxiety, this exercise can be helpful. It can also work with some mild forms of separation anxiety.

**What you'll need:** Food-stuffed chew or interactive toy.

1. Right before you leave, give your dog the food-stuffed toy. If you are going to be gone for a long period of time, such as during a workday, leave him several toys. You can use his breakfast portion to stuff the toys. You can also stuff a chew toy and freeze it to make it last longer.
2. Repeat each time you leave. In time, your dog will associate you leaving with him getting a fun and delicious treat.

NOTE: If your dog still shows signs of stress or does not eat the food in the toy, then his case is more serious and will need additional treatment. Do not just use these specific toys for when you leave. Allow your dog to randomly have them at other times. You don't want him to associate these toys with you leaving. If he does, they might become another departure cue he can worry about.

## Lessening the Impact of Departure Cues

If your dog starts to show signs of stress when you get ready to leave, this exercise can help. The goal is to get your dog to stop associating your departure cues with you leaving, so they don't trigger stress.

What you'll need: A list of your departure cues. You don't have to write them down unless you will find it helpful to remember them. Just think of all the things you do to prepare to leave. For example, put on a jacket or coat, get your keys, get your purse or wallet, put your dog in his crate or a specific room, and so forth.

1. Several times each day, go through your departure cues—and don't leave. For example, put on your jacket, pick up your keys, head for the door, turn around, put down your keys, take off your jacket, and then go back to whatever you were doing previously.
2. Repeat until your dog no longer shows signs of stress.

## Extended Solitude

The first half hour or so of your dog's solitude is the hardest time for him. This doesn't mean that after 30 minutes he's fine. Video surveillance of dogs with separation anxiety shows that, although most of your dog's stress responses will occur in approximately the first half hour after he is left alone, he will continue to be stressed throughout your absence. It's just the first part that is especially rough for him.

*Giving your dog a food-stuffed toy to chew on and play with can lessen the milder forms of separation distress.*

This means that the first part of teaching your dog to be left alone must be done in very small increments, even seconds at a time.

Start by teaching an out-of-sight "Stay." You begin by teaching your dog to "Stay" while you move away from him, then gradually move out of his sight. Once you are out of his sight, you extend the amount of time you are gone.

**What you'll need:** Food-stuffed chew toy, clicker, treats, bed for "Settle," safe confinement area (not a crate).

**Preparation:** Teach "Settle" and "Stay" first, plus lessening the impact of departure cues.

1. When you start work on this exercise, it doesn't have to be solely in the confinement area you use when you leave the house. The goal is to keep training sessions relaxed and fun. Practice in different areas of the house, including your dog's confinement area. For each training session, use one area. Cue "Settle," then "Stay."

2. Take a small step away from your dog. If your dog does not break his stay, immediately return to your dog. Click and give him a treat. If your dog moves, try moving just one leg back a step, then back to its original position. Click and treat. Repeat just moving one leg several times. Then try taking a full, small step.

3. Cue "Settle" then "Stay." Take two steps away from your dog. Immediately return to your dog. Click and treat.

4. As long as your dog can succeed in staying in place, gradually work up to farther steps away from your dog. Always return to your dog, click, and treat. For each session, aim for a total of 10 successful repetitions. It may take you one session to be able to move this far from your dog, or it may take several. Both are normal.

When you can go a room away from your dog, and he remains calm and not stressed, it's time to move out of sight.

1. Cue "Settle," then "Stay." Leave your dog, taking one step out of the room. Immediately return to your dog. Click and treat.

2. Repeat Step 1, but stay out of your dog's view for one second. Return to your dog. Click and treat. If your dog breaks position, do not correct him! He is already afraid of you leaving him, so punishing him, even if you just use a verbal reproof, is going to increase his fear, not help him learn. Just go back to the step in which you were successful. Stay at that level for several more repetitions, then try making it harder again.

3. Repeat Step 2, except stay out of your dog's view for two seconds. Return to your dog. Click and treat.

4. Gradually work up to longer and longer times that you are out of view. Just add one second at a time. Do not always make your absence longer. For example, if you can get up to five seconds, then do a one-second absence. Then go for six seconds. If you always make it longer, your dog could become stressed.

NOTE: Keep these training sessions very short. If your dog shows any signs of stress—lip licking, whining, turning away, tense body—back up your training. The goal is to keep your dog relaxed during the training so that he learns to be relaxed when you leave him for real. It is very normal for this to take many sessions. The biggest mistake people make with their dogs is pushing them too far, too fast. If you do this, you can set back your progress significantly. Again, if your dog has a severe case of separation anxiety, it is best to work with a professional.

# 20
# Shyness

**M**aximus is the most handsome dog Tanya has ever known. A regal Chow mix, Maximus is a large dog, with a thick, luxurious coat the color of cinnamon. He is very affectionate toward Tanya. Tanya adores her 4-year-old dog and wishes she could share him with all her friends. But Maximus is not interested in the least.

When Tanya's friends come over, Maximus hides in another room. She's tried to entice him out with treats; sometimes it works and sometimes it doesn't. When he does venture out, he looks miserable. He sinks to the ground, flinches at every sound, and looks like he wants to run away. Tanya even tried dragging him out on a leash once, and he just fishtailed so badly she let him go. Once, a male friend reached out to pet Maximus and Maximus growled at him.

There is one person Maximus likes, and that's Tanya's sister, Yvonne. Maximus has known Yvonne since he was a puppy. When she comes over, he gets all wiggly and runs right up to her to kiss her face. Tanya wishes everyone could see this side of her handsome boy.

Maximus is a shy dog. Some dogs are naturally reserved. They may have some people they love and enjoy interacting with, but, in general, they are aloof toward others. There is a difference, however, in being reserved or aloof and being afraid. When a dog is frightened of other people, this is shyness.

## Symptoms

Your dog shows signs of stress in the company of other people. This can include lip licking, yawning, cowering, avoidance, whining, clinginess, and trembling. He may try to run away. He may flinch when other people move or when they reach out to him. Dogs who are stressed can also exhibit aggression, such as curling a lip, growling, barking, or biting. This can especially happen if a shy dog feels trapped and unable to escape.

Shy dogs are not always this way with everyone. They may be very loving, outgoing, and social with their families or with certain members of their families. Or, they may prefer one gender to another. Some may be social with adults, but shy and fearful around children.

# Why It Happens

A lot of shyness comes from a lack of proper socialization during a puppy's critical socialization period. Up until about 16 weeks, puppies learn a tremendous amount, including what things in life are wonderful and what things are scary. If a puppy was not properly socialized with a variety of people during this time, he may be shy or fearful of them later.

Proper socialization ensures that each experience is a positive one. So just exposing a puppy to people is not enough. He has to enjoy the experience. For example, you take two young puppy littermates to a child's baseball game. One puppy is alert, tail wagging low and swishy, greeting all the adults and children who approach him. When he hears the crack of a bat, he perks up and he barks at it once, but he quickly moves on to other exploration. The other puppy looks around for a

*When a dog tries to hide from people—or other dogs—this could well be because he is scared and shy.*

little bit, curls up, and goes to sleep. Is the sleeping puppy just exhausted? No. This puppy has shut down. The environment is completely overwhelming him—the crowds, the sounds, the smells. So he has gone to asleep to avoid the scary things altogether. This puppy may later exhibit shyness around children, loud noises, or adults. Many would mistake his sleepiness as just him being tired, but he was really frightened.

Some breeds are naturally reserved with strangers. It's even in their breed descriptions. For example, the American Kennel Club breed description for Shetland Sheepdogs reads, "The Shetland Sheepdog is intensely loyal, affectionate, and responsive to his owner. However, he may be reserved toward strangers but not to the point of showing fear or cringing in the ring." The American Kennel Club also describes the Chow Chow as "Affectionate and devoted to family, the Chow is reserved and discerning with strangers." Research your breed or breed mix. Is your breed supposed to have a huge circle of friends? Some inherently do not. Of course, there are exceptions to every breed. There are Chows who are incredibly social and friendly and Golden Retrievers who are shy. This can be due to genetics and problems with socialization.

Some dogs just don't love everyone they meet. We don't, either! Be sure you are setting realistic expectations for your dog's social nature. If your dog is aloof and doesn't seem to care for other people, that is one thing. But if he is shy, this is a fear issue, and it needs to be addressed. It may be OK if your dog doesn't want to make friends, but it's not healthy for him to be afraid to do so.

While the term "shyness" is generally associated with people, some dogs are also shy and nervous around other dogs. This can be for the same reasons—they may not have been properly socialized to different types of dogs as a young puppy. They may have had negative experiences, or they may just not be fans of other dogs. You can use some of the same techniques to help your dog get better used to other dogs.

# The Training Program

Training to help your shy dog overcome his fear will involve slow steps, ensuring that each is a positive one. Never force your dog to confront what scares him. This is called *flooding*, and it can have some serious consequences. It can increase your dog's fear to the point that he feels he needs to defend himself. It can also make him lose trust in you.

You might also want to check out the Dog–Human Aggression and Phobia chapters of this book for added tips on working with dog fears. If your dog is shy around other dogs, then check out the Dog-Dog Aggression chapter.

With shy dogs, it may sometimes feel as though you are taking three steps forward and two steps back. This is typical. Fighting fear is a challenging battle. You will have days when you make tremendous progress and days when you are disappointed. Don't be discouraged—this is very common with shy dogs. Pocket some extra patience. Your dog can't help it if he is afraid. You just need to be confident for the both of you!

*There are all sorts of reasons why a shy dog hides. Your job is to identify what triggers such behavior and then help him to deal with them.*

## Management

**What you'll need:** Food-stuffed chew toys, safe confinement area, baby gates, leash.

**Safe zones.** If your dog is shy of guests, he will need a safe zone where he can stay while you have guests over. You will be working to help him overcome his shyness, but let's be realistic. You can't work with him all the time. Sometimes, you need to just sit and enjoy being with your friends. So give your dog a safe place away from the action.

This can be a room or his crate in another room. Give him a food-stuffed chew toy as a reward. If he is not so afraid that he will bark or growl, then you can set up baby gates to give him a safe barrier to be behind. This way he can see everyone but isn't forced to interact with them. This also can be a good way to getting him used to your friends slowly.

*Giving your dog a secure, safe place to stay is a sensible precaution to take if he is uncertain with visitors.*

**Leash.** If you go outside, whether it's for a walk in the neighborhood or to the veterinarian's office, always have your dog on leash. The leash is not for corrections. It's to safely keep hold of your dog should he decide he is too afraid and bolts. Some shy dogs can get overwhelmed in the big wide world, and you want to be sure you always have a good hold on your dog just in case he panics and runs.

Also implement as part of your management program:

## Avoidance

This may seem like you're avoiding the issue or in denial, but what it means is that you should avoid the things that make your dog afraid until you can work on his fear during your training sessions. A shy dog who is constantly bombarded with things that frighten him can't catch a break to recover. Is your dog miserable when you go on walks? Skip the walks unless you can specifically use them for training. Does he cower and try to hide when meeting new people? Don't make him meet new

*Giving your dog confidence when out walking can help him deal with the problems that may be worrying him and making him anxious.*

people, unless you are specifically setting up the meeting as a training session—which would not push him to the point where he cowers.

Many think that if they overexpose their dogs to the things that worry them, their dog will "get over it" or become accustomed to them. This is not the case. You could actually be making his shyness worse.

## Education for Others

Make sure you educate anyone who wants to interact with your dog. You may need to tell people to not pet your dog. You are your dog's advocate. It's up to you to keep him safe. He trusts you to keep him safe. So, if he is afraid of strangers, do not let strangers interact with him. For example, children sometimes can be a challenge. Some of them think all dogs are friendly, and they want to pet and hug all of them. If your dog is afraid of children, do not allow this type of interaction. If your dog gets frightened enough to end up biting the child, it's your dog who will be considered the one at fault.

## Foundation Behaviors
### All

Training gives a dog confidence. The more he learns he can earn rewards, the more he wants to learn how. It also improves your communication with each other. So work on teaching your dog all the foundation behaviors. You will end up with a well-behaved dog and a more confident one!

## Pay Attention to Your Body Language: Don't Be Scary

When you are in your training sessions with friends, you will need to guide them on how to interact with your shy dog. Your guests may be trying to be friendly and encouraging, but their behavior and body language could actually be making things worse, so give them these rules:

- No direct eye contact. Some dogs find such contact very assertive. If your friend is staring your dog in the eyes, this can be very intimidating.

- No petting on the top of the head. Many dogs do not appreciate being petted on top of the head. It is another assertive gesture. This is why you sometimes see dogs duck out of the way of an incoming hand.

- No looming over him. Anything that looms over your dog can be scary, especially if you have a small dog.

- Always approach low and under the chin, and only then if the dog is willing and wants to engage. This is a more appropriate greeting gesture.

It can feel awkward educating other people if you're not used to it. But you can do it politely, and it's important so that your dog doesn't feel pushed into defense mode. You want your dog to love your friends as much as you do. So teach your friends not to come across as scary.

## Confident Encounters

You want your dog to be able to see people who scare him without worrying about them. This exercise is especially helpful when you are out for walks where you might encounter strangers. It's for dogs who get nervous at the mere sight of another person. If your dog is OK with seeing people at a distance, but doesn't like them up close, then you may not need this exercise. You can also use this exercise if your dog becomes nervous when seeing other dogs at a distance.

**What you'll need:** Treats, clicker, leash.

1. Have your dog on leash and have treats handy. Be observant of your environment. Ideally, you will spot another person (or dog) before your dog does. You can either take a walk with your dog, or, if you live on a busy street, you can get comfortable on your front porch. Choose whichever scenario you think will make your dog less nervous.

2. When your dog notices a person, stop walking. You'll note your dog's ears may prick or he may tense slightly. Click. Back up a few steps and then treat. If you are on your porch, you don't have to back up. The backing up increases distance between your dog and what makes him nervous and is an added reward for your dog.

3. Repeat every time you see another person (or dog). Keep your session no longer than 15 minutes. You will find that, with practice, your dog will start looking at the scary trigger and then to you for his treat. This is great progress! This means he now associates the scary person or dog with something better—a treat. It doesn't mean he's all ready to make friends, but it is definitely a positive step.

# Hand Touch: Other People

This behavior can give dogs confidence that they can approach other people and not get hurt. This exercise is for dogs who do not have a bite history with people. If your dog has nipped or bitten a person, consult a professional before attempting up-close work. In any event, it is better to try this under qualified, professional supervision.

**What you'll need:** Clicker and treats. For the final steps, you will need another person.

**Preparation:** Teach "Come" first. The hand touch is the beginning of that behavior, so it will be familiar to your dog.

1. Present your hand, palm facing your dog, fingers pointed downward. Your dog should nose your hand. Click and toss a treat to your dog.
2. Cue "Touch" once, in a friendly voice. Present your hand. When your dog noses your hand, click and toss a treat. Repeat for 10 successful repetitions.
3. Repeat Step 2 until your dog is reliably responding to your "Touch" cue.

Now it is time to add another person.

1. Stand close to your friend. Have your friend present his or her hand, just as you have done—palm facing your dog, fingers pointed downward. Point to your friend's hand and cue "Touch." Wait. Don't repeat the cue, just be patient. If your dog noses your friend's hand, click and toss a treat away from your friend. Increasing the distance between the "scary person" and your dog is an added reward for your dog.
2. If your dog will not approach your friend, ask him or her to sit down, facing at a 90-degree angle to your dog, with a hand presented to the side. So, if your dog is looking at your friend, your friend

*Getting your dog to nose your hand is the first step in training him not to be scared of other people.*

would be sitting facing left or right, but with his hand extended toward your dog. Sometimes, having someone sit down is less scary to a shy dog. Cue "Touch." If your dog noses your friend's hand, click and toss a treat to your dog.

NOTE: You should be the one to click and give your dog treats, not your friend. Some shy dogs who are food motivated want a treat so much, they will come right up to a stranger offering one but then get overwhelmed. This can easily turn into a dog bite. By feeding a treat to your dog yourself, you ensure that he stays below his threshold of nervousness.

## Desensitization and Counterconditioning

These two techniques work best together. The goals are to keep your dog at a level where he is not afraid and to change his association with people into a positive one. This may take several or many sessions, and that is normal. Aim for 15 minutes maximum at a time. You don't want to overwhelm your dog. This example uses guests to your house. At the beginning stages of this exercise, guests should completely ignore your dog. This includes not making eye contact with him.

What you'll need: Treats, baby gate. Use the baby gate to block your dog from coming into the guest area, but keep him where he can still see them and you.

1.  Have the baby gate up and treats handy. As your guests settle in, just randomly toss treats over the baby gate to your dog. Look for signs of canine stress—lip licking, whining, yawning, and turning away.

2.  If your dog stays at the gate and is not exhibiting signs of stress, remove the baby gate. This may take one session, or it may take several. This is normal. Randomly toss treats to your dog.

3.  If your dog is coming into the room of his own volition, then it's time for this step. Give your guests

## Non-Treat Alternatives: Petting Depends on the Receiver

Your dog likely enjoys when you pet him. You probably know all his favorite spots. When you pet your dog, it's a reward. When someone he doesn't know pets him, however, that is very different.

It can be hard for a dog lover to accept that a dog is frightened of him or her. It may or may not be something the person is doing, but the bottom line is that if a dog is shy around a person, the dog has the right to be afraid. It's not personal. Dog lovers want to pet and cuddle with dogs, but this is not rewarding to a dog who is frightened of them.

Imagine being terrified of clowns. A giant clown comes to you and wraps you in a big hug, then starts stroking your hair. Yikes! This will not help you love the clown. You may like hugs from people you know. You may like it when your significant other strokes your hair. But for a scary clown to do it is another story. It's an invasion of your personal space. It's not rewarding. Frankly, it's more than a little creepy!

For a shy dog, being petted by a stranger is not rewarding. So when working with your friends—and even with strangers you may encounter while you are out with your shy dog—do not let them pet him. Hopefully, if you work at his shyness, he will learn to enjoy affection from others.

treats. They should not feed your dog directly. They can roll treats to your dog along the ground, but they should still ignore your dog.

With practice and time, you may find your dog is now looking forward to your guests arriving. This is great progress! He may want to start engaging with them. Here's how to do it safely, so your dog doesn't get overwhelmed.

1. Your dog should only approach your guests on his own terms. Just be patient and let him proceed as he wants. If he approaches a guest, the guest can drop treats for him. Guest should not feed him directly to mouth.

2. If your dog approaches a guest and starts sniffing him or her, the guest should drop a treat and then leave his hand out, held low, for your dog to sniff. If your dog engages, the guest can pet him for three seconds on the chest, not on top of his head. After three seconds, the guest should stop. This gives your dog a brief engagement with a "scary" person, but then it quickly gives him a break. If the dog wants to engage more, the guest can pet for another three seconds. Your guest should pause every couple of seconds to see if your dog still wants to be petted. Some dogs can handle one engagement and will then leave, but this is still progress! Some will stick around for more. It should be up to your dog. This is empowering for him. He'll learn that he has a choice on whether he engages with someone new.

NOTE: The desensitization part of this exercise is keeping your dog below threshold at a level where he is not stressed. The counterconditioning part is the association of treats with your guests.

*If your dog feels ready to sniff people, he is making good progress at coming to terms with their presence.*

# 21

# Whining

Gerald wishes Molly, his 4-year-old French Bulldog, would bark. He wishes she would howl. He wishes she would make just about any other noise than whine. But Molly is a whiner.

When Molly gets excited about anything, she whines. She whines in the car. She whines when Gerald is getting her food ready. She whines if he ignores her when he's watching TV. When they go to the veterinarian's office, she tries to get into his lap, whining the entire time they are in the lobby. It drives Gerald crazy. There's just something about the pitch Molly reaches with her whining that rattles his ears. You'd think with those big bat-like ears of Molly's, it would bother her, too!

Molly is a multi-purpose whiner. She gets excited about car rides and food, so she whines. If she wants attention, she's whining for that, too. At the veterinary clinic, with Molly trying to climb into Gerald's lap, her whining probably a nervous or frightened. For some pet parents, whining can be the ultimate in annoyance.

## Symptoms

Your dog whines. It can vary in volume and frequency. Some dogs only whine in certain situations, while others seem to be prone to whining quite a bit.

## Why It Happens

Whining is a form of canine communication. It can indicate stress or excitement. If it is due to stress, you will likely also see other stress behaviors, such as lip licking, ears back, turn-aways, yawning, clinginess, or trembling. Not all dogs will exhibit all stress signals.

Whining will increase if the dog is rewarded for it. For example, if your dog whines to go outside and you let her outside, she will likely continue to whine when she wants to go outside. She may also learn that whining gets a nice paycheck, so she will begin whining for other things she wants. This doesn't mean your dog is deliberately being a whiny brat. It means you paid for whining, so you indicated to your dog that whining is successful. You probably did not intend to do this!

*Dogs whine for all sorts of reasons. Sometimes, they are just excited!*

# The Training Program

Whining has some similarities with barking. Both of them are natural canine behaviors, but they can become annoying.

## Research

**Goal:** To determine your dog's whining triggers.

**What you'll need:** A list of whining triggers. Before you choose a training exercise, you need a list of what makes your dog whine. Is it excitement? Is it only when he's frightened or worried?

## Management

No matter what kind of whiner your dog is, a good management program can help.

**Goal:** To prevent your dog from experiencing triggers for whining.

**What you'll need:**

**Blinds, drapes, doors, window film.** Use these to block your dog's view of items that trigger his whining. For example, does your dog only whine when he sees another dog outside? A person? A squirrel? Remember, the more your dog practices whining at triggers he sees outside, the better he will get at the behavior. Blocking his view will lessen the chances that he will whine.

## Foundation Behaviors

**"Down," "Settle"** Some dogs find it harder to whine when they are lying down. For others, it doesn't stop them.

*Teaching your dog to hush when you cue him can help deal with unwelcome whining behavior.*

## Hush

Teaching your dog to be quiet on cue can be extremely useful. This exercise is useful if your dog is whining from excitement. It will not be as helpful if your dog is whining because he is anxious or afraid.

**Goal:** Your dog will stop whining when you cue him.

**What you'll need:** Clicker, treats.

1. Do something that is likely to get your dog whining. This sounds odd, but if you don't get your dog whining, you can't teach him the opposite!

2. When your dog is whining, wait for him to be quiet. Even if it's just for a second. As soon as it happens, click and treat. Repeat. You will find that your dog stays quiet for longer periods as he recognizes he will be rewarded if he does so.

3. When your dog starts to quiet on a regular basis, start cueing "Hush" just before you think he will be quiet. Say it once and don't yell it. As soon as your dog quiets, click and treat.

## Counterconditioning

If your dog is whining because he is anxious or nervous, then counterconditioning can help him become more confident when faced with the triggers that are frightening him. Once he gains more confidence, the whining should cease. If your dog is afraid, don't scold him for whining. He is trying to tell you that he's scared, and scolding him for communicating with you won't make his fear go away.

**What you'll need:** Treats. You'll also need a trigger for his whining. This example uses a veterinary clinic. Please note that this is a great exercise to do to help any dog get used to the veterinary clinic, whether or not he is whining about his visits.

1. On a day that you do not have a veterinary appointment, take your dog to the clinic. Have a seat in the lobby and feed your dog treats. It's OK if he whines a little at this point. For this exercise, you are simply trying to associate the scary clinic with happy treats. If he will not take the treats at all, this

means he is really stressed. Please review the chapter on Phobias for help.

If your dog is social and the veterinary staff can spare a minute, ask them to give your dog treats. Stay for about 15 minutes, then leave.

2. Repeat at least twice a week for several weeks. If you can do it more often, you will extinguish the behavior more quickly, but this may not be practical. Your goal is to make the veterinary clinic a place that your dog looks forward to visiting.

When your dog can go to the veterinary lobby and not whine during your sessions, ask the veterinary staff if you can borrow an exam room. Be sure to call ahead and arrange this, as all rooms could be occupied with sick animals needing care. Explain that you are getting your dog used to the veterinary clinic, and many vet offices will want to help you. You may need to visit when they are light on appointments.

*Getting a veterinarian to give your dog a treat can help him feel better about vet visits, and therefore whine less.*

## Small-Dog Options: Bath Mat Advantages

If your small dog whines at the veterinary clinic because he is afraid, one thing that might be adding to his concerns is the slippery examination table. When you put him on the table, do his little legs splay out? Does he flatten like a pancake? These can be signs he is nervous. Plus, he has no traction on that table.

To help your dog be more comfortable at the veterinary clinic, purchase a rubber-backed bath mat. Get one large enough so that your dog can fit on it while lying down. Then, teach your dog to love his bath mat.

Store the bath mat up high, so your dog doesn't chew on it or eliminate on it. For every meal time, bring out the bath mat and put your dog's food bowl on it. After he's done eating, put the bath mat away.

Randomly throughout the day, place the bath mat on the floor and drop a small handful of treats on it. After your dog has eaten all the treats, put the bath mat away.

Teach your dog "Settle" on the bath mat. By the time you are done with all of this, he should love his mat!

The next time you go to the veterinary clinic, take your dog's bath mat with you. Place it on the scary table, then put your dog on the mat. He loves his mat by now, so he should find it reassuring. The rubber back of the bath mat prevents it from sliding, which also gives him a more stable surface to stand on. This will help his confidence. And, since it is machine washable, you can wash it when you get home. You may find your dog gets quite attached to his blankie!

3. Go to the veterinary lobby. Have a seat and give your dog treats.

4. After about 5 minutes, go to your assigned waiting room. Feed your dog treats. Stay about 10 minutes, then leave. During this visit, if veterinary staff is available, they can also give your dog treats.

5. Repeat Steps 3–4 until your dog no longer whines at the veterinary clinic. This may take a few sessions or many, depending on how stressed your dog is and how long he has been practicing this problem behavior.

You can also use these visits to help your dog feel more comfortable with other veterinary clinic situations, such as getting on and off the scales, being on the examination table (for small dogs), and the like. Keep a close eye on your dog for signs of stress. If your dog is stressed, slow down your training and allow your dog to get used to things. Be sure you are using delicious treats.

NOTE: It is best to start this training long before your dog needs to visit the veterinarian for his annual wellness check-up. Of course, accidents and illnesses happen. Your dog may need to visit the veterinarian sooner than you would like. But taking the time to prepare your dog for a vet visit can stop his whining and make him more comfortable with getting health care for the rest of his life.

## Substitute a Quiet Behavior

If your dog is whining, and you are paying him for it, then you are rewarding the behavior. It will continue and likely get worse. It's time to train you! If you don't change your habits, your dog will never change his.

Cueing your dog to sit can distract him from whining.

Once your dog quiets down, it's time to give him a reward in the form of a treat or some playtime with you.

At first, the whining may get worse. This is normal. It is because your dog is confused—you just changed the rules on him, and he doesn't understand. His whining always got him what he wanted before. He can't see why it's not working now. He may whine louder, trying to get what he wants. You can work through it. If you revert to your previous actions, you will just make the problem more cemented and harder to fix.

**Goal:** To teach your dog that his whining does not result in a desired reward.

**What you'll need:** Items your dog finds rewarding and that he usually whines to get. Clicker. You'll also need resolve to stop paying your dog for whining. If you stick with your plan sometimes, but give in at others, the whining inevitably will get worse.

**Preparation:** Teach "Sit" and/or "Down" first.

1. When your dog starts to whine for something, such as his food bowl, your attention, for you to throw his ball, or whatever, wait. Wait for him to be quiet, even if only for a second.

2. The second he is quiet, cue him to do something else, such as "Sit" or "Down." If he keeps whining, wait, then try again when he is quiet. If he complies but still whines, cue him to do something else. The goal is to cue him to do another behavior that you can reward him for. It doesn't really matter what it is, but it should be done without whining.

3. When he performs the behavior you've requested and he's quiet, click. Then you can give him what he wants, if it's appropriate. For example, if he's whining for you to throw his squeaky hedgehog and you don't mind throwing the toy, throw it once he's quiet and sitting. If he's whining to be given some of your pizza, you don't have to give him the pizza! Give him a more appropriate reward.

NOTE: You may wonder why you don't just immediately give your dog what he wants

A trained dog is a happy dog, but you must be clear in your cues so that you don't confuse your dog.

*The ultimate aim of training is to establish mutual love, trust, and understanding between you and your dog.*

when he is quiet. If your dog has been paid for whining, it can be easy for him to chain the behavior. Here's the chain: the dog whines to get a valued item, he is quiet, and then he immediately gets the valued item. What he learns is that he still needs to whine to get what he wants. This is why we insert a different behavior in between. It's better for him to learn to be quiet and sit or lie down in order to earn his reward.

## The Easy Dog: Is There Such a Thing?

Dogs who never bite, bark to excess, pee or poop inside, love everyone and every other creature they meet, don't steal food, never dig, and only chew on their toys do exist. Mainly in memory. We often have wonderful, loving memories of dogs we've had in our past that were poster perfect. Memories are funny that way. The love we had for great dogs overshadows the times they did something naughty or needed extra training.

Any time we bring a dog into our home and our hearts, we risk frustrations. The reason that there are professional dog trainers, veterinary behaviorists, and certified applied animal behaviorists—and training books, classes, and DVDs—is because it can be so challenging to bring humans and dogs together in one household. So don't feel alone.

Working with your dog and improving your relationship with him can offer you amazing rewards. When you finally understand each other and your dog starts to respond to you positively, it's a magic moment. Hopefully, with your efforts and continued dedication, your dog will end up being a cherished family member for years to come. And later, when you look back on your dog in loving memory, you'll believe that the work you put into fixing his problem behaviors was worth every minute.

# RESOURCES

**Author: Teoti Anderson, CPDT-KA, KPA-CTP**
Website: www.teotianderson.com
Facebook: www.facebook.com/teotianderson
Radio: http://petliferadio.com/getpawsitiveresults.html

**American College of Veterinary Behaviorists (ACVB)**
College of Veterinary Medicine, 4474 TAMU
Texas A&M University
College Station, TX 77843
Website: www.dacvb.org
Find a veterinary behaviorist: www.dacvb.org/about/member-directory/

**Animal Behavior Society – Certified Applied Animal Behaviorists (CAAB)**
2111 Chestnut Ave
Suite 145
Glenview, IL 60025
Website: www.animalbehaviorsociety.org/
Find a CAAB: http://www.animalbehaviorsociety.org/web/applied-behavior-caab-directory.php

**Association of Professional Dog Trainers (APDT)**
2365 Harrodsburg Road
A325
Lexington, KY 40504
Website: www.apdt.com
Find a trainer: https://apdt.com/trainer-search/

**Certification Council for Professional Dog Trainers (CCPDT)**
Administrative Office: Professional Testing Corporation
1350 Broadway, 17th Floor
New York, NY 10018
Find a training and behavior consultant: http://ccpdt.org/index.php?option=com_certificants&Itemid=102

**Karen Pryor Clicker Training: Academy-Certified Training Partners** (KPA-CTPs)
49 River Street
Waltham, MA 02453
Find a KPA-CTP: www.karenpryoracademy.com/find-a-trainer?source=kpctnavbar

**International Association of Animal Behavior Consultants (IAABC)**
565 Callery Road
Cranberry Township, PA 16066
Website: www.iaabc.org
Find a consultant: http://iaabc.org/consultants

**National Association of Dog Obedience Instructors (NADOI)**
7910 Picador Drive
Houston, TX 77083
Telephone: 972-296-1196
Website: www.nadoi.org
Find a trainer: www.nadoi.org/instructors.htm

# GLOSSARY

**Aggression:** Hostile or violent behavior toward others; a readiness to attack or confront. Some examples of how dogs exhibit aggression are by growling, lunging, barking, snapping, and biting.

**Behavior:** Any action that an animal does.

**Bite inhibition:** A behavior in which an animal learns not to bite down hard.

**Classical conditioning:** The process of associating a neutral stimulus with an involuntary response, until the stimulus triggers the response.

**Clicker:** A box-shaped tool that emits a "click" sound when you press it on one side.

**Clicker training:** A system of teaching that uses a clicker to mark desired behavior, followed by positive reinforcement.

**Counter-conditioning:** The process of pairing a stimulus that causes a response with another stimulus that causes an opposite response.

**Cue:** A word or physical signal you use to ask a dog to perform a specific behavior.

**Dominance:** A relationship between individuals that is established by force, aggression, and submission in order to determine who has priority access to multiple resources such as food, preferred resting spots, and access to mates. Dominance is not a personality trait.

**Flooding:** A behavior therapy technique in which the dog is exposed to the objects that frighten him to a maximum intensity.

**Fluency:** Training behaviors so that your dog will perform them with distractions, in different environments, under different conditions.

**Luring:** A hands-off method of guiding a dog through a behavior.

**Marker:** A signal used to mark a desired behavior the second that it occurs. The "click" sound is a marker.

**Pheromones:** The chemicals dogs excrete to attract other animals.

**Phobia:** An extreme fear.

**Piloerection:** A condition in which the fur on a dog's shoulders, and sometimes back, rises. This can be due to aggression, fear, or high excitement.

**Positive reinforcement:** Something favorable added after a behavior, which causes the behavior to increase.

**Separation anxiety:** A condition in which a dog becomes traumatized when left alone. Symptoms include drooling, elimination, destruction of exits, anorexia, and self-injury.

**Target:** Something an animal is taught to touch with a part of his body, such as his nose or paw.

# ACKNOWLEDGMENTS

I'm a problem solver. It's my nature, and it's what I love doing, especially when it comes to helping people solve problems with their canine companions. Thanks to the wonderful I-5 Publishing team for working with me on this book, which I hope will help keep more dogs in their lifetime homes.

Thank you to all my clients who have trusted me to help them with their dogs. You are the reason I keep learning and loving what I do! Special gratitude to the professionals who have educated and inspired me—Dr. Ian Dunbar, Dr. Patricia McConnell, Terry Ryan, Sue Sternberg, Karen Pryor, Ken Ramirez, Ken McCort, Ray Coppinger, Pat Goodmann, the late Dr. Sophia Yin, and Dr. R. K. Anderson.

Many thanks to my parents for their faith in me, and to the rest of my family and friends for their love and unwavering support. To my dearest friend, Phyllis Beasley, thank you for sharing this training journey with me. To my sweetheart, Tim Mullally, a heartfelt thank-you for being my No. 1 fan. And special love and thanks to my boys, Finian the Papillon and Sawyer the Belgian Tervuren, who want readers to know that the problem behaviors in this book in no way resemble them at all.

# INDEX

# PHOTO CREDITS

# Teoti Anderson, CPDT-KA, KPA-CTP

**Teoti Anderson**, a Certified Professional Dog Trainer and Karen Pryor Academy Certified Training Partner, has been a professional dog trainer for more than two decades. She is the owner of Pawsitive Results, LLC, in Lexington, South Carolina (www.getpawsitiveresults.com) and is the author of several dog training books, including the Dogster *Ultimate Guide to Dog Training*. She also has a radio show, Get Pawsitive Results, on Pet Life Radio, is a regular columnist for *Modern Dog* magazine, and has appeared in *Southern Living*, *New York Times*, *DogFancy*, *Puppies USA*, *Whole Dog Journal*, and other national publications. A popular workshop presenter, she has given presentations to pet owners and other canine professionals across the United States and in Japan.

Teoti is Past President of the Association of Professional Dog Trainers (APDT). She also serves as a consultant on canine training and behavior for local and national dog rescue organizations. Teoti's canine family includes Finian, a Papillon who is a registered therapy dog, and Sawyer, a ridiculously handsome Belgian Tervuren.